Hardy in History
A study in literary sociology
Peter Widdowson

D1226975

Thomas Hardy is a significant cultural figure – widely published and read, filmed and televised, taught and examined, and an asset to the English tourist industry. Who invented this Hardy and why? What are his characteristics and what do they mean? In this study Peter Widdowson investigates Hardy not so much in terms of his novels but as he has been constituted as a major figure in English literature. Using Hardy as a case-study, he looks at how a 'great writer' is produced in sociological terms, analysing the critical, cultural, and ideological factors involved.

Widdowson explores the way Hardy's fiction has been moulded and formed by criticism, education, publishing, and the media to forge the 'Hardy of Wessex' within a conventional English national culture. In the course of exposing this construction, Widdowson also seeks to release Hardy – and by implication any other 'great writer' submitted to these processes – from the constraints imposed by orthodox literary history.

Peter Widdowson is Professor and Head of the School of English at Middlesex Polytechnic.

Hardy in History

A study in literary sociology

Peter Widdowson

Routledge
London and New York

First published 1989
by Routledge
11 New Fetter Lane, London EC4P 4EE
29 West 35th Street, New York, NY 10001

Printed in Great Britain by
TJ Press (Padstow) Ltd, Padstow, Cornwall

British Library Cataloguing in Publication Data

Widdowson, Peter
  Hardy in history. A study in literary sociology.
  1. Fiction in English. Hardy, Thomas,
  1840–1928. Criticism
  I. Title
  823'.8

  ISBN 0-415-01330-5
       0-415-01331-3 Pbk

Library of Congress Cataloging in Publication Data

Widdowson, Peter.
    Hardy in history: a study in literary sociology
  Peter Widdowson.
      p. cm.
    Bibliography: p.
    Includes index.
    ISBN 0-415-01330-5. — ISBN 0-415-01331-3 (pbk.)
    1. Hardy, Thomas, 1840–1928 — Criticism and interpretation —
  History. 2. Hardy, Thomas, 1840–1928 — Political and social views.
  3. Literature and society — Great Britain. 4. Social problems in literature.
  5. Wessex (England) in literature — Sociological aspects. I. Title.
  PR4754.W46   1989
  823'.8 — dc19   88-37441

For Patrick
    Emily and
    Thomas
            with love

Contents

List of plates

Acknowledgements

I would like to express my gratitude to a number of individuals and institutions without whose help this book would not have been possible. As I indicate more specifically in notes to the chapters, I received crucial assistance from the British Film Institute Library, from the Department of Education and Science Library, from the BBC Library, from the University of Cambridge Local Examinations Syndicate archive, from 'Carrie' of the BBC's Drama Department, and from the Libraries at Thames and Middlesex Polytechnics. My thanks, too, to the many groups of students, mainly at Thames, but also latterly at Middlesex Polytechnic, who found themselves involved in the working-out of parts of this book, and to colleagues and friends – especially in the School of Humanities at Thames Polytechnic – whose intellectual stimulation enabled me to write it. A term's sabbatical leave in the early 1980s got the book started – for which I am indebted to Valerie Pitt (amongst other debts); and four months as a visiting research fellow at the Humanities Research Centre, the Australian National University, Canberra in 1984 helped another chapter to emerge: my thanks to the staff there for that marvellous opportunity. Early versions of parts of the book resulted from these sabbaticals in the shape of two essays already published elsewhere: 'Hardy in history: a case-study in the sociology of literature', *Literature and History*, 9, 1, Spring 1983; and 'Hardy, "Wessex" and the making of a national culture', in Norman Page, ed., *The Thomas Hardy Annual*, no. 4, 1986. For permission to reproduce materials for the plates, I am indebted to Penguin Books, Macmillan, the BBC, Columbia Pictures TV, Weintraub Entertainments, and the West Country Tourist Board.

But my biggest thanks go to Valerie Osborne, of Thames Polytechnic's School of Humanities, who typed reams of appalling manuscript with unflagging good humour and a sharp eye for the ridiculous – this book is as much hers (poor thing) as it is mine; to Jean Tonini, secretary of the School of English at Middlesex

Polytechnic, for typing the Notes and References, for unfailing support, and countless other good offices; and finally, to Jane, who has lived with it and helped it take shape.

Introduction: Literature, criticism, and history

If I begin this book by suggesting that Thomas Hardy's novel *The Hand of Ethelberta* is as significant as *Tess of the d'Urbervilles*, I will immediately create a number of problems – or rather, one problem in several guises. First, quite a number of readers who would otherwise consider themselves Hardy fans may never have heard of it, let alone have read it. Others, who have read it, will almost certainly join 99 per cent of the Hardy Critical Industry in thinking I am either stupid or perverse. They will regard *Ethelberta* – or perhaps *A Laodicean* – as Hardy's worst novel, whilst *Tess* will represent the acme of his achievement in fiction: his fullest, most tragic, and most characteristic work. What will lie behind this certainty is a great web of discriminations and evaluations spun over the last hundred years or so: by Hardy himself, by reviewers, critics, teachers, publishers, examination boards, students, and ordinary readers. We will, in fact, have a concrete example – at its simplest and crudest – of that hoary old theoretical problem of 'literary value': the ranking, that is to say, of literary works into hierarchies of value. At one end of the scale, we will have 'major', 'serious' or 'great' works of art, 'masterpieces' or 'classics', which are ranged with others similarly evaluated to constitute a 'tradition' or 'canon' of 'Literature' (as distinct from the generic 'literature' – meaning the whole corpus of imaginative writing), which itself represents 'the best that has been thought and written in the world' and which – so the argument runs – it is proper civilized people should read and be able to read. At the other end of the scale, we will have 'minor', sometimes trivial or slight, often 'popular', works which are deemed to have little merit: ones which were once perhaps widely read but are now only of 'period' interest, or are the 'lesser' works ('juvenilia' or 'failures') of some major writer; but all of which, for whatever reason, have been marginalized, lost, forgotten, dismissed, or suppressed by literary history, let alone by literary criticism and literary education.

1

How this process works – so that it appears natural and self-evident that *Tess* is 'great' and *Ethelberta* is not – is complex and wide ranging in its implications, and it is the purpose of this book to unpack some of those implications. But one thing can be stated immediately and with confidence: the process, and indeed the whole edifice of 'Literature' and 'literary value', is neither self-evident nor natural – although it has, crucially, been naturalized. Notions of organic taste, of the self-revealing greatness of a masterpiece instantly and incontrovertibly striking the eye of the receptive reader, are the naturalized myths of a particular cultural ideology which constructs and reproduces artificial mechanisms of perception as surely as general social ideology constructs unseen a world view as natural, common sense, and 'real'. *Tess* is not self-evidently 'better' than *Ethelberta*, except to the 'educated eye', nor does it intrinsically contain its value – any more than ivory or silver do in their ante-social, pre-utilized state. Value – and thence hierarchization – is the result of processes of discrimination (and we may note how the word holds two senses), education, and evaluation which are brought to literary works by active readers who themselves individually construct a version of the text – one which we might call 'My Thomas Hardy', or MYTH for short. This is not to suggest, however, that each such individual response is purely subjective, unilateral, and transitory; rather the reverse, since the reader will be functioning within a critical mindset constructed around her or him by prevailing cultural institutions and discourses, themselves already deeply naturalized ('fully-developed characters' and a 'plausible plot', for example, are still generally regarded as a good thing in novels, films, and television serials), and the individually perceived 'version' of the text is therefore likely to coincide, or 'fit', with other similarly constituted versions of this text or others, and with the values enshrined in the 'tradition' or 'canon' of 'great works'. This consonance of evaluations results, of course, not in *a* version of the text in question but in *the* version, naturalized in the hierarchy as 'self-evidently' a great work. This process of constructing 'literary competence' (that is, of being able to read such a work 'properly') is, then, both produced and reinforced – by an apparently natural 'recognition' of consonance – in the literary culture of its historical period. My point is simply that it is a *process*, not a static, universal, and immanent truth. *Tess* is only 'better' than *Ethelberta* because historically-positioned readers, bounded by certain parameters of perception and intelligibility, construct it as such, and impute 'its' value to it. A friend of mine, in a letter, argues another line:

I think there's one very obvious point you skip over. It surely isn't enough to say that *The Hand of Ethelberta* is ignored because it doesn't fit into a particular way of thinking about the novel. That may be so, and indeed it probably is, but . . . the truth is surely that Hardy's readers don't go for the novel. Those readers aren't ones who are critically subdued by any orthodoxy: Hardy has replaced Jane Austen as the novelist most teenagers/ adolescents read, and it seems to me pretty obvious that the novels they tacitly agree to prefer are the ones that form the canon. I mean by this that Hardy's readers are on the whole entirely innocent of any critical presuppositions about what they are supposed to like/dislike (even if some of them have to play examination games about his imperfections). The majority read Hardy because they want to not because they have to.[1]

This is a telling point, much of which I can concur with; but it seems to me quite wrong to hypothesize readers who are 'entirely innocent of any critical presuppositions'. Of formal, academic criticism, perhaps; but no one able to 'read' a nineteenth-century novel is without certain learnt competences which are themselves critically inscribed and deeply naturalized. And these for the most part, I would suggest, can be described as 'realist expectation'; which means that when confronted by a novel which thwarts this expectation, the wrong set of competences is being deployed. The normal 'critical' response to such a dilemma is to describe the offending text as a 'bad' novel, a 'failure', 'deeply flawed', and so on.

If I suppose a 'common reader' and ask them why *Tess* is a better novel than *Ethelberta*, I will probably receive an answer which comprises references to the power of the protagonist's characterization, to the author's skill in depicting the natural environment and relating it to the main character and the action, and to the tragic force of the novel's theme. *Ethelberta*, on the other hand, will be: outside Hardy's true ambit (about London 'society' and not rural Wessex) and therefore an oddity in his *oeuvre*; perhaps a poor pastiche of Meredithian comedy; certainly trivial, clumsy, and improbable. Well yes, that response makes sense if we start from there – from all the literary and critical assumptions and criteria which are implicit in a 'realist expectation' process of evaluation. But if, as the old joke has it, we wouldn't have started from here in the first place – if, indeed, we don't even start from a position of wanting to rank them at all (and the ranking is usually done on unspoken premises, which the critic could not articulate if asked) – then the entire naturalized edifice of established critical orthodoxy collapses, and a vast unfamiliar landscape opens out in front of us.

3

In no sense, however, is this book an attempt to 'correct' the relative status of two of Hardy's novels, to prove that *Ethelberta* is 'better' than *Tess* if read with a (my) more discerning eye. Nor is it, indeed, yet another critical monograph on Hardy, offering an extensive re-reading of his fiction – although examples and suggestions for this will come into it. It is rather an exploratory essay in a kind of historical criticism – or perhaps better, a sociology of literature – which involves current debates about literature and its social relations, and which takes Hardy as an empirical focus or case-study. It alludes to such questions as: what constitutes received and naturalized notions of 'Literature'; how and why is 'Literature' read and valued in the ways it commonly is; what is its place and function within our culture generally and, more particularly, within the education of its members; what are the strategies and effects of a professional literary criticism in these contexts; and what has been the impact on Literature and literary criticism of recent developments in cultural and critical theory. At its centre lies a challenge to the orthodoxies of 'literary value', the 'canon' and 'tradition' of 'Literature'; to the place of author, text, and textual analysis which underpin these concepts, and which so limit our cultural perspectives. The book does not do this by way of extensive theoretical expositions; but rather, by exemplifying their implications in an empirical methodology applied to a specific body of writings: Hardy's fiction, and the cultural accretions which effectively are now a part of its fabric.

Why, then, Thomas Hardy? Why take a single late nineteenth-century author who is an established constituent of the canon of English Literature? Does this not in itself reinforce the accepted tradition and practice of literary studies? And even if this book were to be a radical re-reading of Hardy's fiction – at once rejecting the critical stereotype of the tragic annalist of human nature at work in rural Wessex, and critical practices which mine 'the text in itself' for its essential meaning and unique value – what would be the point of studying Hardy in this way in the 1980s? Would we, for instance, be regarding his work as a historical source for better understanding the ideological contradictions of late nineteenth-century society and culture? But if so, why look at Hardy, and not at other documents – literary and non-literary – from that period? Would there still be some special value inherent in Hardy's work which distinguishes it from all other documents? And would not that then return us – despite all the initiatives of marxist, structuralist, post-structuralist, and deconstructionist theory and practice – to a notion of a 'metaphysics of the text', to the hierarchies of 'literary value', and to the great trans-historical 'genius' of the author?

The answers to these questions, this book proposes, lie in the empirical, but theory-informed, reshaping of the study of a writer *in history*. It attempts to provide in detailed terms what Terry Eagleton in his book on Walter Benjamin has called a 'revolutionary criticism': one which elucidates the historical processes of the production and reproduction of meaning, status, and value in the specific case of a writer who is both an established 'classic' and widely read now in our own historical period. Eagleton, too, observes the

> process whereby a certain set of texts are grouped, constructed, and endowed with the 'coherency' of a 'readable' *oeuvre*.
> 'Thomas Hardy' denotes that set of ideological practices through which certain texts, by virtue of their changing, contradictory modes of insertion into the dominant 'cultural' and pedagogical apparatuses, are processed, 'corrected' and reconstituted so that a home may be found for them within a literary 'tradition' that is always the 'imaginary' unity of the present.

And Eagleton also, as this book will confirm, sees the process for Hardy as one of 'struggle, outrage, and exasperation', marked by all the contradictions of his being 'a major realist' who is also 'scandalously nonchalant about the "purity" of orthodox verisimilitude, risking "coincidence" and "improbability"'; a writer who 'with blunt disregard for formal consistency . . . articulate[s] form upon form', and who has had 'a profoundly unnerving effect upon the dominant critical ideologies'.[2] To put it oversimply for the moment, a 'revolutionary criticism' replaces writers not in their period history, but in the history which has carried them down to us in the present as 'readable' and 'profitably' readable.

Hardy is an especially good case. He is extensively read by the general public and widely studied on the secondary and tertiary education syllabuses (indeed, he seems to be the current favourite, among students, of the 'modern classics'). His life and work is widely reproduced by the publishing and tourist industries, and by radio, television, and film. As the 'poet of Wessex', he is a figure who transcends the boundaries of literary discourse and has become, like Shakespeare and Dickens, a component of the national cultural heritage. But he is also a 'world writer': translated into many languages; widely read in France and Japan; on the education syllabus wherever English Literature is taught; part, indeed, of English cultural imperialism (nineteenth-century novels, and especially Hardy, have been very popular in India for example, where they were originally deployed as 'useful tools for extending the imperialist ideology').[3] He has had a chequered critical history (a 'genius' riddled with 'flaws') in which it is possible to perceive the complex processes of construction by which a writer is shaped and appropriated for the canon. And finally, for me personally, but also, I presume, for many other readers, his work is so resistant to simple explanation, in form and effect, that it remains to be engaged with in any understanding both of its own historical conjuncture and its contemporary 'readability'. In other words, 'Thomas Hardy' is a cultural figure of the present: a figure who has already been constituted and appropriated for many readers and students but one who needs to be explained and (possibly) recuperated: at the very least, we need to know the reasons (and purposes behind) why we rate this particular figure so highly. A single author of this kind allows access, in an empirical and palpable form, to the processes which go to the making of 'Literature' and 'literary value', to the creation of a 'great author' in the treasury of the nation's culture; but it also offers an arena in which to combat and demystify other related critical, cultural, and ideological practices. 'Thomas Hardy' has been produced and reproduced in history in a certain guise and for certain purposes by the dominant cultural apparatuses – not, of course, consciously and conspiratorially, but in the silent and naturalizing processes which tirelessly confront us with the images of human life and experience we genuinely believe to be true. This book attempts to deconstruct some of these processes – in part to expose their workings, but also to reveal how, paradoxically, the very fact that their practices are shown to be artificial legitimizes other reproductions of Hardy in different guises and for different purposes.

I wish, then, to present 'Thomas Hardy' as a cultural figure in the late twentieth century, as well as of the late nineteenth century. In order to do this, the first half of the book offers what I shall call a *critiography* of the main constitutive discourses within which 'Hardy the novelist' is produced and reproduced in the period between his present and our present. This is to show how meanings and evaluations are constructed on a writer's works and are not intrinsically and determinately contained in them; to show how variable they may, therefore, be and how they depend on tacit assumptions about the nature, social place, and function of 'Literature' and literary criticism; and to show how these assumptions are historically and ideologically determined. First of all, I consider the way in which Hardy has been shaped by criticism, both by the early reviewing of his novels and later by academic criticism. In each case, of course, this discourse affects the accessibility of his texts by deciding which is important and which insignificant; and, by way of its unspoken presuppositions about what comprises 'good' and 'bad' fiction, establishes the parameters within which texts may be read, understood, and appreciated. I shall examine some of the reasons behind the relegation of nearly half of Hardy's fiction to the status of 'minor novels'; and in this context I shall glance at the effects of this critical process on the publishing of Hardy's works, and also, conversely, at how far publishing interests themselves determine the reception and comprehension of a writer's production. In addition, I will offer a specific critiographical case-study of the way Hardy has been formed and canonized as the supreme literary celebrant of 'rural England', and thence incorporated as a central figure in the ideological discourse of 'the national culture'. Second, I will survey the place of Hardy in education where criticism reproduces itself and the texts it favours as 'the syllabus', and where both the literature selected for study and the associated pedagogic and critical practices are naturalized – the locus, in fact, in which the social construction and appropriation of 'Thomas Hardy' is most dynamic. Finally in Part I, I shall consider the reproduction of Hardy by the media – most particularly in television and film versions – for it is here, after all, that many people will first be exposed to Hardy's 'works', and may well learn to read them later in book form only because of, and already predetermined by, that initial visual reproduction. (We might say, for instance, that in the 1980s *Tess of the d'Urbervilles* is indelibly intertextually inscribed by Polanski's film, *Tess*.) I want to suggest, in these ways, that Hardy's work in the 1980s only exists as 'meaning' within the weave of this complex pattern of interrelated determinants.

In the second part of the book, having exposed the fabric of Hardy's constitution as a 'great writer', I attempt to release him from the discursive set in which he is constrained. This involves the 'reading' of texts which are not normally regarded as his major fiction, and starts with what I want to suggest is Hardy's last completed novel, *The Life of Thomas Hardy* by Florence Emily Hardy – ostensibly a biography written by his second wife but in fact written by Hardy himself in old age and passed off after his death as the definitive account of his life by someone who knew him intimately. By way of this reading it is possible to reveal another Hardy – one for whom social class and class relations, for example, were of obsessive interest and significance. From there, it is only a short step to recuperating the 'minor' and vilified novel *The Hand of Ethelberta*, which in some senses may be regarded as the 'true' 'Life of Thomas Hardy' and a novel in which the fictiveness of a class society and of realist fiction are counterpointed in a deeply alienated discourse. And thence, in the final chapter of the book, I hope to point to the implications of this process for literary study in general, and for Hardy in particular, by proposing the production of a different Hardy – I shall briefly reconsider novels like *Tess of the d'Urbervilles*, freed of the circumscriptions imposed by being the 'great work' of 'Thomas Hardy' and reorientated by the indicative case of the so-called 'minor novel', *The Hand of Ethelberta*. *Tess*, in other words, is reconstructed in my critical discourse as a novel permeated by the issue of class and gender relations, and in which the so-called 'faults' and 'flaws' of Hardy's writing rejoin the substantive discourse of the novel as indices of an attempt to fracture the illusions of a common-sense humanist realism which obscures the contradictions and tensions of a system where people 'pay' with their lives for inequality, prejudice, and injustice. No longer, then, can *Tess* be seen as an elegy for rural innocence, but instead as the product of a fiercely alienated consciousness. This process of deconstituting the naturalized 'Hardy' enables us, first, to perceive the (unadmitted) partiality of the factors involved in his constitution, and then to offer an openly and unequivocally *partial* version of his work in its place – a version which admits that Hardy's 'meaning' for the reader/critic of the 1980s is a reflex of an active participation in her or his own historical conjuncture. And recognizing the processes involved in constructing social consciousness – even by way of a literary education – is one centrally important aspect of that participation.

But this book is neither a blueprint for 'how to study Hardy' nor a draft syllabus, although it could be used to those ends. It is rather an attempt to explore, explicitly and in full view of the student, the social implications of 'Literature' and of studying it. In this sense it suggests a trajectory well beyond 'English' or 'Literary Studies', with their primary interest in authors and texts and the education of their reading subjects. In itself, of course, this short book can only touch on the sociological dimensions as they bear most directly on the literary domain and the individual subjects ('common readers', critics, and students) interpellated within it. But literature, for all its problematic status in a late twentieth-century society in which other media are the dominant cultural forms, remains a crucial factor in the hierarchization of social relations (literacy, 'literary competence', 'taste', 'cultivation', examination success, are all social markers). And the exposure of its social meanings as an institution is just as – if not more – important than the reappropriation of particular texts and writers by radical re-readings of them. Yes, I may conclude that *The Hand of Ethelberta* is as 'significant' as *Tess*, and *Tess* may indeed be remade as a new novel in the perspective of the 1980s; I might even claim that MY('different')TH is a preferable reproduction. But that is not really what the present book is about.

Part I

Making 'Thomas Hardy':
A Critiography

1

The critical constitution of 'Thomas Hardy'

What is a critiography?

'Historical criticism' is neither a common nor a precise concept. It might be, but is not, criticism which dates from an earlier historical period; nor is it a form of analysis of written history. Neither is it necessarily, although it might sometimes appear to be so, a materialist, not to say marxist, criticism hiding behind a less provocative title in a time of right-wing offensives against the ideologically unsound, especially within education. Most recognizably and simply, perhaps, it defines a kind of literary criticism which favours a sense of history in the study of literature, in contradistinction to more formalistic or philosophical approaches. But even so, this definition would include several different kinds of critical enterprise. First, there are those now long-established studies of 'literature, life, and thought' or 'literature and its social background' which seek to sketch in the general social and cultural 'context' within which literary works were produced and within which, it seems to follow, they can best be understood. Second, there is an older, often marxist, form of criticism which reads literature as an expression of the history of the period of its production. Third, there is an empirical sociology of literature which assembles the social facts of literary production in the writer's period – printing and publishing, audiences and readerships, forms of patronage, and so on. And fourth, there is a more recent and radical 'sociology of literature', better known perhaps as marxist/structuralist criticism, which seeks to theorize the social relations of literary texts, finding in them inscriptions of the ideological matrix in which they were produced, these 'marks' then offering a unique and defamiliarizing perspective on Ideology.

Now each of these studies of 'literature in history' – whether bourgeois or marxist, and leaving aside their own inherent problematics – has two related features in common: they are concerned with the original production of the text; and they tend to

11

take for granted the primacy of the 'primary material', literature, as though this exists objectively and independently of the attention criticism pays to it. (We all construct our bibliographies with the texts sectionally privileged as 'primary sources'.) In comparison to History, 'Literary Studies' have been naïve, or disingenuous, to a degree. They lack what I want to call, on the analogy of historiography, a *critiography*. Now it may be argued that the 'history and theory of literary criticism' is Literary Studies' equivalent, but I mean rather more than the academic process of historicizing, demarcating, and challenging different schools of criticism in different periods – necessary and hygienic as this is. I mean, first, the extrinsic study of the discipline itself – its history, its institutions, its practices, its theoretical premises, and its social relations (what is the place and function of the criticism and teaching of literature in the 1980s; what is its 'politics'?). And second, I mean a consciousness of the constitution of the material which criticism takes as 'primary': literary texts – the 'facts', if I may for a moment appropriate the word, of Literary Studies. But it is here that criticism – however 'historical' it may be – can and should learn a salutary lesson from historiography, which recognizes that its 'facts' – the documents, the primary sources, 'the Past' – are not permanent and palpable, but are constituted in the process of writing history; that they are discovered, selected, suppressed, interpreted, produced, and reproduced by historians who are themselves historical and political subjects interpellated into certain subject positions in a particular historical conjuncture – 'the Present'. E. H. Carr's still sharply corrective book *What is History?* (1961) is helpful here. He reminds us:

(i) that 'the facts speak only when the historian calls on them: it is he who decides to which facts to give the floor, and in what order or context';[1]

(ii) to 'study the historian before you begin to study the facts' (23), because the historian 'is also a social phenomenon, both the product and the conscious or unconscious spokesman of the society to which he belongs; it is in this capacity that he approaches the facts of the historical past'. (35)

This results, of course, in 'some measure of interpretation' and in the making of 'value judgements' (79):

the abstract standard or value, divorced from society and divorced from history, is as much an illusion as the abstract individual. The serious historian is the one who recognises the historically-conditioned character of all values, not the one who claims for his own values an objectivity beyond history. (84)

(Such a perception of the historically-determined nature of 'value' would be an encouraging sign in many a 'serious' literary critic.) What Carr thus recognizes is that, as 'the historian has no excuse to think of himself as a detached individual standing outside society and outside history . . . [he] *can and should know what he is doing*' (139, my italics); which, for Carr, is 'to master and understand [the Past] as the key to the understanding of the present' (26). Historians, in other words, quite literally *write* History, constituting it in those discourses which are available to them, and in which they can 'realize' the past in order to understand, and hence shape, the present and the future. This, let us be clear, is a *political* activity; and History, because of its apparent closeness to the domain of the politically 'real', has more fully recognized its political function than criticism, which has tended to claim for itself the ideologically inno-cent activity of reading its 'natural' primary material, 'the literary text in itself', for its intrinsic, 'abstract' value, 'divorced from history'.

But what is, I hope, already clear is the consonance between history and criticism as regards a problematical 'primary material' – the difference being the absence of a critiography which confronts the partiality of critical practice. Extrapolating from Carr's historio-graphy, however, we can readily see that 'Literature' is constituted by criticism (and other related social processes), as much as 'the Past' is by history. Literary-critical notions of canons and traditions of great literature; of inherent meanings and intrinsic value; of hier-archies of major and minor, classic and popular, texts and writers; of evaluations and discriminations of acceptable and unacceptable works within or between writers' *oeuvres*; of objective readings and definitive interpretations and editions – all these are historically determined and historically variable. The critic, too, is a 'social phenomenon' who selects and organizes the facts/texts according to his/her positioning in history: who (pre-eminently) makes 'value judgements'; who, in effect, 'writes' Literature from the perspective of a historical and ideological present. As with a 'historical fact', the 'primary text' is continually reconstituted by the historically chang-ing critical attention paid to it. Neither the moment of production nor the text itself is ontologically stable, ultimately explanative, or definitive. Its 'meanings' lie not within the text, nor within past history, but in the determinate and changing sets of discursive and social relations in which they are continually reproduced in present history.

In his essay, 'Text and history', Tony Bennett clarifies positions he outlined in *Formalism and Marxism* (1979), and it is interesting to notice how similar his remarks on the literary text are to Carr's

on the historical fact. He points out how both bourgeois interpretative and structuralist criticism have succumbed to 'the seductive
facticity of the text', and how marxist criticism has done the same
by its concern with the 'conditions of production'. All, however,
have 'fetishise[d] [the text] in abstracting it from the concrete and
historically varying relationships in which it is inscribed during the
successive moments of its history as a culturally active, received
text'. He adds:

> A condition of any text's continuing to exert long-term cultural
> effects within any society must be that it is constantly brought into
> connection or articulated with new texts, socially and politically
> mobilised in different ways within different class practices or
> educational, cultural and linguistic institutions and so on . . . It is
> only in the light of such historically concrete, variable and
> incessantly changing determinations – determinations which so
> press in upon the text as fundamentally to modify its very mode
> of being – that it is possible to assess, at any given moment, the
> effects that might be attributed to any given text or set of texts.[2]

Drawing on Derrida, Bennett suggests that a text's 'iterability' (its
capacity to be constantly 're-read' and 're-written', with 'diverse
meanings' and 'plural effects' beyond 'any particular set of author-
reader relations' (226–7)) proscribes any notion of intrinsic meaning;
that a text and its meanings are produced in the process of its
consumption by variable historical readers in variable historical
conjunctures and, in particular, within the discourses of criticism and
education which 'especially since the nineteenth century . . . have
constituted a privileged site for the circulation of those texts which
have been regarded as of special value; that is as "literary" in a
specialised and restricted sense' (230). This *consciousness* of
literature as historically determined and variable, Bennett argues,
enables us to 'redetermine its connections with history' (235), to free
it from existing discourses and to mobilize it on behalf of the present
and the future. In recognizing the essentially political nature of the
critic's practice, this is not at all unlike Carr's perception of the role
of the historian, who 'can and should know what he is doing' and
what he is doing it for. Whether this does actually describe the
average critic in the 1980s is highly debatable – although the gender
pronoun there is significant. If instead of 'he', I had said 'she', then
an explicitly conscious, strategic function for criticism might not
now be in question: feminist critics (as well as feminist historians)
have, far beyond their male colleagues, deconstructed the myths of
abstract 'value' and apolitical 'objectivity' or 'disinterestedness' in
their respective subject areas.

I would propose, therefore, that if there is to be a 'historical criticism' which is genuinely historical and empirical, and which 'knows what it is doing and why', it must necessarily involve a conception of critiography. This means a study of texts *in history*; not merely as productions of their 'period', nor as receptacles of historical messages from that period which criticism decants, but as cultural productions of their long history since first appearing. A critiography, then, is a study of the process by which 'literature' becomes 'Literature' (just as historiography studies the process by which 'the past' becomes 'History'). That long process, and thence the received artefacts available to us in the 1980s, are inscribed by the incessant operation of reproducing literary texts as cultural meaning. And this meaning is only meaning*ful* when comprehended in its ideological location within society. 'Literature' is valued not because it is 'self-evidently' Literature and therefore good for us, but because it signifies values – values which have been ascribed to it in the course of its reception and reproduction in history. Reviewing, literary criticism, publishing, education, the advertising and tourist industries, adaptation into other media, are all *loci* in which this ascription of value goes on. So that to 'read' Hardy in the 1980s is to consume the product of these processes with all their material and ideological determinants embedded in it. 'Hardy' *means* (is reproduced as) what these processes and determinants have constructed him as. A critiography, therefore, studies the historical construction of this product as an essential prerequisite of understanding what it currently means, and of fashioning other meanings for it. In this respect, critiography must always precede criticism in order to establish the composition of the object of attention, for the notion of 'the text in itself' (as with the 'pure' historical fact) is a chimera. We can, in a sense, only study the discursive set in which it has meaning. This implies, of course, a displacement of the apparently neutral 'primary material' from the central focus in favour of the constitutive social discourses which make it available in a determinate form as a present cultural fact. It is for this reason that I have entitled my project a 'literary sociology', since it represents a more accurate description of the practice than the ambiguous term 'historical criticism'. Hardy's fiction (and I limit myself here to this genre only) is very much present in the 1980s – and it is present as the construct 'Thomas Hardy': that is, as a cultural phenomenon defined by its place, function, and parameters of intelligibility within the contemporary social formation. What one should immediately be forced to ask, therefore, is how 'Hardy' got here; which texts constitute 'Hardy'; what 'his' place in the social process may be; how those texts have been, and are, read; what, indeed, 'Hardy' means in our culture.

In the subsequent sections of this chapter, then, I offer an analysis of literary criticism as a major constitutive discourse in the making of 'Thomas Hardy', and in the following ones I fill out my critiography with other modes of production and reproduction which relate to this process. But for any writer of Hardy's stature criticism remains the primary shaping *locus*.

To 1914

To read straight through the *Critical Heritage* (1970) volume on Hardy is to be struck by the patterns, stereotypes, and commonplaces of criticism which accrete around his work in the course of his novel-writing career, and the strong sense that these remain, even now, as much a part of the construct 'Hardy' as the works themselves. A hint of this fusing of discourses is suggested unwittingly by R. G. Cox in his introduction to that volume, when he writes of the critical reception of Hardy's first published novel, *Desperate Remedies*: 'All the reviews agree in selecting for praise those parts of the novel which point forward to Hardy's most characteristic later work; their censure is directed against sensationalism and an over-complicated plot.'[3] Self-fulfilling prophecies! Cox is only able to perceive this 'agreement' because he too 'agrees' as to the 'most characteristic' features of Hardy's work. This shaping of the 'characteristic Hardy' as an acceptable 'great writer' takes two major forms: one, the discrimination of 'the excellent' (and therefore 'the characteristic') in his work (and the rejection consequently of that which is not as 'faults' and 'flaws'); and two, the ranking of the works into categories of 'major' and 'minor' importance, which means the excision of the latter from the canon and the syllabus. These processes, though naturalized, are by no means natural; so we must ask: what features are conceived to be good or bad, and why?

The rapidly established positive commonplaces about Hardy's work in his own lifetime are strikingly familiar. These are his descriptions of 'peasant life' and his 'Shakespearian' rustic characters (see below, pp. 58–66); his creation of the myth of 'Wessex'; his description and deployment of the natural environment; his nostalgia for a passing rural world; his poetic style; his 'Greek' conception of tragedy, tragic characters, and Fate ('the dramas themselves have an elemental largeness which befits their background. They are tense and simple, like the dramas of Sophocles.');[4] and the 'universal' significance of his characters and settings. This is, of course, the Hardy of the 'novels of character and environment', and it is worth remembering that this is his own designation – in the General Preface to the 'Wessex Edition' of his works in 1912 (of which more below, pp. 48–9) – of certain of his novels, in contradistinction to others defined as 'romances', 'fantasies', 'novels of ingenuity', and 'experiments' (like *The Hand of Ethelberta*). Hardy, in other words, himself encourages the categorization of his work and the establishment of a selective 'canon'; his emphasis may only echo the reviewers' discriminations and rankings hitherto, but it also helps to reinforce them. By 1914, for example, Harold Williams in a long survey article for the *North American Review*, 'The Wessex novels of Thomas Hardy', had already appropriated Hardy's terms as his own. Having confidently established that 'the signal and final test of genius in the writer of fiction' lies in 'two faculties . . . the gift of visualizing characters who belong to the real world . . . and the power of placing them in an (appropriate) environment', he continues, as though Hardy had never written the General Preface, 'if we begin to measure Mr. Hardy's novels by this standard, the necessity of uncompromising differentiation becomes apparent'; he distinguishes 'five novels, in which the author keeps himself to life on the soil of Wessex, [which] stand in a distinctive place above Mr. Hardy's other books; they are *Far From the Madding Crowd*, *The Return of the Native*, *The Mayor of Casterbridge*, *The Woodlanders* and *Tess of the d'Urbervilles*'.[5] Reinstate *Jude the Obscure* and we have the novels dealt with by Ian Gregor in *The Great Web* in 1974 as 'Hardy's major fiction', and indeed the core works in most other assessments of his achievement.

The 'characteristic' faults or flaws in Hardy's work were again rapidly established by the reviewers: violent sensationalism; artificiality of plot ('are they the faithful rendering of real events taking place from time to time in the South Western counties, or are they not imaginary creations?');[6] chance and coincidence; 'melodrama' ('inevitably repugnant to our sense of the probable');[7] 'flat' and unconvincing characterization; awkwardness and pedantry of style ('the imperfect digestion of certain modern science and philosophy [which] could not more potently destroy our illusions if they were steam whistles');[8] 'fashionable pessimism' or 'gloom';[9] didacticism (or 'ideas'); and Hardy's attempts to write about any society other than rural 'Wessex'. Fundamentally, these are all reflexes of a dominant – but unspoken – predilection for a realism defined by notions of 'plausibility', 'probability', 'conviction', 'credibility', and 'naturalness'. Indeed the frequency with which the words 'probable/improbable' occur in Hardy criticism (and elsewhere) encourages coinage of the term 'probablism' for the orthodox critical discourse of realism against which Hardy is measured. (Notice above the critics' 'inevitable repugnance' for the improbable, the serious anxiety about 'the faithful rendering of real events', the obtrusive style which 'potently destroys our illusion'.) But what is interesting is how the critics deal with these 'faults' so that the disturbance they cause can be 'written out' of the construct 'Thomas Hardy', just as, as I shall indicate later in this chapter, the 'minor novels' are excised from the canon because they challenge its organic coherence. *Tess* is a good example, in so far as, for many late nineteenth-century critics, it is the last of Hardy's great 'tragic' novels, while already evincing the tendentiousness which was to make *Jude* a disastrous failure ('the worst novel he has ever written', L. W. Phelps wrote in 1910).[10] Edward Wright in 1904 makes a significant comparison with George Eliot (a matter I shall return to): he finds *Tess* more tragic than *Adam Bede*, but

> George Eliot's story is more simple, more natural and far more probable. If her fault is want of Art, Mr. Hardy's is artificiality. Too much machinery is employed in *Tess* to bring about the catastrophe; and in the latter part of the tale especially, disaster follows disaster in so close and yet disconnected a manner that all sense of verisimilitude is destroyed.

Equally, Hardy 'was unable, in creating his characters, to preserve the balance and the general truth to nature which is found in *Adam Bede*', these being of such 'nefarious or brutal, vicious, weak, or scornful natures' that the credulity of the most sympathetic reader is 'dispelled'.[11] And Harold Williams, in 1914, justifies the inclusion of *Tess* in *his* 'Hardy' by acknowledging that it is flawed – 'its worst faults lie in the author's obvious didacticism'; but since questions of a writer's 'philosophy' have 'nothing to do with our judgment of imaginative writing', it can still be claimed as a great 'work of art'. In effect, he excises the whole intransigent dimension of Hardy's 'pessimism' because it does not fit his conception of a romantic-humanist Hardy opposing the 'old wisdom' of the rural world to the 'desolating influences' of 'modern civilization'. Indeed, a quotation from Williams's essay may serve as a fair synthesis of the critical consensus which constitutes 'Hardy' by 1914:

> The scene is laid in a secluded agricultural country where the noise of the great industrial centres hardly comes as a distant murmur, the characters belong to the simplicity of an older and less sophisticated world than most of us are condemned to live in; but in these novels life is greater, nobler, more tragic, more fraught with tremendous issues . . . Whatever may be the limitations of Mr. Hardy's insight . . . or the improbability of plot

in his minor books, he can claim to have invested the tragedy of the individual with a note of universal significance as only the great masters have done. . . . That the individual existence is 'rounded with a sleep' is less to Mr. Hardy than the knowledge that the essential elements of human life and character are not mortal; they endure unchangeably through the centuries.[12]

Williams's stance, of course, is that of the Victorian liberal-humanist opposition to industrialization and urbanization which was to continue into the twentieth century with, amongst others, D. H. Lawrence and F. R. Leavis at its head, and which a later Williams, not entirely free of it himself, was to call the 'Culture and Society' tradition. Whether Hardy is part of it is more problematical than Harold Williams's critically processed 'Hardy' would allow, but to produce this model at all it was necessary to discard his 'philosophy' – a good proportion of his work – and to suppress those aspects of his 'true achievement' which might put it in question.

It is worth pausing here to pick up one specific element in this nineteenth-century construction of 'Hardy', so that I can return to it later in discussing Leavis and other twentieth-century critics: that is, the relation in criticism between Hardy and George Eliot. From the beginning, George Eliot is invoked in reviews of Hardy's novels: there is a passing reference in the *Saturday Review* notice of *Desperate Remedies*, and *Under the Greenwood Tree*, with its sub-title, was immediately seen as rivalling 'the most admirable rustic pieces of George Eliot herself'.[13] With *A Pair of Blue Eyes* the comparisons develop further, although discriminations of real difference begin to emerge. But it is with the serial publication of *Far From the Madding Crowd* in 1874 in the *Cornhill* magazine that the comparisons climax – the *Spectator*, for example, suggests that the novel might be by George Eliot herself. Others disagreed: *The Times* thought it good, while suspecting conscious or unconscious imitation of Eliot, but the *Athenaeum* 'cannot conceive' how it 'could ever have been supposed to be written by George Eliot . . . we should say, on the contrary, that some of the scenes . . . are worthy, in their extravagance, of Mr. Reade', thus first drawing attention to 'improbablism' as an aspect of Hardy's unlikeness to Eliot. The *Westminster Review*, while finding Hardy her equal in the rustic scenes and in the character of Gabriel Oak (especially in comparison with Adam Bede), also criticizes the novel for its 'sensationalism' and decides that Hardy 'has not reached the splendid heights which George Eliot has attained, nor sounded her spiritual depths'. R. H. Hutton in the *Spectator* (after the book publication), and a major proponent of 'probablism' throughout his reviewing, asks if Hardy's

descriptions are 'trustworthy', notes his 'incredible' picture of the
farm labourers, and sharply distinguishes him from George Eliot –
one passage striking Hutton 'as in the nature of a careful caricature'
of her: a perception which points unwittingly, as we shall see later,
to a real and unsettling possibility in the dynamics of Hardy's
fiction. But perhaps the most famous (and influential) critical
comparison of the two novelists is Henry James's review of *Far
From the Madding Crowd* in the *Nation*. James immediately suggests
that Hardy is imitating Eliot and is found wanting – capable only of
'cleverness' which is a sign of 'the difference between original and
imitative talent'. In particular, it is Hardy's lack of 'reality' and
'humanity' (those pre-eminently Eliotean virtues in humanist realism)
which damn him:

> this is Mr. Hardy's trouble; he rarely gets beyond ambitious
> artifice – the mechanical simulation of heat and depth and wisdom
> that are absent. . . . Everything human in the book strikes us as
> factitious and insubstantial; the only things we believe in are the
> sheep and the dogs. But, as we say, Mr. Hardy has gone astray
> very cleverly, and his superficial novel is really curious imitation
> of something better.[14]

The 'something better' is, of course, George Eliot: her presence as
the ultimate touchstone broods behind the entire review, and there is
no sense that Hardy's 'ambitious artifice' might be not imitatively
worse than, but strategically different to Eliot's practice. Indeed, it
will be worth considering later how far James influences F. R.
Leavis's total exclusion of Hardy from his 'great tradition' of
English fiction, in which, of course, 'reality' and 'humanity' –
exemplified most fully in the novels of James and Eliot – are crucial
concepts.

As Hardy's career progressed, his negative ranking with George
Eliot diminished, so that by 1881, in a survey article in the *British
Quarterly Review*, he is seen as having taken 'the falling mantle' of
'greatest living novelist' after Eliot's death. Significantly, this appears
to be because he has joined that select band (Shakespeare, Fielding,
Richardson, 'Miss Burney, perhaps', Scott, Jane Austen, Dickens,
Thackeray, Eliot) who have 'the power of creating personages which
live, and become even more real than many historic phantasms'.
Such a selective realist-humanist emphasis on 'character' (together
with the 'rural idyll' and other 'characteristic' Hardy virtues) enables
this serious non-conformist periodical reviewer to ignore all the
controversial religious and moral aspects of Hardy's fiction up to
that point, and find 'his whole influence . . . pure, ennobling and
gracious'. He hopes more people will 'steep themselves in the fresh

healthy air of Dorset, and come into contact with the kindly folk who dwell there, through these pages'.[15] Other critics began to discern the dissimilarities between the two novelists – positively or negatively; although it is worth noting that George Eliot's 'humanity' and humanism remain a touchstone for Hardy's deeper pessimism. Edward Wright, for example, thought that in *Jude the Obscure* Hardy was saying that 'the travail of the whole human race, of the whole world, leads in the end to nothing; duty, morality and life itself . . . are nothing',[16] and, as we saw earlier, he critically compared *Tess* with *Adam Bede* in terms of the former's 'artificiality'. In this, he more or less recognizes the consonance of anti-humanism and non-realism as the 'problem' in Hardy's work.

Hardy's own response – one of considerable irritation – to this emphatic comparison of his work with George Eliot's is interesting. It reveals itself in an odd, pawky little paragraph in 'Florence Emily's' *The Life of Thomas Hardy*:

> In the first week of January 1874 the story was noticed in a marked degree by the *Spectator*, and a guess hazarded that it might be from the pen of George Eliot – why, the author could never understand, since, so far as he had read that great thinker – one of the greatest living, he thought, though not a born storyteller by any means – she had never touched the life of the fields: her country-people having seemed to him, too, more like small townsfolk than rustics; and as evidencing a woman's wit cast in country dialogue rather than real country humour, which he regarded as rather of the Shakespeare and Fielding sort. However, he conjectured, as a possible reason for the flattering guess, that he had latterly been reading Comte's *Positive Philosophy*, and writings of that school, some of whose expressions had thus passed into his vocabulary, expressions which were also common to George Eliot.[17]

It is also apparent in the suggestion – happily and continually taken up by critics – that he wrote his next published novel, *The Hand of Ethelberta*, on the rebound from the reception of *Far From the Madding Crowd*; which, *The Life* says, 'had nothing whatever in common with anything he had written before', and which gave him 'the satisfaction of proving, amid the general disappointment at the lack of sheep and shepherds, that he did not mean to imitate anybody'.[18] In fact, as we shall see later, *Ethelberta* has a great deal 'in common' with other of his writings, and his tone and vocabulary here suggest that he has James's review in mind while writing this passage (over forty years later). The fact that he wrote

Ethelberta immediately after *Far From the Madding Crowd* – in part
to 'prove' how dissimilar his work was to that of George Eliot –
suggests that *Ethelberta* should be afforded a more significant place
in the comprehension of Hardy's fiction than merely being dismissed
as an impetuous deviation from his 'characteristic' line, and it might
also direct us to just how overtly conscious was Hardy's reaction to
Eliot's work. If he were, indeed, setting his face against both realism
('reality') and humanism ('humanity'), then it would begin to explain
his reconstruction by nineteenth-century criticism in the terms we
have seen above; his later exclusion from 'the great tradition'; and
his partial, pruned, and uneasy status as a tragic modern master in
the canons of other critics.

In this context, and before moving on to the critical reproduction of
Hardy in the twentieth century, it is worth noting that there were
some dissonant voices in nineteenth-century reviewing of Hardy's
work who directed attention towards different aspects of it. Havelock
Ellis, for example, in two essays (1883, 1896) and amid many
commonplace judgements, perceives Hardy's obsession with the
nature of women, his concern to render the psychic in physical
terms, and his fierce irony. He also observes that despite the 'facile
brilliance' of *Ethelberta*, Hardy seems 'to have devoted more
elaboration to her than to any other of his heroines' (except Eustacia
Vye); and he regards *Jude* as a great novel, one which may well be
a 'farce', but a farce used for a truly serious purpose.[19] Or again,
there is the anonymous reviewer in the *Saturday Review* (1896) who
values *Jude* as follows:

> For the first time in English literature the almost intolerable
> difficulties that beset an ambitious man of the working class – the
> snares, the obstacles, the countless rejections and humiliations by
> which our society eludes the services of these volunteers – receive
> adequate treatment.

The same reviewer recognizes the 'reality' of *Jude*'s autodidacticism
and launches a scathing attack on the British higher education
system:

> It is impossible by scrappy quotations to do justice to Mr. Hardy's
> tremendous indictment of the system which closes our three
> English teaching Universities to what is, and what has always
> been, the noblest material in the intellectual life of this country –
> the untaught.[20]

Even more interesting, perhaps, is the first 'survey' review of
Hardy's work to date in the *New Quarterly Magazine* of 1879, and

which, in effect, has as a theme its ambiguity and uncertainty of direction. It is significant that this perceptive reviewer, writing at a point before Hardy's career as a novelist was half over and before criticism had established an orthodox formulation for it, was able to enunciate features of his fiction which are largely occluded later: problems about class in *A Pair of Blue Eyes*; Hardy's 'genius' as 'gothic in expression'; his obsessive and ambiguous fascination with women; the irrelevance of 'probablism' as a measure of Hardy's fiction; the sense, most tellingly, that he 'not only cannot be compared with other writers, but cannot be classified under any known formula of literary art'.[21]

Such perceptions – of Hardy's interest in class, sexuality, education, 'consciousness', and non-realist modes of presentation – are absent, of course, from the established 'Thomas Hardy', and we may ask why they receive so little attention in the process of constituting him. The answer, again, alludes to the 'realism/humanism' problematic, and to the fact that significant elements of Hardy's writing simply will not fit ('cannot be classified under any known formula of literary art'). In other words, his work – unmanipulated or recuperated by criticism – subverts the realist-humanist enterprise, challenges and destabilizes it. For realism, as we shall see later, is not merely a literary mode but a crucial representation of bourgeois individualism, and any disturbance of the realist discourse implies a disturbance of its informing liberal-humanist ideology. An early hint of this – and an index of why Hardy had to be 'rewritten' by criticism to protect the realist/humanist ideo-aesthetic – is offered in a curiously obsessive review by Frederic Manning in the *Spectator* in 1912, after Hardy's General Preface to the 'Wessex Edition' had appeared. The whole purport of it – despite, or perhaps because of, Manning's admiration for Hardy's 'greatness' – is to attack the central 'flaw' in his work: its didacticism and moral pessimism, or anti-humanism. The review is a sophisticated synthesis of long-standing elements in Hardy criticism, and it brings into sharp relief the correlation between the ideology of humanist individualism and 'artistic truth'. Manning states at one point:

> Whether the notion of ourselves which we have gained from experience in practical affairs be true or false, it is at least sufficiently true to say that we regard ourselves as active agents to whom is allowed a certain freedom of choice, and upon whom ultimately falls the sole responsibility for the choice. Possibly this notion of ourselves may be an illusion, but it is an illusion which life compels us to accept.

It is the *illusion* of freedom which Manning wishes to retain, and it is this that Hardy jeopardizes. So that, for Manning, *Tess* and *Jude*, though remarkable when 'considered purely as works of art', are not his 'best novels'. They are too singularly focused on one aspect of life; after quoting a 'fatalistic' passage from *Tess*, Manning comments:

> thus to shift the responsibility for the catastrophe to God, or Nature, or Fate, or Chance, is a fault in art. The passage may be admirable as a criticism of life, or as an expression of feeling; but it destroys the illusions of an individual will and of individual activity. Sympathy is not regulated by any considerations of justice, of which it is quite independent; but we do require that the person or character with whom we are asked to sympathize should be a responsible agent.

This then leads him to regard *The Return of the Native* as 'more complete as a representation of life' because it has more 'human warmth', and he adds:

> It is by this intuitive sympathy with humanity in all its moods that Mr. Hardy is great. His pessimism, after all, is only a habit of thought, a weariness with life that comes upon all of us sometimes, if it does not remain with us always; and that, too, springs from his sympathy with mankind, from the depth and richness of his emotional nature.[22]

What Manning in fact perceives is the way Hardy's work undermines his own world view, and he neutralizes this, in 'artistic' terms, by elevating *The Return of the Native* and *The Mayor of Casterbridge* over *Tess* and *Jude*. It is a reaction and a process which has been repeated many times since.

To the present

By the First World War, then, we can see that 'Hardy' is already cast as a great modern tragic humanist and rural annalist, flawed by perverse tendencies, but whose five or six major 'novels of character and environment' represent his 'true' achievement. It is a 'Hardy', I suggest, who is reproduced time and again, with subtle variations, in teaching, criticism, journalism, and other discourses right up to the present. I cannot, of course, chart the entire post-First World War map of Hardy criticism, but I will sketch in some lines here (and below, pp. 58–72) to substantiate the general point.

Let me start with what may appear too much of a sitting duck, but which remains a highly influential text: Lord David Cecil's *Hardy the Novelist* (1943). Cecil reproduces more or less exactly the late nineteenth-century version of Hardy, admiring all the same qualities (he is 'built on the grand Shakespearian scale'),[23] and recognizing that though a 'great writer' he is also a 'faulty writer' (111). The 'faults' are precisely those I have noted above – pessimism, preaching, clumsy style, melodrama, coincidence, and so on – and the 'minor novels' are indisputably failures. 'Improbablism' is a major flaw: *Tess*, despite its greatness, is 'disastrously' marred by it – 'these crude pieces of machinery, tearing the delicate fabric of imaginative illusion in tatters' (116); and in *Jude*, Hardy 'breaks with probability altogether' (118). These faults, however, are insignificant in the light of Hardy's 'real' achievement, which is, of course, Cecil's own constitutive 'reading' or 'production' of Hardy: 'it is a tragic theme' (19); 'a struggle between man on the one hand and, on the other, an omnipotent and indifferent Fate – that is Hardy's interpretation of the human situation. . . . Man in Hardy's books is ranged against impersonal forces' (26); 'man's struggles as a political and social character seem too insignificant to fire his creative spark' (35);

> We are shown life in its fundamental elements, as exemplified by simple, elemental characters actuated by simple, elemental passions . . . And the fact that they are seen in relation to ultimate Destiny gives them a gigantic and universal character. Nor is the universality of this picture weakened by the fact that Hardy writes only of country people in nineteenth-century Wessex. On the contrary . . . concentrated in this narrow, sequestered form of life, basic facts of the human drama showed up at their strongest. (32)

Lest anyone believes that Cecil is now disregarded and that I am loading the odds in favour of my argument by elevating this *passé belles-lettrism* to representative status, let me point to the school examination questions adduced in the next chapter, behind many of which, even now, Cecil's ghostly presence lurks. The reason is not far to find: his book is still the single most recommended secondary reading in many contemporary student 'study guides'. For example, in Methuen's 'Study-Aids' (first published in 1971, but continually reprinted) it is the only substantial critical monograph in the 'suggested reading' section; in the Pan 'Revision Aids' series 'Brodie's Notes' (first published in 1977), and in the two Macmillan 'Master Guides' on Hardy so far available (first published in 1985 and 1986), it is still included in the short lists of 'further reading'. More generally, these 'study guides', in their recounting of the plot and their analysis of 'themes', 'characterization', and 'style' – however 'neutral' and 'descriptive' these may appear to be – have a substantial effect in reproducing 'Hardy' in conventional terms and in perpetuating the literary-critical and pedagogic praxis which underpins it.[24]

Cecil's 'elemental' tragedian of Fate and Nature, however, is somewhat displaced in the middle decades of the twentieth century by a Hardy who becomes the elegist of the passing rural 'organic community' of England – at its centre another profoundly and persistently influential book by Douglas Brown (*Thomas Hardy* (1954), see below, pp. 64–5).[25] Given this development, one of the strangest (and most negatively influential) phenomena in criticism is F. R. Leavis's almost total ignoring of Hardy, and his absolute rejection of him from *The Great Tradition* (1948). As Raymond Williams remarks in *Politics and Letters*, it is almost inconceivable 'why he should have adopted that particular tone towards Hardy': even Leavis's 'faulty formulations' – 'his emphasis on Englishness or on particular kinds of rural community – should at least have directed his attention towards Hardy, rather than excluding him from the very tradition in which they were being urged'. Williams's interviewer at this point suggests a sharp and pertinent solution to the puzzle: 'Isn't the answer that he must have felt very threatened by the radicalism of Hardy?' (on 'the realities of class and power' Hardy is more 'explosive' than D. H. Lawrence). And Williams himself picks this up: 'the explanation of the paradox is that Hardy is very disturbing for someone trying to rationalize refined, civilized, balancing judgement. Hardy exposes so much which cannot be displaced from its social situation, particularly in the later books.'[26] The discussion remains inconclusive in *Politics and Letters*; but Terry Eagleton has also suggested that Leavis (as part of 'a predominant critical strategy') 'writes him out' of the tradition of nineteenth-century realism because of his subversive implications. I will return later to what this 'radicalism' and 'subversion' may consist of, and why Leavis was 'threatened' by it, but first it is worth establishing just how strikingly little Leavis says about Hardy the novelist.[27]

There is, first of all, the significant substitution of Conrad for Hardy in the list of 'major instances' of 'the artist' between the publication of *Mass Civilization and Minority Culture* in 1930 and its reappearance in *Education and the University* (1943); there is a passing reference in *The Common Pursuit*; two insignificant mentions in *D. H. Lawrence/Novelist* (nothing on his *Study of Thomas Hardy*); and there are the two or three dismissive remarks in *The Great Tradition* itself. There Leavis, in denying Hardy's reputation as a 'great novelist', significantly confirms Henry James's famous judgement: 'The good little Thomas Hardy has scored a great success with *Tess of the d'Urbervilles*, which is chock-full of faults and falsity, and yet has a singular charm'; offers a back-handed accolade to *Jude*; and dismisses the early 1920s claim that Hardy is 'pre-eminently the representative of the "modern consciousness" or the modern "sense of the human situation"'. Later, at the end of his section on George Eliot, in talking about 'her rank among novelists', Leavis takes to task Oliver Elton. The latter, whilst discussing the '"check to George Eliot's reputation"' brought about by 'the coming into "fuller view" of "two other masters of fiction" – Meredith and Hardy', had criticized Eliot for restricted vision compared to theirs: '"one of her greatest deficiencies [is] that while exhaustively describing life, she is apt to miss the spirit of life itself."' Leavis comments:

> I can only say that this, for anyone whose critical education has begun, should be breath-taking in its absurdity, and affirm my conviction that, by the side of George Eliot – and the comparison shouldn't be necessary . . . Hardy, decent as he is, [appears] as a provincial manufacturer of gauche and heavy fictions that sometimes have corresponding virtues.

Hardy also, in comparison this time to Conrad, is not a novelist whose work is truly addressed to 'the adult mind'.[28]

That is all there is on Hardy in Leavis's writings about the English novel. By 1948, Hardy's work had been on the school curriculum for at least twenty years; *Tess* had been reprinted in England alone forty times between 1900 and 1930;[29] there was already a powerful body of criticism acclaiming Hardy's greatness in the terms we have noticed earlier – as lyrical and tragic annalist of the English rural community; Leavis himself would obviously have known of *Far From the Madding Crowd*'s early comparison with George Eliot (if only because of his interest in Henry James (cf. the latter's review quoted above p. 20)) and of Lawrence's *Study of Thomas Hardy* (which he refers to in *The Common Pursuit*)[30] written at the crucial point when Lawrence was beginning the work which became *The Rainbow* and *Women in Love* and which is a companion to it. But in effect Leavis ignores Hardy: there is silence rather than a substantial swingeing attack. I will return more fully to the possible reasons for this later, but for now we may merely remark that there is some connection between that silence and the crucial trio of 'the great tradition' (Eliot, James, and Lawrence), with Hardy's relationship to George Eliot at the centre of it. Leavis perhaps had to write Hardy out of 'the great tradition' because, in some way, he destabilized it and because he seemed to counter everything Eliot stood for. Hardy, indeed, may be seen as threatening Leavis's whole literary-ideological project (of which Eliot and Lawrence are the fullest expression), in which the vague but crucial notion of 'Life' is opposed to the deadly processes of a 'technologico-Benthamite' mass civilization by way of the concrete, experiential 'reality' of a literature which is the product of mature and discriminating intelligence playing over and evaluating empirical experience. But as Raymond Williams says, Hardy 'exposes so much' – both in content and in fictional form – which challenges and endangers the humanist-realist pastoral of Leavis's world view that he could not be shaped and recuperated – he had to 'disappear' in silence. Williams also confirms the centrality of *The Great Tradition* in mid-twentieth-century literary-critical discourse: 'by this time [late 1960s][31] . . . he had completely won. I mean if you talked to anyone about the English novel, including people who were hostile to Leavis, they were in fact reproducing his sense of the shape of its history.' It seems likely, if this is true, that one of the factors in the continuing uncertainty about Hardy's 'greatness', his 'flawed genius' and his uncomfortable place in the realist canon, has been Leavis's need to secure 'the great tradition' against the enemy within.

But as Leavis's influence waned, and the Hardy industry opened up in the 1960s and 1970s, the approaches to Hardy's fiction multiplied and diversified dramatically. Terry Eagleton, in his book on Walter Benjamin, offers his own highly compressed critiography of Hardy which parallels the lines of the analysis which follows here. (So, too, does George Wotton in an interesting recent study, *Thomas Hardy: Towards a Materialist Criticism* (1985) which, in its later chapters, also charts the appropriation of 'Hardy' by liberal-bourgeois critical and educational discourse, and to which further reference will be made *passim*.) Eagleton discerns several phases in the trajectory of Hardy criticism: first, the 'anthropologist of Wessex', followed by 'the melancholic purveyor of late nineteenth-century nihilism' (see above, pp. 16–24 for accounts of these earlier stages). Largely ignored by Leavis and the New Critics in the mid century when 'Anglo-Saxon criticism [was] increasingly controlled by formalist, organicist and anti-theoretical assumptions', Hardy is recovered in the fifties by a sentimental sociological criticism which regards him as the apologist of the passing rural order (see pp. 64–5 for examples of this). Eagleton concludes:

> safely defused by such mythologies, Hardy could now for the first time merit the attention of critics more preoccupied with colour imagery than with the Corn Laws or the Immanent Will; and the sixties and seventies witnessed a steady recuperation of his texts by formalist criticism. Hardy has been phenomenologized,

Freudianized, biographized, and claimed as the true guardian of
'English' liberal-democratic tendencies against the primitivist
extremism of emigré modernists.[32]

A great deal of this criticism, however, is no more than a conventional re-reading of the novels from the sophisticated angle of the
'approach' taken. In this respect, it is, as with most literary
criticism, a vapid and self-regarding exercise, at once purporting
ontological certitude while necessarily acknowledging its relativist
pluralism. Its general effect is by no means to neutralize or discard
the conventional 'Thomas Hardy' (which remains, in any case, a
powerful critical and pedagogic discourse), but to reinforce the
author's stature, the 'complexity' and 'richness' of his work, to
underwrite its value as Literature and, most importantly, to
emphasize the humanism of the author's profound vision of life's
experience. 'Thomas Hardy of Wessex' has simply become a larger
and denser figure than hitherto. In the following pages I attempt not
only to expand and extend Eagleton's phases and categories, but
also, and more particularly, to direct attention to the dominant continuing reproduction of Hardy as humanist realist, and to the effect the
disregarding of his 'minor novels' has in this incorporation of his
oeuvre.

The painstaking biographies of Hardy by Michael Millgate and
Robert Gittings contribute to the process. At one level they do this
by portraying Hardy as a man of complex and contradictory make-
up, both in his relations with women and in terms of his class position; at another, by nevertheless working within highly conventional
parameters of literary-critical practice and judgement. In a sense,
then, Hardy's 'greatness' – as evidenced by the 'mature', 'major'
works – is explained by the psychology of the author, as indeed are
the characteristic achievements and 'flaws' that criticism descries in
it. Millgate, for example, in the 'Prelude' to his earlier critical
biography *Thomas Hardy: His Career as a Novelist* (1971), writes
emphatically of Hardy's 'inequalities' as a novelist, of 'his persistent
failure, as an artist, to learn from his own past experiences'; and
puts his real achievements down to 'creative accident' in his
'imagination' when it was 'seized by a central dominating figure, or
by an overpowering movement of human compassion'.[33] As a
reflex of this, Millgate states that 'Wessex' and 'the fate of the
agricultural community . . . had relatively little significance in socio-
political terms', and that Hardy was 'reluctant to venture into the
areas of politics and social policy' (24). This perception of Hardy's
innate liberal humanism further allows Millgate to recognize *Far*

From the Madding Crowd as 'unmistakably a major work' in which Hardy 'begins to realise his *proper* subject' (79–80, my italics); and later to present 'Wessex', the centre of Hardy's achievement, as 'an autonomous world essentially outside of time and space, pastoral in its setting and in its implications, permanently eloquent of permanent truths' (351). The problem, of course, with biographical criticism is that, under its façade of scientific scrupulousness and facticity, it purveys just such subjective critical observations of the conventional kind (Hardy as asocial, apolitical humanist), but which, because of their context, take on the semblance of impartial and objective truth.

A not unrelated effect is produced by the textual and archival work of the Hardy 'scholars'. This ranges from the accumulative research of men like R. L. Purdy and F. B. Pinion, who bring together assorted materials to do with Hardy's life and times, through editions of his non-literary writings (letters, essays, journals, etc.), to the textual scholarship of the 'standard editions' and the fascinating work of critics like Chase, Paterson, Ingham, and Laird who trace the process by which a novel arrives at its finished form.[34] This is, indeed, a highly revealing sociology of literature and of publishing which shows how a writer like Hardy had to adapt, edit, rewrite, and cut for serial publication in nineteenth-century 'family journals' and then reconstitute the novel for book publication. My point, nevertheless, is that such work continues to substantiate the figure of 'Thomas Hardy' within the discourse of conventional literary criticism. For example, Laird's (1975) account of the 'gradual evolution' of *Tess* to its final form is painstakingly and impressively scholarly, but its effect is at once to take for granted critical commonplaces about the novel, and seem to definitively underwrite them by way of its 'scientific' method. Hardy's changes, for example, occasionally 'led to effects that were sentimental, melodramatic, or improbable'. This is stated incontrovertibly, as is the view that the novel developed into 'a richly imaginative and genuinely tragic exploration of a number of significant themes – all revolving around the general concept of the fate of natural innocence adrift in a world without order or justice'. The advantages, ironically, of Laird's 'genetic approach' over 'the more traditional, impressionistic approach' are that, by allowing the reader to study 'the author's creative processes it eventually leads to a surer and deeper understanding of the meaning of the definitive text' (which meaning Laird's approach, of course, both defines and then 'discovers'). His approach also illuminates 'the reasons for the uneven quality of the writing . . . helping the reader to perceive the causes of both strengths and weaknesses in a novel which, in spite of its deserved reputation as Hardy's masterpiece, remains a singular mixture of artistry and clumsiness'.[35] We have, of course, heard it all before, and modern scholarship in this guise, enmeshed in a methodo-logically self-fulfilling process, simply 'proves' by science what 'traditional, impressionistic' criticism had long established and naturalized.

As one might expect, many of the earlier strains of Hardy criticism are still heard in the post-war period, albeit with modern inflections, and some of these are glanced at later in this chapter (pp. 64–72). But in most cases, and whatever the new 'slant' on Hardy, the burden of the criticism is to shape his work so that it expresses the (often quietist and defeatist) humanist values of the critic. Perhaps this is best articulated by the concluding sentence of Carl Weber's *Hardy of Wessex* (rev. edn 1965) – one of the most highly regarded pieces of American Hardy scholarship: 'He has taught them [readers] how the spirit of man can persist through defeat, and he continues today to inspire readers to strive towards noble conduct in an imperfect world.' (It is worth noting, in passing, that Weber completely accepts the dismissal of *The Hand of Ethelberta* as a failure, and is himself puzzled in this context that Hardy did not take the *Spectator*'s conjecture that *Far From the Madding Crowd* was by George Eliot 'as a compliment'.)[36]

However, as Eagleton has indicated, the commonest critical approach to Hardy in the post-war period is formalistic, but this does not belie the fact, as I shall hope to show, that this usually works – intentionally or unintentionally – on behalf of humanist ideology. Early but influential essays of this kind are those by John Holloway in *The Victorian Sage* (1953) and *The Charted Mirror* (1960) which, by way of a close, New Critical analysis of the words on Hardy's page, show that his work is an equivocal elegy for the passing rural world, and that in it his characters are locked into a deterministic natural order. Ironically, Holloway's work was subjected in 1965 to devastating counter-analysis in another influential (if wayward) book, Roy Morrell's *Thomas Hardy: The Will and the Way* (reprinted 1978). In effect, Morrell offers a limited but revealing critiography of the way a seemingly impartial close reading of Hardy's words actually constructs the critic's own deeply partial (ideological) version of Hardy's 'vision' as though inscribed in his work. This is in part the result, says Morrell, of modern critics 'in all good faith [being] unable to set aside the bulk of established criticism';[37] so that Holloway, despite all the appearance of newly 'proving' Hardy's meaning on the incontrovertible evidence of *the text itself*, is inescapably conditioned by this long process (for Morrell) of misrepresenting Hardy. Morrell's whole project is to deny the various inflexions of the Hardy-as-determinist line of criticism which

31

sees his characters as inevitably controlled by Fate, whether metaphysical or sociological. Ironically again, however, in my context here, what Morrell wishes to replace this Hardy with is one of definitively existential/humanist aspect; so that, once more, 'the novels and stories are much more intimately concerned with personal and human dilemmas than with the documenting of social conditions' (xiii). 'Hardy's humanism' (16) is apparent, *contra* Holloway, in not 'denying a margin for the exercise of human intelligence or freedom' (ibid.) and in seeing 'point in exploring where the possibilities of freedom and happiness may lie' (17). For Morrell, then, Hardy is 'more tolerant than George Eliot . . . For while she saw an order which mysteriously and arbitrarily survived the divine order in which she no longer believed, Hardy saw none. He held fast to the one fact of human kinship, and the human kind's chances of creating something out of life's difficulties' (170) – a position which may at once explain Morrell's radical rejection of so much Eliot/Hardy criticism, and his book's continuing presence at the centre of it. It is a further sign of this contradictory position that Morrell rejects the 'popular fallacy' that Hardy's novels comprise 'inspired master-pieces' and 'dismal failures' (173); he finds 'good things even in *The Hand of Ethelberta*', while nevertheless regarding it as 'the worst of Hardy's stories', and then goes on to offer a recuperative reading of *A Laodicean* – albeit on a humanist ticket (173ff.).

There are several other influential books of a formalist/humanist slant which appeared in the 1960s and early 1970s. There is, for example, Richard Carpenter's *Thomas Hardy* (1965, reprinted 1976), in which the stated interest is Hardy's 'imagery' and the 'basic mythic structure' of his work, and in which the 'minor novels' are to receive more than usual attention. Nevertheless, Carpenter's account remains securely within the confines of conventional views of Hardy. 'Minor novels' like *A Laodicean* and *The Well-Beloved* are 'fiascos',[38] while *The Hand of Ethelberta*, 'if not the most vapid, is the most brittle and superficial of his works' (54). There is 'well-nigh universal consent' that there are 'six major novels' and then the rest (38), and that the former, while having 'undeniable weaknesses . . . cannot hide the work of genius'; 'the flaws become insignificant' and 'we know that we are encountering the work of a master who is striking the major chords on a rich and powerful instrument' (80–1). Certainly Hardy tends 'to encumber his living tale with philosophical language, much of which might be jettisoned without any loss', but his 'great faults' are not 'crippling'; and after all

> there remain the universal qualities. . . . Hardy wrote novels of
> tragic power and poems of austere severity that deal with 'love

and honor and pity and pride and compassion and sacrifice'.
Especially did he write of love and sacrifice, knowing full well in
his artistic intuition that these are eternal. (204–5)

This, then, is not such an unfamiliar 'Hardy' – even though one
read, as the Preface claims, 'with the eyes of the mid-twentieth
century'. A second highly regarded and much recommended book[39]
is Jean Brooks's *Thomas Hardy: The Poetic Structure* of 1971, the
title indicating its orientation, and which, like Carpenter's, purports
to emphasize new things, but only within a heavily circumscribed,
received version of Hardy. What has recently been under-emphasized
in Hardy, says Brooks, is 'the poetic power' which 'make[s] real
those great commonplaces of heroic, though doomed, human
nature'.[40] We will not be surprised to find that David Cecil lurks
closely behind this work – albeit with a dash of existential absurd for
good post-war measure: 'the predicament is tragic'; 'man's predicament as a striving, sensitive, imperfect individual in a rigid, non-
sentient, absurd cosmos, . . . rewards him only with eternal death'.
But it is the protagonists' 'endeavour to stamp a humane personal
design on cosmic indifference [that] makes them nobler than what
destroys them' (14–15). In this universe, Fate, Chance, and Coincidence work inexorably to destroy characters of 'simple epic and
tragic strength' – a process observed and commented on by a
'peasant chorus' (17–18). But it is 'Hardy's emotionally charged
poetic pattern [which] integrates all his personal interests into a new
artistic unity' (23). This is never entirely absent from his fiction,
although at times it is only there 'in flashes' (147) – these, of
course, are in the 'minor novels' like *The Hand of Ethelberta*, which
according to Brooks suffers from a confusion of modes (151). But
in the 'major fiction' it is constant, making *The Mayor of Casterbridge* a 'cosmic tragedy' which will 'stand comparison with the
Greeks and Shakespeare' (215); infusing the whole of *Tess of the
d'Urbervilles* with its heroine's 'vibrant humanity, her woman's
power of suffering, renewal and compassion' (253); and allowing
Jude the Obscure – 'this epic of modern existentialist man' – to
affirm 'a memory of [Jude and Sue's] love, ennobled by its
comparative freedom from physical grossness' and 'their courageous
assertion of Hellenic joy and meaning and human dignity against the
abstractions of society and the looming dark of death' (274–5). We
should note the enfeebling anti-materialism of this 'humanism' here;
and finally, in this context, that Hardy, in his influence on a contemporary poet like Philip Larkin (see pp. 70–2), has 'played a vital
though unobtrusive role in educating us to an awareness of the
common human predicament' (303). That last phrase, indicating the

apparent absence of any historical sense, enables a critic like Brooks at once to sound like so many earlier critics and yet appear to be erecting a sixties existential version of Hardy.

But perhaps the single most highly regarded book of its period (and since) is Ian Gregor's *The Great Web: The Form of Hardy's Major Fiction* (1974). As its title implies, the 'minor novels' are not within its purview (although a passing comment refers to *The Hand of Ethelberta* as a 'dubious experiment in social satire'),[41] and the book consists of a careful and sensitive reading of the form of Hardy's 'major fiction' as a metaphor for his metaphysical vision – 'one great network or tissue' (33, 40–1). Significantly, this notion of the 'interrelatedness' of things is overwhelmingly reminiscent of George Eliot – although Gregor scarcely refers to her in the entire book. Indeed, it becomes obvious that the real thrust of Gregor's work is precisely to establish this humanism of 'human relatedness' (135) as the true philosophical burden of Hardy's 'major fiction', by way of a formalistic reading of the 'poetic structure' of the works. Certainly that is what is claimed for the novels from *The Woodlanders* on, and the project thus at once proscribes any treatment of the 'minor novels' and makes for difficulties of argument with *Jude the Obscure*:

> In the pages that follow I would like to argue that the power of Hardy's last singular achievement was shaped by a conflict between a kind of fiction which he had exhausted and a kind of fiction which instinctively he discerned as meeting his need, but which, imaginatively, he had no access to. (209)

And Gregor's ideological sub-text can be perceived most clearly in the claim for *Tess* (cf. Brooks, above), where 'Hardy finds women expressive, in the purest form, of the human capacity for endurance and the steadfast refusal to be overcome' (208). A similar manifestation of this formalist/humanist correspondence is apparent in another highly regarded work of the same year (1974) – Penelope Vigar's *The Novels of Thomas Hardy: Illusion and Reality*. Emphatically concerned, as the Preface states, only with 'Hardy's technique as a novelist', but nevertheless intended to 'show how profoundly these elemental principles ["the concepts on which Hardy based his literary style"] affected his artistic vision as it is projected in the novels', Vigar's book is essentially a descriptive account of the 'fluctuations', 'tensions', and 'complexities' of Hardy's art.[42] Like Gregor, Vigar is attempting to answer the question: 'what kind of fiction did Hardy write?'[43] Nevertheless, the 'minor novels' are bundled together in a chapter entitled 'Experiments and mistakes' (*The Hand of Ethelberta* being elsewhere referred to as 'frivolously stylized' (146)), and

Vigar's work, while self-designedly an attempt to consider the various, tense, and often highly artificial features of Hardy's fictional technique as it plays out the 'seemings' of illusions and realities, still cannot break out of the dense thickets of conventional Hardy criticism. It remains within the humanist/realist paradigm, in which, for Vigar, Hardy is a superior realist paradoxically *because* 'his picture of "truth" gains in force from its conjunction with deliberately artificial representations of caricature and fantasy'; what he gives us is merely 'an impression, an artist's view which displays the distortions and illusions and absurdities in man's vision as accurately as possible' (215–16). Here, Hardy has become the *realist* purveyor of a humanist/existentialist vision.

There are many other works of the 1970s and 1980s which fall within this humanist/formalist paradigm. I am thinking, for example, of David Lodge's essay on language and style, 'Tess, Nature and the voices of Hardy' (1966); or Tony Tanner's on imagery, 'Colour and movement in *Tess of the d'Urbervilles*' (1968); or the other essays in the Macmillan Casebook: *Hardy: The Tragic Novels* (ed. R. P. Draper, 1975). In addition, there is J. Hillis Miller's *Thomas Hardy: Distance and Desire* (1970), which finds 'a single design in the totality' of Hardy's work, and which traces a correlation between theme and structure in terms of the motifs of 'desire' and 'distance' throughout the *oeuvre*. (Significantly, *The Hand of Ethelberta*, mentioned in passing only as 'that strange novel', receives no treatment although it perhaps fits Hillis Miller's theory most exactly.[44]) There is Dale Kramer's *Thomas Hardy: The Forms of Tragedy* of 1975, which again focuses on 'form or structure' in the novelist's work (without mentioning *The Hand of Ethelberta* or *A Laodicean* at all) as the precondition for the vitality of his tragedy – a tragedy which has 'a universality' in terms of the 'large questions . . . posed about man's relationship with the universe he must live in and with the other humans who in personal and social relations constitute his ties to humanity'.[45] And there is John Bayley's subtle and wide-ranging meditation on 'texture' in *An Essay on Hardy* (1978), a book which by its own humane tone and manner at once illuminates Hardy brilliantly and polishes away the jagged contradictoriness of his work. More recently, we might adduce Peter Casagrande's *Unity in Hardy's Novels: 'Repetitive Symmetries'* (1982) which again, as the title clearly announces, is concerned to show the repeated patterns of structure and motif throughout Hardy's fiction, and especially those of 'return and restoration'. Nevertheless, even here, we return finally to the stereotypes of Hardy criticism: 'his carefully delineated world and its people are intensely English, intensely West Country, and uniquely his at the same time they are universal [sic]'; and these, as well as expressing Hardy's sense of the absolute pastness of the past, also 'reflect a nostalgic sensibility and a traditional upbringing violated by "change and chancefulness"'.[46] Finally there is J. B. Bullen's recent book, *The Expressive Eye: Fiction and Perception in the Work of Thomas Hardy* (1986), which takes Hardy's phrase 'visible essences' and studies his 'pictorialist techniques' in relation to his knowledge of and interest in the visual arts of his own day. It is an indication of the control which conventional critical parameters of Hardy exert, that, apart from in one instance, *The Hand of Ethelberta* – a novel spectacularly 'visual' and 'pictorialist' in technique – is dismissed as 'a weak novel' which it was 'fortunate' Hardy had 'enough self-criticism' to recognize as being a 'wrong direction'.[47]

All these books and essays do not, of course, constitute an undifferentiated mass; nor do I mean to imply that, within their terms of reference, they are inadequate – some, indeed, are full of fine critical *aperçus*. My point simply is to demonstrate that in their pursuit of 'pattern' and 'unity' of formal structures and motifs – and despite their sophistication – they merely reproduce generically conventional literary-critical versions of Hardy. On the whole, they reinforce notions of Hardy's humanism, in terms of 'universal tragedy' and realism, and in particular they seek to establish the homogeneity of Hardy's work, rather than recognizing its fractured and dissonant discourses. This has the effect of smoothing and refining his *oeuvre*, both in terms of the 'major' texts themselves and, of course, also with regard to the status of the 'minor fiction'. There is one further strand in formalistic post-war Hardy criticism which I want to identify – if only because of its significant scarcity – before moving on to briefly survey the few more radically 'alternative' initiatives of the last twenty years or so. This strand I will call the 'anti-realist' or 'fictionalist' Hardy.

In an early and equivocally-regarded study, *Thomas Hardy* (1949, revised 1964), Albert J. Guerard floats the idea that Hardy, despite being 'a dogged, leisurely, old-fashioned storyteller . . . was a sufficiently conscious artist consciously to rebel against drab and placid realism . . . [and that] his symbolic use of mischance and coincidence carry us no small distance toward the symbolic use of the absurd in our own time'.[48] Guerard's general project is to release Hardy from a 'generation' of critics which 'is not ours' (2). That generation he calls 'post-Victorian' (from Lionel Johnson to David Cecil), one which

looked upon its everyday experience as placid, plausible, and reasonably decent; it assumed that the novel should provide an accurate reflection of this sane everyday experience and perhaps a consolation for its rare shortcomings. It assumed that realism was the proper medium of fiction – and that to see a preponderance of evil and brute chance in life was to be unrealistic. (2)

'We', Guerard suggests, belong to a different world – one in which Hardy's 'deliberate anti-realism' tunes in with 'the actual and absurd world', where 'our everyday experience [is] both intolerable and improbable, but even more improbable than intolerable' (3). (Writing in 1949 after World War II, Auschwitz, Hiroshima, and Nagasaki, Guerard states that 'we have rediscovered . . . the demonic in human nature as well as in political process' (3).) And he wants to associate Hardy's work with 'the increasing sensationalism of serious modern fiction' (4). Guerard is too early to have in mind the 'neo-gothic' and 'fabulation' of especially American post-war fiction, but Vonnegut, Heller, and Pynchon amongst others would recognize an 'improbable' real experience as somehow outdoing fiction and the need, therefore, for fictional forms which break with realism. Of Hardy, Guerard claims:

> We are in fact attracted by much that made the post-Victorian
> realist uneasy: the inventiveness and improbability, the symbolic
> use of reappearance and coincidence, the wanderings of a macabre
> imagination, the suggestions of supernatural agency; the frank
> acknowledgement that love is basically sexual and marriage
> usually unhappy; the demons of plot, irony, and myth. And we
> are repelled or left indifferent by what charmed that earlier
> generation: the regionalist's ear for dialect, the botanist's eye for
> the minutiae of field and tree, the architect's eye for ancient
> mansions, and the farmer's eye for sheepshearings; the pretentious
> meditation on Egdon Heath; the discernible architecture of the
> novels and the paraphrasable metaphysic; the Franciscan
> tenderness and sympathy – and, I'm afraid, the finally unqualified
> faith in the goodness of a humanity more sinned against than
> sinning. (6)

The irony of it is that Guerard's 'post-Victorian generation' of critics did not end, in the terms of this passage, with Cecil, but continues, as I have tried to demonstrate, up to the present day. 'We', indeed, did not perceive things (including Hardy) in the way Guerard predicted, and 'we' have tended to ignore Hardy's fictive anti-realism, together with everything else that that implies. Guerard, in fact, produces a critiographical perspective which goes far beyond 1949, and which underwrites my own:

Hardy's post-Victorian critics, confronted by their own very
strong affection for his books, have tried to find academic,
formal, respectable reasons for this feeling; they have tried to
discover not merely a philosopher and a realist but a minute and
subtle craftsman. . . . Criticism has refused, in its devotion to
realism, to recognise the strength and validity of Hardy's anti-
realistic aim and has often deplored his imaginative heightenings
of reality. (11, 13)

'The strength and validity of Hardy's anti-realistic aim' is a notion
which I want to pull sharply and clearly into view, so that I can
return to it in the final section of this chapter and in Part II.

In the event, Guerard's own work on Hardy is disappointing, failing to work through *in extenso* the implications of an 'anti-realist'
perspective on the fiction, and too ready to present Hardy as a naïve
and unserious novelist whose 'failings' and 'weaknesses' are
everywhere apparent – despite the fact that these might represent
aspects of Guerard's 'anti-realist' theory. (*A Laodicean* and *The
Hand of Ethelberta* are 'failures' for Guerard too, the latter being
full of 'lifeless satire' and 'melodrama' (51).) Nevertheless, it is
worth noting that Guerard gives full cognizance to Hardy's persistent
'unrelaxed consciousness and resentment of class feeling' (41) – not
least in *The Hand of Ethelberta* and *A Laodicean* where it is dealt
with 'in other than conventional terms' (26); and that he prob-
lematizes the notion of 'character' in Hardy's fiction, questioning
whether that is an appropriate term for the kinds of psychological
delineations we find there (see his chapter, 'Of men and women').
In this, as in the concern with class and anti-realism, Guerard draws
a sketch for a non-humanist and materialist reproduction of Hardy
which has seldom emerged since. Indeed, I want to draw attention
here to two indices of the failure to follow Guerard's lead. First:
there is, as I have implied throughout the above, a striking absence
within formalist-humanist criticism of work dealing with Hardy's
manifestly non-realist discourses. Penelope Vigar (see pp. 34–5) is
an exception, but, as we saw, even there such elements were rein-
corporated within a realist paradigm; and Hillis Miller, in the Introduction to the 'New Wessex' edition of *The Well-Beloved* (1975),
offers a subtle analysis of Hardy's 'fictiveness' in relation to that
text. But there is little else that I am aware of, within the dominant
critical mode (which is perhaps to be expected, as I shall hope to
establish in the final section of this chapter). Second: there is equally
little address to the anti-realism issue, as we shall see in a moment,
in the sparse materialist criticism so far devoted to Hardy. It simply
has not been recognized that the potentially subversive nature

of his fiction – its non- (sometimes anti-) humanist trajectory – is articulated or enacted in strategically non- (or anti-) realist modes. Guerard's study was salutary in its implications; we have failed to learn from it for too long.

In the last part of this section, I will briefly survey some of the Hardy criticism which challenges, or runs athwart, the dominant critical conventions and ideologies presented above – criticism which derives principally from marxist and feminist (or, more generally, 'materialist') positions. It is not my intention here to offer an extended critique of such work – some of it, indeed, is referred to elsewhere in this book – but merely to draw attention to it and some of its characteristics.

It is immediately striking, amongst the huge mass of Hardy criticism, how little of it has considered him seriously and historically as a social novelist concerned with the composition of the rural economy, with class, property, and gender relations. Of course half the critical monographs on Hardy talk about 'Wessex', the 'rural order', and 'peasants', and Douglas Brown's *Thomas Hardy* (1954) (see pp. 64–5) has been extensively influential in establishing the critical tradition of Hardy mourning the destruction of a rural community by the dehumanizing processes of nineteenth-century industrialization. It has been the subject of some debate within Hardy criticism (cf. J. C. Maxwell's 1968 essay 'The "sociological" approach to *The Mayor of Casterbridge*' and Roy Morrell's work cited pp. 31–2), but it has never been more than a quasi-historical reworking of the traditional version of Hardy as rural annalist. More 'marxist' – and hence more subject to critical rubbishing (cf. Maxwell and Morrell again) – was Arnold Kettle's earlier essay on *Tess of the d'Urbervilles* in *An Introduction to the English Novel* (1953), in which he categorically claims that *Tess*'s theme is 'in fact . . . the destruction of the English peasantry'; that the novel is a 'moral fable'; and that its major weaknesses derive from Hardy's 'conscious philosophy', while its major strengths are the product of his 'social understanding'.[49] It was indeed a crude claim, and symptomatic of a marxist–humanist criticism which forces together 'social history' and bourgeois literary-critical praxis in contradictory amalgam. In fact, thirty years later, in an Open University unit on the novel, Kettle offers a characteristically disarming apology for the earlier essay, and produces instead a text-orientated, rather than 'sociological', approach.[50]

A rather more extended, although still simplistic work on the relations of Hardy's fiction to the historical rural economy of Dorset, was Merryn Williams's *Thomas Hardy and Rural England* (1972).

To my knowledge it still remains one of the very few full-length studies of Hardy in a specific and material historical context. It was, nevertheless, criticized in a bibliographical essay in 1980 by Richard H. Taylor for its 'emphatic left-wing subjectivity [which] clouds interpretation of some of the evidence'. (Taylor, who awaits 'the definitive work [of criticism on Hardy] that has yet to appear', states that 'despite his deep empathy, artistically Hardy saw Wessex and its peasantry as raw material for the portrayal of elemental passions in a circumscribed scene'.[51] With guards like this defending the Hardy Critical Edifice, it is not surprising that Ms Williams is seen as a threat!) I would suggest that her book is marred rather by a theoretically naïve critical and historiographical view of Hardy as 'recording' the 'real facts' of the world he saw about him with accuracy and insight, so that his novels represent the 'highest kind of realism'.[52] It is still a sharply corrective study, and its claims for Hardy's achievement are by no means misplaced, but its failure to perceive the ideological refraction consequent on both Hardy's exact historical position and the complex deployment of fictional discourse in the novels, indicates again that literature, literary criticism, and history cannot sit in any simple correlation: of 'background' or 'context', of 'reflection' or 'recording the facts'. Realism indeed – 'telling things as they really are' – is the trickiest of all literary modes.

Raymond Williams has also written on Hardy: most extensively in *The English Novel from Dickens to Lawrence* (1970) which at once positions the novelist at a *locus* of literary and sociological transition and recuperates the positive values of Hardy's writing from 'the alienation, the frustration, the separation and isolation, the final catastrophes'[53] – a deliberate strategy on Williams's part to resist liberal-humanist cultural pessimism. There are, in addition, some interesting comments on Hardy in *Politics and Letters* (1979), (see p. 26) and a joint essay with Merryn Williams on 'Hardy and social class' in *Thomas Hardy: The Writer and His Background*, edited by Norman Page (1980). It is a useful attempt (see pp. 130–2 for further reference to this essay) to specify accurately the class fraction from which Hardy springs and which is central to his fiction, but it has two serious omissions: first, it does not take into account the class position Hardy occupies when he becomes a metropolitan man of letters; and second – in common with Williams's other work, but more serious here – it ignores the minor fiction, which is deeply marked by a consciousness of class (particularly *The Hand of Ethelberta*). So, too, does Mary Eagleton and David Pierce's chapter on Hardy in *Attitudes to Class in the English Novel* (1979), a disappointingly descriptive account of *Tess* and *Jude* and their presentation of sexual marital ideology rather than an analysis of social class in any direct sense.

The most incisive and stimulating writing on Hardy from a marxist perspective is by Terry Eagleton, but it is brief and suggestive rather than worked through. His Introduction to the 'New Wessex' edition of *Jude the Obscure* (1974) is the only one of that series to present Hardy from a materialist literary-critical perspective, and it remains almost the only widely accessible countering of the conventional critical 'Thomas Hardy'. Most importantly, perhaps, Eagleton has emphasized the formal disjunctions of Hardy's texts – the ideological significance of the clash of modes and of the 'anti-realism' which is its result. This is the thrust of a synoptic paragraph on the trajectory of Hardy's fictional career in *Criticism and Ideology* (1976), and of the brief account of him in the same book as 'a literary producer . . . ridden with contradictions' whose work is marked by 'the peculiar *impurity* of his literary forms (pastoral, melodrama, social realism, naturalism, myth, fable, classical tragedy)'. Eagleton, indeed, perceives *Jude* as 'a calculated assault' on its audience: 'What have been read as its "crudities" are less the consequences of some artistic incapacity than of an astonishing raw boldness on Hardy's part, a defiant flouting of "verisimilitude" which mounts theatrical gesture upon gesture in a driving back of the bounds of realism.'[54] In addition, as we have seen earlier, Eagleton, in *Walter Benjamin or Towards a Revolutionary Criticism* (1981), has offered a critiographical account of the constitution of 'Hardy' within bourgeois criticism, recognizing that Hardy's anti-realist subversiveness has to be 'expelled' or incorporated in order to sustain the humanist-realist critical/ideological project.[55] I will return to this in the final section of this chapter. It is a small, but perhaps indicative, criticism to add that nowhere as yet has Eagleton recognized how central the case of the 'minor novels' – and especially *Ethelberta*, *A Laodicean*, and *The Well-Beloved* – is to his argument. However, it is appropriate to note here that the one full-length study of Hardy which operates within the paradigm that Eagleton outlines is by an ex-pupil of his, George Wotton, and that *Thomas Hardy: Towards a Materialist Criticism* (1985) is, in effect and especially in its third part, a companion volume to the present book.

By nature of its project, feminist criticism challenges the politics and the ideology of most other literary criticism, if in no other way than by admitting that it is political, and by making its politics its *raison d'être*. It follows, therefore, that feminist criticism of Hardy can avoid the stereotyping and conventions of the 'Thomas Hardy' which I have been extrapolating so far. This is not to say, of course, that the vast amount of criticism concerned with 'Hardy's women' is in any sense radical. On the contrary, as George Wotton shows in his critiographical chapter, 'The production of meaning: "Hardy's women" and the Eternal Feminine', most criticism of this kind 'is based on a reading determined by a dominant gender ideology'.[56] Even as subtle and 'social' a critic as John Lucas in his long essay 'Hardy's women' in *The Literature of Change* (1977), which Wotton fails to mention, is held within it – most particularly in his criticism of *Jude* as 'something of a muddle, at least as far as Sue is concerned',[57] and in his resolute refusal to deal with either *A Laodicean* or *The Hand of Ethelberta*, both of which have powerful female protagonists who are amongst the most 'successful' survivors in all of Hardy's fictions. However, it is Lucas's determined and self-confident evaluation of some literature as unequivocally 'bad' which accounts for his missed opportunity here.

But a feminist criticism, of course, is not one which merely focuses attention on Hardy's women; it is concerned, rather, with the sexual/textual politics of the novels. An early and still very radical initiative of this kind is John Goode's essay 'Women and the literary text', which proceeds from the notion that texts are not 'representations' but processes of signification,[58] and that 'we can only see the political importance of a text by attending to its formal identity as the object of an act of production' (255). In relation to *Tess*, Goode briefly suggests that what we watch (and are implicated in) is 'the objectification of Tess by the narrator which is acted out in the novel' (253), so that we feel the guilt of the 'object images' imposed on her by (patriarchal) society (254). She is, as it were, composed of all the images she is subjected to bearing (by male 'lookers'), and it is this process of objectification, Goode claims, which means that whatever was Hardy's own 'ideological commitment, no frame will hold his novel in place' (255). The discourses of the text, in other words, have to be accepted as contradictory. This approach is refined and extended in Goode's essay on 'Sue Bridehead and the new woman', where he suggests that the radicalism of *Jude* lies in its 'taking of reality apart', in its 'exposure of its flaws and its mystifications', and that Sue's function in the novel is to articulate this – as an 'exposing image' – in relation to notions of love, marriage, and other heterosexual relations. This, he suggests, is why she has mystified and alienated so many readers and critics: 'the incomprehensibility of Sue . . . is one way at least in which the incomprehensibility of the world (i.e. bourgeois ideology) is offered.'[59] As a literary function Sue, in her incomprehensibility, exposes the mystifications of sexual ideology. In Goode's work, it is important to understand the emphasis on the radical nature of the

formal operations of Hardy's texts, not merely their 'representa-
tional' historical/political/ideological messages. It is a key aspect of
Hardy's subversive anti-realism.

Excellent though Patricia Stubbs's book *Women and Fiction:
Feminism and the Novel 1880–1920* (1979) generally is, it is limited
in its study of Hardy by the absence of this sense of the complex
formal tensions and contradictions of his fictions. There is gestural
reference to the 'breakdown' of realism under pressure of his social
analysis, but Stubbs's readings of the novels are relatively conventional formal accounts – albeit within a salutary sexual/social
framework. They are also restricted to the 'major novels' – no
reference being made to the 'experiments' – and this, again, limits
her argument. What Stubbs does provide, however, is an interesting
thesis on Hardy's central 'contradiction': that is, between his
'intensely modern, even feminist consciousness' and his residual
acceptance of conventional character 'types' with regard to women
– which belies his imprisonment within patriarchal ideology.[60] This
contradiction I shall return to in my final chapter. Lastly, I should
mention Penny Boumelha's *Thomas Hardy and Women: Sexual
Ideology and Narrative Form* (1982) which does attempt to correlate
the 'experimentalism' of Hardy's fiction with a radically subversive
presentation of sexual relations. Interestingly, Boumelha deploys the
'minor novels' (although they do not receive the full-chapter treatment of the others), and they become, therefore, a substantive part
of a body of writing which is studied for its political significance,
released from their marginalization by literary-critical 'discrimination'. If Boumelha is to be criticized, it is for her failure to
distinguish clearly whether 'Hardy's radicalism' is to be seen as
Hardy's own, or whether it is activated in the texts by the strategic
reading of a modern feminist critic. If it is the former, then she
needs to engage Stubbs's 'contradiction' head on; if it is the latter,
then it should be enunciated clearly as the proper function of a
political cultural criticism.

Modern Hardy criticism, then, generally reproduces a 'Thomas
Hardy' whose lines were drawn early: a tragic humanist-realist,
marred by 'flaws', but represented by six or seven 'masterworks'
which rank, in their grasp of the (universal) human condition, with
other great literature in English. Some attempts have been and are
being made to liberate a different 'Hardy' from this powerful critical
creation, but too often they are implicated in the discourses they
intend to challenge – in particular by their tendency to continue to
privilege those works which are central to the humanist-realist
canon, and so to ignore their subversive textuality. It is this,

amongst other things, which 'minor novels' like *Ethelberta* and *A Laodicean* bring into view, and it is to the significance of this 'neutralized' sub-group that I now turn.

A note on the case of the 'minor novels'

The fate of Hardy's so-called 'minor novels' may act as a specific exemplum of the preceding critiography. Two essays in contemporary collections of critical essays on Hardy make a similar point about the 'minor novels' with reference to Macmillan's publication of the 'New Wessex' edition in 1974–5. Richard H. Taylor remarks: 'Not the least virtue of the New Wessex Edition is its disinterment of the lesser novels, long denied the critical attention (and paperback publication) they deserve.'[61] And Irwin and Gregor, noting how 'the New Wessex Edition has restored the "minor" novels to general currency', continue: 'Critical concentration on the six famous "Wessex" novels has made his art appear simpler and more homogeneous than it was. To study the minor works is to be reminded that Hardy's creative talents involved tensions and contrarieties not easily or always reconciled in fictional terms.'[62] Neither essay does anything to correct the balance, and neither seems to question the categorization 'minor'. Taylor, indeed (whose later book on 'The Neglected Hardy' is discussed on pp. 52–3 and 174–6), happily accepts Hardy's own classification of his fiction in the 1912 'General Preface': 'The implication of these divisions must direct our understanding of Hardy's aims, and concomitantly perhaps the nature of his achievement, in different modes of fiction. More generally, the essay is essential reading if we are to read Hardy aright.'[63] Whatever happened, we might ask, to the intentionalist fallacy? Irwin and Gregor's point about the homogenizing effect on Hardy's writing of ignoring the 'minor' fiction is an important one, although it reinforces the fact that criticism has made the 'art' of the 'major' novels 'simpler' by implying that the 'tensions' and 'contrarities' are to be found only in the 'minor novels' and not in the major ones themselves. In other words, it leaves the ranking, and therefore the general consensus about Hardy's 'art', undisturbed. Nevertheless, both essays do draw attention to the fact that Hardy has been commonly represented by only a proportion of his fiction, that the 'New Wessex' paperbacks put the missing novels back into circulation, and that this, willy-nilly, alters our perception of 'Thomas Hardy'.

It is worth a parenthesis, in this context, to notice the significance of the publishing industry as an aspect of critiography. I cannot here outline and analyse the long, complex history of the relationship between Macmillan and Hardy – although I recognize that a full account of the material determinations which shape, produce, and reproduce an author would need to include it. However, we may note in passing that for many years Macmillan effectively 'owned' or controlled Hardy's appearance in the public world. They turned down his first novel, but became his publishers from *Far From the Madding Crowd* onwards, buying the copyright outright from Hardy's estate in the early 1940s. This did not expire until 1978 – a date I will return to in a moment. Given that from the outset *Tess* was an outstanding commercial success; that in 1967, Macmillan were quoted as saying that *Under the Greenwood Tree* sold about 10,000 hardback copies a year and 20,000 paperback, while the 'better known' novels sold in 'vast quantities' all over the world (they had five different editions of *Tess* on offer);[64] and that in 1983 *Far From the Madding Crowd* and *Tess* were two of their six best selling novels[65] – Macmillan have made a great deal of money out of Hardy. Even in 1985, with the copyright gone, they put out a pamphlet which read: 'MACMILLAN – Hardy's own publishers are pleased to announce TWO *NEW* WORKS BY THOMAS HARDY.' (These turned out to be *The Life and Work of Thomas Hardy*, edited by Michael Millgate – a 'restored' version of 'Florence Emily's' *The Life*, and *The Literary Notebooks of Thomas Hardy*, edited by Lennart Björk.) It is further worth remarking that Macmillan have been at the forefront of the Hardy critical industry, publishing a good proportion of the books available on him. How far Macmillan's investment in publishing Hardy's own work has affected their attitude to criticism of him – how far, for example, house editors have a particular approach to Hardy scholarship, and how far, therefore, Macmillan can be seen as controlling and shaping the critical reproduction of 'Hardy' – are interesting, if unanswerable, questions.

What is clear, however, is that they have, in effect, had a critical function in the constitution of 'Thomas Hardy' in relation to the 'minor novels'. Although Macmillan had had a paperback Hardy in print for many years ('St Martin's Library', then 'Papermac'), this did not comprise the complete set of novels. In other words, for the vast majority of readers the 'minor novels' did not exist, and in terms of public accessibility Hardy existed solely as the novelist of 'character and environment'. My general point here is a simple one: publishers, almost certainly in relation to established critical opinion, materially affect the status and constitution of a writer. Hardy without the minor novels is a different Hardy to one with them; teaching him is different when one can, if one chooses, 'set' *The Hand of Ethelberta* for study – just as so many radically new syllabuses could be on offer if the books to be taught were in print. Availability is a crucial critical term. In 1974–5, then, 'Hardy' changed: Macmillan produced the 'New Wessex' edition, including all fourteen novels with new introductions, notes, and prefaces; and in 1975 they also published a 'students edition' – aimed primarily at schools and differently packaged. This edition, significantly, contained none of the 'minor novels'. Nevertheless, in the mid 1970s two cheap and attractive paperback editions of Hardy with modern introductions and explanatory notes were available. It is a moot point, of course, whether it is now possible to teach *The Hand of Ethelberta* or *Desperate Remedies* solely because, in 1978, Macmillan's control of the Hardy copyright fell in and they had to flood the market before others could join them. My point again simply is that a 'great writer' is not naturally present, but is determined in shape and status by many material processes which do not immediately appear to have very much to do with 'intrinsic' literary value.

Not surprisingly, perhaps, the first editions of the 'New Wessex' novels were adorned with pictorial covers (see plate 1 on p. 67) – modern photographs which pose mock-Victorian 'characters' in an emphatically rural 'environment', while the covers of the later Penguin (see plate 2 on p. 68) and Oxford 'World's Classics' editions have English landscape paintings on theirs. Once again we can see how, even in the physical packaging, 'Hardy' is being subliminally constructed in conventional critical terms. More importantly, perhaps, the novels – as with so many modern paperback editions – are 'framed' by a critical introduction. This is not to complain – as some critics and teachers do – that this gets in the way of a student's/reader's 'spontaneous' engagement with 'the text itself', since 'the text itself' is no more directly accessible or autonomous than the reader's engagement is free of critical presuppositions. Rather, it is merely to draw attention to a most obvious instance of the way criticism constructs or 'writes' the object of its attention, since the novel must, in some sense, be read 'through' its (authoritative) critical frame. In the case of Hardy's 'minor novels' this is particularly significant. For what we invariably find, despite the introducer's enthusiasm at 'recovering' a forgotten work, is a residual damning-with-faint-praise, an apologetic tone, a reserve of position, never perceived in the introductions to the major 'Wessex' novels. Barbara Hardy's extremely interesting introductory essay on the 'feminism' of *A Laodicean*, for example, nevertheless opens with the words: '*A Laodicean* is certainly not one of Hardy's great novels',[66] and C. J. P. Beatty's introduction to *Desperate Remedies* is full of references to 'flashes of the *real* Hardy here and there' (my italics) and to 'truly Hardyan themes', as compared to 'sensationalism' and 'melodrama'. In one classic formulation, he notes that *Desperate Remedies* is classified in the 1912 'General Preface' as a 'Novel of Ingenuity' and adds: 'an *inevitable* designation if the novel is to be considered as a whole. Yet for some two-thirds of its length *Desperate Remedies* surely deserves the attention *normally* given to a Novel of Character and Environment.'[67] Equally Ronald Blythe, in *A Pair of Blue Eyes*, assures us that this is not a 'slight work', despite finding it 'luridly invaded by melodrama'[68] (in the 'World's Classics' edition (1985) Alan Manford, although generally positive, is much concerned with it as an 'apprentice novel' and with the 'flaws' in its 'craftsmanship');[69] and Robert Gittings's introduction to the 'New Wessex' *The Hand of Ethelberta* (see pp. 173–4) while full of interesting information, still presents the novel as 'the joker in the pack' of Hardy's fiction, a 'comparative failure' and riddled with 'improbabilities'.[70] The effect of this kind of presentation, of course, is at once to make available the 'missing' novels of the Hardy *oeuvre*, with all the razzmatazz of publishing enterprise, and to effectively institutionalize their predetermined critical status. They are, ironically, now republished, but as 'Hardy's second best'.

I can return from here to consider how these novels originally achieved their 'minority'; why they might have done so; why this marginalization has been accepted and perpetuated for so long; and what might be the implications of restoring the 'minor' novels to a Hardy *oeuvre* free of any preconceived hierarchical shape. If a critical enterprise centred on 'literary value' is set aside, then the notions of 'value' and 'majority' which it constructs and naturalizes wither away and the writings are left clear for alternative constructions to be placed upon them. What is of primary interest for the moment, however, and essential if such a deconstructive turn is to be convincing, is a clear understanding of how the taxonomy of writings is arrived at: in this case, how 'Hardy' is perceived, understood, and valued only with six of his fourteen novels omitted.

The six novels normally regarded as 'minor' are *Desperate Remedies* (1871), *A Pair of Blue Eyes* (1873), *The Hand of Ethelberta* (1876), *A Laodicean* (1881), *Two on a Tower* (1882), and *The Well-Beloved* (1892/7). The first thing to notice is that they are not Hardy's 'early' fiction or juvenilia; they are spread throughout his publishing career. *Desperate Remedies* is his first published novel (although not his first written one); *A Pair of Blue Eyes* follows *Under the Greenwood Tree*; *The Hand of Ethelberta* follows *Far From the Madding Crowd*; *A Laodicean* and *Two on a Tower* follow

The Return of the Native and *The Trumpet-Major*; and *The Well-Beloved* follows *Tess* in its periodical publication and *Jude* – Hardy's last novel – in its heavily revised book form. However, they are all included in the second and third groups of Hardy's own 'classification' of his novels in the 1912 General Preface to the 'Wessex' edition of his work. It is worth noting here how Hardy distinguishes them, and what he says more generally about his fiction, although not in the spirit of simple intentionalism recommended by Richard H. Taylor above. Indeed, a letter to Sir Frederick Macmillan (2 April 1912), in which Hardy writes that 'the advantage of classifying the novels seems to be that it affords the journalists something to discuss',[71] should alert us to both the self-defensive irony Hardy continually deployed in writing about his own work, and to his sharp consciousness of the processes of critical reproduction. In the General Preface, then, Hardy writes: 'the first group is called "Novels of Character and Environment", and contains those which approach most nearly to uninfluenced works; also one or two which, whatever their quality in some few of their episodes, may claim a verisimilitude in general treatment and detail.' As with so much of Hardy's explanative writing, this appears simple, clear, and helpful, but is, in fact, the reverse. What exactly are 'novels of character and environment'? Novels which focus on characters (or people 'of character'?) and on the physical world which determines their being, and which are thus in the great tradition of humanist realism? Or are they novels about 'great' characters set against the universe (in the tragic Greek mode he praises later in the Preface)? Or do the terms mean something different again? What does the odd phrase 'approach most nearly to uninfluenced works' mean? That the novels are original? But why does Hardy need to specify this, what does it add to 'novels of character and environment', and what are the others 'influenced' by? Why can only 'one or two' of this group 'claim a verisimilitude in general treatment and detail', and which ones are they? Criticism may have followed, and still follow, Hardy's 'directions', but it can only have done so because it wanted to be led blindfold.

Hardy continues: 'The second group [*A Pair of Blue Eyes, The Trumpet-Major, Two on a Tower, The Well-Beloved*, and *A Group of Noble Dames*] is distinguished as "Romances and Fantasies", a sufficiently descriptive definition.' Quite why it is 'sufficiently descriptive' is wonderfully unclear; nor is it apparent why *The Well-Beloved*, for example, should be here and not in the third group, 'Novels of Ingenuity'; nor, vice versa, why *A Laodicean* should not be with *Two on a Tower* in the second. The third group is defined more fully, although in the end no more definitively:

The third class – 'Novels of Ingenuity' – show a not infrequent disregard of the probable in the chain of events, and depend for their interest mainly on the incidents themselves. They might also be characterised as 'Experiments', and were written for the nonce simply; though despite the artificiality of their fable some of the scenes are not without fidelity to life.

Hardy then proceeds, very quietly, to admit that 'these differences are not distinctly perceptible in every page of every volume. It was inevitable that blendings and alternations should occur in all.' In other words, the classification is basically factitious. Neither is the third group readily distinguishable from the others: do *Tess* and *Jude* not show 'a not infrequent disregard of the probable in the chain of events'? In what sense is *Jude* or *The Well-Beloved* not an 'experiment'? And what does 'written for the nonce simply' mean? Which of his novels was not – if we are to understand it as meaning written out of immediate material necessity? Nevertheless, Hardy does distinguish, and he does impute a superiority or seriousness to the first group above the other two, and that distinction is, as far as it is possible to guess, based on notions of 'verisimilitude' *contra* 'artificiality' and on 'realism' ('novels of character and environment') *contra* 'romance', 'fantasy', 'ingenuity', and 'experiment'. What is puzzling, however, is that towards the end of the Preface Hardy insists that there is no coherent 'consistent philosophy' running through his work, and that the 'following pages have been stated truly to be mere impressions of the moment'. Earlier, after a long list of 'Wessex' places and their 'real' equivalents which he pretends 'discerning people have affirmed in print', Hardy gently mocks 'these keen hunters for the real'. Such remarks are clearly reminiscent of the many references throughout his non-fictional writings (especially in the individual prefaces to the novels and in *The Life*) to the 'unreality' of fiction, to his novels being a series of 'seemings', 'mental impressions', and so on, which suggest that he certainly did not regard himself as a simple realist who 'photographically' reproduced reality in fiction as his Victorian 'probablist' critics demanded, and that he had instead a sophisticated sense of the artifice of fictional discourse (see pp. 159–64). The General Preface, in other words, is part of that mystifying and ironic strategy Hardy so constantly deployed – and of which *The Life* is the classic instance – to protect himself and his work from the (mis)representations of biography and criticism.

Whatever Hardy may have meant, however, two points are worth making in this context. First, most of his remarks about his work in 1912 had already been made many times in the reviews over the years since his first novels appeared. The passing reference, for example, to Greek tragedy echoes several comparisons of his work to classical literature; his emphasis on Wessex as a source of 'human nature', and his suggestion that the 'local' Wessex characters contain elements which are 'really universal', were already critical commonplaces; his emphasis on the real and fictive Wessex in the long list of place-names picks up the reviewers' major fascination from the earliest days with Hardy's loving exploration of the little-known life and lore of 'Wessex'; and the comments on his 'pessimism' are in direct response to one of the commonest debates in Hardy criticism of the late nineteenth century. More particularly, in my context here, Hardy's novels were already being ranked according to 'probablist' criteria well before he wrote the General Preface. In the first survey of Hardy's work (up to and including *The Return of the Native*) in the *New Quarterly Magazine* (October 1879), *The Hand of Ethelberta* is already regarded as 'a fantastic interlude to his more serious work'; while reviews of *Two on a Tower* in the *Saturday Review* (November 1882) – which also includes a side-swipe at *A Laodicean* ('very queer people doing very queer things') – and in the *Spectator* (February 1883), attack it fiercely for its lack of 'probability' and 'plausibility', the latter finding it 'melodramatic without strength, extravagant without object, and objectionable without truth'. Coventry Patmore, in *St James's Gazette* (April 1887), omits *The Hand of Ethelberta* from a list of novels containing Hardy's heroines – 'the most original and delightful' feature of his work – and later comments that it 'was signally below his true mark'.[72] J. M. Barrie and Edmund Gosse (both friends of Hardy) wrote general reviews of his work in 1889–90 in which *The Hand of Ethelberta* and *Two on a Tower* were ranked lowest. Barrie described the former as a double disappointment – 'it is not a comedy, and its London life is preposterous', and the latter (along with *A Laodicean*) as 'dull books: here and there, nasty as well, and the besom of oblivion will soon pass over them'.[73] Gosse offers 'four classes' of novels (*Far From the Madding Crowd* and *The Return of the Native* are first), and while admitting the 'cleverness' of *Ethelberta* and *Two on a Tower*, regards them as 'partial failures', putting them in the fourth class.[74] It is noteworthy that Gosse is already explicitly 'classifying' the novels. Finally, in two general essays on Hardy in 1904 and 1910, the process is largely completed – certainly as far as *Ethelberta* is concerned. Edward Wright, finding like so many other critics that only the truly 'Wessex Hardy' will do, fiercely dismisses *Jude* and *The Well-Beloved*, and notes that his 'society novels' are 'rather successful essays in the art of sinking'; and W. L. Phelps, offering a hard sell on Hardy to the

American public, finds *Far From the Madding Crowd* and *The Return of the Native* Hardy's finest works and 'Wessex' his greatest achievement, mentioning every other novel but *The Hand of Ethelberta*. There is some doubt as to whether he has even heard of it; but if he has, he ignores it.[75] I shall return in a moment to the implications of this critical consensus for Hardy's own view of his fiction in 1912.

My second point in relation to the categorization of the 'minor novels' is that most criticism since then has, of course, followed Hardy's own ranking, has concentrated on the 'novels of character and environment', and has continued to ignore or belittle the 'fantasies', 'romances', and 'novels of ingenuity'. A brief glance at literary history starkly reveals this. Two of the earliest surveys of his work following the publication of the General Preface endorse Hardy's classification. Charles Whibley in *Blackwood's Magazine* (June 1913) immediately notes Hardy's 'own wise classification', and confirms that 'the best of his works are ranged under the title of "novels of character and environment"'. In the course of this facile and derivative encomium on Hardy, all the novels in his groups two and three have become irretrievably 'minor', although the jejune Whibley finds that even the slightest of these works is touched by the master's hand.[76] And Harold Williams (as we saw on p. 17) had already hijacked Hardy's categories as though they were his own, thus allowing him to rank the novels so that all but five could be ignored – *A Pair of Blue Eyes*, *A Laodicean*, and *The Hand of Ethelberta* being especially marked down: 'the characters are unconvincing and the plot improbable.'[77] These tendencies, attitudes, and evaluations, as we have remarked in the previous section, are reproduced time and again in later literary history and criticism. A few further examples may, however, clinch the point. B. Ifor Evans's *A Short History of English Literature*, published by Penguin in 1940 and reprinted many times, refers only to those novels 'most memorable by common consent', and Harry Blamires in a later *Short History of English Literature* (1974) mentions that Hardy had to pay to get *Desperate Remedies* published, notes the appearance of *A Pair of Blue Eyes*, comments 'after [it] the pattern of the great Wessex novels is laid down in *Far From the Madding Crowd*', and ignores any of the other 'minor novels' thereafter.[78] In Albert C. Baugh's mammoth, standard *A Literary History of England* (1967) all the minor novels are named and receive a comment: *Desperate Remedies* is 'a highly improbable tale of mystery and murder'; *A Pair of Blue Eyes* 'combines sensational intrigue and incredible coincidences'; with *The Hand of Ethelberta* Hardy 'achieved only a negligible piece of frivolity'; and *The*

Well-Beloved 'shows a temporary exhaustion after the profound emotional effort called forth by *Tess*'. But the most devastating comment is reserved for *A Laodicean*: 'Criticism . . . is disarmed by the fact that, having been contracted for, it was composed during convalescence from a severe illness. It is quite worthless.'[79] Even the *Critical Heritage* volume on Thomas Hardy (1970) – in which the editor notes that he has included 'representative reviews of each of the major works',[80] and which has small sections on each of the other 'minor novels' – excludes *The Hand of Ethelberta* altogether. Equally symptomatic of the continuing construction of 'Hardy' as the novelist of 'character and environment' is the fact that in at least three major collections of essays on Hardy published in the last ten years[81] none of the 'minor' novels – apart perhaps from *The Well-Beloved* – receives any substantive treatment at all. But what is further apparent in critical orthodoxy is that, even amongst the 'minor novels', there is a pecking order. Where *The Well-Beloved* and *Two on a Tower* are sometimes seen as 'ingenious' fictions, and *Desperate Remedies* and *A Pair of Blue Eyes* as interesting 'juvenilia' or prototypes, *The Hand of Ethelberta* and *A Laodicean* are thoroughly disliked and rejected. 'Worthless', 'lifeless', 'frivolous', 'trivial', 'failures', and, of course, 'improbable' are the words most commonly associated with them.

Finally in this context, I should draw attention to a recent book devoted entirely to the 'minor novels': Richard H. Taylor's *The Neglected Hardy: Thomas Hardy's Lesser Novels* (1982). Taylor's project, while pre-emptively recognizing that 'no revaluative process could elevate them to the stature of the major works',[82] is to bring these novels back into view, since they all have the 'stamp of greatness' even when most wayward. It is a strangely revealing book, because Taylor both registers several significant points (Hardy's fiction 'resists classification'; half of the *oeuvre* is dismissed by critical orthodoxy; certain critical preconceptions about his writing have 'hardened into myth'; the minor novels affect our reading of the major ones) and is at the same time deeply diffident about his material and his enterprise. There is no doubt in Taylor's mind that the 'great novels of character and environment' (the phrase is not attributed to Hardy) are superior, indeed it is partly because of their 'remarkable qualities' that the lesser novels are regarded as lesser. (The circularity of argument in much conventional literary criticism here becomes strikingly apparent.) In fact, perversely, Taylor seems mainly to want to establish 'the nature of each novel's deficiencies and . . . the circumstances which may have contributed to their lesser stature', while rescuing them from oblivion: in other words, to prove definitively why they are 'lesser'. While 'recognising' that even Hardy's major works are 'flawed', that he was really a poet writing pot-boiling fiction in order to live and that he was often affected by the exigencies of the Victorian literary market-place, Taylor, in his conclusion,[83] struggles to establish 'the artistic reasons why the lesser novels fail to attain the stature of the others'. Hardy's own categorization of his fiction is supposed to assist him in this task, but he can only repeat that it is 'exactly the psychic interplay of "character" and "environment" that sustains the reader's deeper interest in the major novels', and admit that while the 'Novels of Ingenuity' are interesting experiments and significant precursors of *Tess* and *Jude* in their exploration of the 'incipient psychic fragmentation' of the protagonists, Hardy's 'shot is scattered too wide' and their effect diffused. Equally, Taylor at once feels that Hardy is most at home with the 'psychic completeness' of Wessex, but also that 'we' as readers imprison him there, thus depreciating his treatment of other milieux; or again, that while Hardy's 'emotional commitment always vitalizes the narrative', there is, in the lesser novels, too much 'biographical reality'. In the end, Taylor can't really find any solid reasons for 'their being lesser works' (he suggests that their titles may contribute because Hardy's best titles are 'straightforward' – like *The Return of the Native* or *Jude the Obscure*?), and he recognizes that they are boldly experimental, highly revealing 'pivots' on which Hardy's career turns. Taylor's problem is that, writing within the confines of conventional Hardy scholarship as he is, he cannot abandon the superior hierarchization of the 'major novels'. Despite the fact that he cannot establish what makes the 'lesser novels' lesser, and despite his perceptions about their qualities and their similarities to the big seven, he cannot confront the implications of his own work: that the hierarchy is a factitious construct, and that he does not need it at all. Instead, he reasserts critical orthodoxy in the very process of appearing to revise it.

We may now ask: first, what was the significance for Hardy of classifying his novels; and second, what is the significance of the 'minor novels' as a critiographical exemplum here? In the first case, there is, of course, no answer: Hardy doesn't say, and what he does say in *The Life* and in his prefaces is part of the ironic and deceptive screen he so painstakingly erects around his life and work. In one sense, the General Preface could suggest that Hardy thought the reviewers by and large correct in their assessment of his fiction (although the evidence of his extreme sensitiveness to criticism militates against this); in another, it might suggest that he was content, for whatever reasons, to maintain the general critical consensus by 1912 – indeed, even to reinforce it with his own classification. But why? Because by then he was a poet, and no longer interested in fiction? Because he was a successful man of letters and a familiar of the best society who wanted his reputation as a novelist to remain intact? Or because he could hide uncomfortable areas of his work behind the irony of a spurious 'classification'?

Three interrelated features of the 'minor novels' may point towards an answer, and also provide one for my second question above. First, like the mysterious 'lost' first novel *The Poor Man and the Lady*, all of these novels are sharply conscious of social class and of the difficulties, in particular, of sexual relationships across class divides. Indeed in some cases, and especially *The Hand of Ethelberta* as we shall see, they are obsessed by it. Second, they are all novels in which 'writing' – or more generally 'art' – is brought into the foreground: either because characters are writers/artists and there are discussions about writing/art (*Ethelberta, A Pair of Blue Eyes, An Indiscretion in the Life of An Heiress* (all that remains of *The Poor Man*), and *The Well-Beloved*); or because the artifice and fictionality of the writing itself is so obtrusive and self-conscious (producing those very factors, indeed, which have caused the heaviest criticism – artificiality, farce, melodrama, pedantic or overwritten style, implausibility, improbability, and so on). The third feature, which in a sense subsumes the other two, is the 'autobiographical' content: in other words, those issues which *The Life* was designed to obscure – questions of the writer's social class and career, and of his ideas and practice as a novelist. The novel in which these three elements inhere most emphatically is also the one that criticism has most despised and disregarded, *The Hand of Ethelberta*. *Ethelberta* tells us more about Hardy as man and writer than *The Life* ever does.

What, then, is the significance of the 'minor' novels? I am not concerned here with their 'meaning' or 'intrinsic value' – which literary criticism demands and my whole project disputes; nor do I wish to propose that these novels have been mis-ranked (that they are 'major' rather than 'minor'), since that would be to reinstate the fallacy of evaluative hierarchies. All I wish to indicate is what happens when 'minor' novels are reassembled with a writer's 'major' ones, with the evaluative categorizations removed. First, the process of doing so itself exposes how the discrimination of 'major' from 'minor' texts is achieved, and how a 'great writer' is constructed: quite simply, criticism 'perceives' those texts which most fully satisfy its norms and assumptions, and excises those which do not. The lack of any objective or absolute status for the evaluative hierarchy is, thus, immediately apparent. Second, and in conjunction, the replacing of 'minor' texts in juxtaposition with 'major' ones shows how criticism also suppresses those features of the 'major' texts which do not square with its preconceptions (hence the 'flaws' in the otherwise 'great' *Tess*, for example), and foregrounds these 'faults' in the 'minor' ones; both of which without the evaluative and comparative categories could be regarded as modal features ('melodrama', for instance). Third, the process raises questions as to why it was necessary to excise the 'minor' texts in the first place, and hence to a recognition of the partial nature of criticism's aesthetic, and more importantly, social predispositions. Fourth, once the evaluative categorization has gone, *all* the novels are freed for much more various and open reading: the closures of the 'major/minor' opposition do not merely exclude certain texts from the agenda, they limit the ways in which the 'major' texts may be read. Fifth, the relocation of the 'minor' texts may pull into relief aspects of the other texts which have before been minimized: for example, the obsession with social class and gender relations in Hardy's 'minor novels' forces these elements in the 'major' ones into much greater prominence.

By rejecting the 'major/minor' classification we expose the premises and presuppositions on which it is constructed in the first place, the determining factors – aesthetic, material, and ideological – which naturalize some writing as 'great literature', and in the process we liberate that writing from precisely those constricting determinations. Hardy may be no more interesting, significant, or representative than any other writer in the last quarter of the nineteenth century in Britain, but constituted as 'Thomas Hardy' his work is at once a present cultural force and one delimited by its very constituents. Part of the enterprise of exposing and understanding the social and cultural field in which 'Hardy' operates as a force, is to perceive how and why 'Hardy' has been constructed as he has and to reappropriate the potentialities of that discursive site.

We may now turn, as a further dimension of this critiography, to a case-study of the ways in which, and the reasons why, the dominant cultural ideology had needed to reproduce and appropriate 'Thomas Hardy' as the 'poet of Wessex', as a great English writer, and as a 'component of the national culture'.

Hardy, 'Wessex', and the making of a national culture

The blurb on the back of a lavishly illustrated biography by Timothy Sullivan (1975) tells us that Thomas Hardy is 'the supreme poet of the English landscape'.[84] It is not a statement that many who are familiar with English literature would think twice about. Some might say 'what about Wordsworth?' – but on the whole there would be assent. Over the hundred years or so since Hardy was producing his earliest novels of 'Wessex', the sentiment has acquired something of the status of a myth. But what does it mean, and is it as natural a judgement as it seems?

I will begin by unpacking the phrase itself. First of all, 'poet' here does not mean only 'the writer of poetry' – it certainly also includes Hardy as novelist. In which case, does 'poet' mean 'celebrant of' or does it contain the Greek sense of 'maker'? My guess is that it signals the former; but that other sense nevertheless still lurks there making for complications which I shall return to. 'The English landscape' is equally problematical, for Hardy's work focuses almost exclusively on his native Dorset and its environs in other west-country counties. In what sense, then, does this 'landscape', and Hardy's 'poetry', represent 'the English landscape' in all its diversity – say, from Kent through Warwickshire to Lancashire, Yorkshire, and Westmoreland? Even more to the point: does it subsume the industrial 'landscape' of Birmingham, Manchester, and Newcastle-upon-Tyne? Of course not. So 'the English landscape', here, calls up a notion of a natural rural environment which is somehow quintessentially 'English' – a non-urban, non-industrial England which itself has mythic force in its implication of an ultimate and irreducible reality: an 'essential England'. Again, I shall return to this.

But it is not even Dorset that Hardy's work represents: it is 'Wessex' – which he himself in the 1895 Preface to *Far From the Madding Crowd* (and elsewhere) ambiguously admits is a 'fictitious' construction. He refers to 'the horizons and landscapes of a partly real, partly dream-country'; later he adds: 'The description of these backgrounds has been done from the real – that is to say, has something real for its basis, however illusively treated.'[85] 'Wessex' is an imaginary area, a landscape of the mind. And this perhaps calls up again that second meaning haunting the word 'poet' – the maker, one who forges. With that in view, we may next interrogate the term 'landscape'. In the context of the publisher's blurb, it certainly means the perceptible physical characteristics of the countryside; it means, to put it simplistically, 'Nature'. But 'landscape', too, also has connotations of aesthetic making: from the verb 'to landscape' in the physical sense, through to the noun for verbal or pictorial representation: 'a landscape.' Artists don't copy landscapes, they make them in the discourses of their work. 'Truth to Nature' may be preceptive, but 'the landscape' is constituted and exists only in its artificial image. So we may say that Hardy 'the poet' creates an English landscape – 'Wessex'.

But there are two words, finally, which I haven't yet considered: 'the supreme.' This is, of course, the ultimate value judgement, placing Hardy above all other contenders for the title 'Poet of the English Landscape'. It is an interesting instance itself of a process of 'making'. First of all it has to construct a notional category or frame of reference: 'poetry of the English landscape' (this is, of course, a naturalized assumption – the reason for its necessity I will return to); and then it has to erect a hierarchy in which it can place Hardy as 'top poet' (the criteria which govern this structure and the ranking within it are, of course, tacit – assuming, again, an unquestioning agreement as to their necessity and common currency). Hardy, then, is positioned as representing the acme of a set of discourses – of genre and evaluation – which have become so naturalized that they can remain unspoken. Indeed much of their force is drawn, precisely, from that silence.

What we have got from this deconstruction of seven words of a publisher's blurb is a great deal about 'making', 'construction', 'artifice', 'representation', 'reproduction', and 'evaluation'. There are two main aspects of this. First, there is Hardy the maker of a landscape ('Wessex'); and second, there is the making of Hardy into the supreme exemplar of a genre – itself artificially constructed – 'the poetry of the English landscape'. My purpose here is to focus primarily on the second of these considerations, but in the process to see what effect such an enterprise has on our understanding of the first. For my central premise is that the two are not, in fact, separate or separable. 'Hardy', as we have him, is so inscribed with the processes of the consumption and reproduction of his work in history that it is now, as it were, a palimpsest of the perceptions, evaluations, readings, re-readings, and rewritings of a particular literary and aesthetic – not to say national – tradition. Hardy is now the product of the process of his reproduction. And it is a 'Hardy', as I have suggested in earlier sections, limited, manipulated, and constrained by the parameters of intelligibility which that process erects. This is not to say, of course, that I have access to the 'real' Hardy – that would be to admit the central tenet of most of the criticism I wish to challenge: that there actually is an antecedent, intrinsic, and essential 'meaning' which criticism prospects for, washes clean, and hallmarks with value. Rather it is to reiterate the two projects of this book: one, that the processes of reproduction are the constitutive discourses of meaning in which any artwork is intelligible, and that they should be as much the focus of study, therefore, as the notional 'text-in-itself'; and two, that – precisely because this is so – literature can be released from the dominant traditions of reproduction, in the very process of their deconstruction, and reproduced differently and strategically on behalf of other interests. This is a 'politics of culture': and a salutary lesson of these deconstructive procedures is to perceive that all cultural production is always political. But the ramifications of this politics, as I hope to show, take us well beyond the hushed and rarefied realms which 'Culture' is conventionally held to occupy.

First, then, I shall explore critiographically the ways in which Hardy has been reproduced in one of his principal modes as 'the poet' of Wessex and the English landscape, and what that implies. Thereafter I will relate this to the process of constructing a national identity, by way of a national culture centred on notions of England and an essential Englishness, which is also structurally related in the twentieth century to the place and function of 'English' in school and tertiary education, and which, as it were, demands 'supreme poets' for its canon. These two processes work hand in glove, at particular historical moments especially, to make, mould, or forge Hardy in such a naturalized image.

If anyone is in any doubt about the shape and place of 'Hardy' in English culture, let me adduce two minor instances of his reproduction in the 1980s. In 1982, in the column he wrote for the *Guardian* each Saturday, Roy Hattersley, a senior Labour Party politician, wrote of his sense 'never quite destroyed . . . that Hardy is the novelist of England, Home and Beauty', and went on to admit that in Reykjavik during the Cod War with Iceland he turned one night to *The Mayor of Casterbridge* 'for consolation and solace'.[86] And in 1983, in the National Trust shop at Blickling Hall in Norfolk, the Macmillan paperback Hardy was on sale beside the glossy books of wholefood recipes and coffee-table editions of country houses. No other novels were to be found on those shelves.[87] But the implications, here, of Hardy as wholesome, homely pastoralist, offering a retreat from a brutal and over-civilized world to a 'real' rural England are not solely the result of fishy politics or consumerist overkill.

From the earliest reviews of his work there are signs of a particular casting of Hardy in these terms. The *Athenaeum*, reviewing *Under the Greenwood Tree* in 1872, noted that he 'has worked principally that vein of his genius which yields the best produce . . . graphic pictures of rustic life somewhere in the West Country. . . . Here the author is clearly on his own ground'; and the *British Quarterly Review* of 1881 comments on the general popularity of that novel, adding: 'the book . . . is a most delightful idyll. . . . [Dorset] is lovingly presented in all its pleasant aspects, its rough frank life, its genuine English language, the fair scenery of its woods and wolds. In it Mr Hardy has laid down the lines of his work.'[88] Already, too, his 'peasants', with, in Edmund Gosse's phrase, their 'exquisite dialogues of rural humour', are attaining a 'Shakespearian richness'[89] – a critical commonplace by the Edwardian period and beyond, which I shall return to. It is no surprise, then, as we have seen (pp. 16–17, 50), to find critics, after Hardy had ceased writing fiction, elevating those novels which contain his most 'characteristic' excellences. Indeed, there is something plaintively telling about W. L. Phelps's remark in 1910:

> one reading of *Jude* suffices, while we never tire of re-reading *Far From the Madding Crowd* and *The Return of the Native*. Probably no publishers' announcement in the world today would cause more pleasure to English-speaking people than the announcement that Thomas Hardy was at work on a Wessex novel with characters of the familiar kind.[90]

Hardy himself, of course, had encouraged this 'ruralizing' process in the General Preface of 1912 by privileging the Wessex novels, by giving credence to the 'reality' of Wessex in listing his fictitious places' 'real' equivalents; and by suggesting that an important aspect of his purpose in writing this fiction was 'to preserve . . . a fairly true record of a vanishing life'. Whatever Hardy intended, his remarks have subtly and substantially underpinned the predilections of his critics before and since. 'Wessex' very rapidly becomes – not Mixen Lane in Casterbridge, not Flintcomb Ash in *Tess*, not the knacker's estate in *The Hand of Ethelberta*, not Marygreen or Aldbrickham in *Jude*, not lifehold leases falling due followed by evictions, not the penetration of machinery and the railways into Dorset, not the extreme poverty of farm labourers, not sexual and economic exploitation, not the tensions of inter-class relations, not the effects of different levels of education on the community, not the workings of a double sexual morality: 'Wessex' becomes 'the true romance of country life', as Edward Wright put it in 1904, where Hardy's real heroes are all on the model of Gabriel Oak – 'country-men in whom the dumb passiveness of the peasantry under affliction rises into a moral grandeur of resignation' (the politics involved in 'making' Hardy a rural idyllist are sharply apparent here). On the strength of this, Wright helpfully points out: 'the truth is that "Merrie England" is a land that still exists, though hidden for some centuries in obscurity'; and it allows him to contrast these 'peasants' with 'men of a meaner sort . . . either townsmen or persons of urban culture', while recognizing that changing conditions 'have obliterated so much of the old romance of Wessex'.[91] 'The old romance of Wessex': this is what is being mined out of Hardy's work, and by 1914 at least, it is well established as having 'elemental' and 'universal' significance. Harold Williams, in that year, represents Hardy's true achievement as those novels characterized by the same type of hero: 'the strong, patient, thoughtful and upright man belonging to the soil' who is brought into conflict with people representing 'the artificial world of modern civilization'. In order to counteract 'the desolating influences of the great industrial cities', Williams constructs a Hardy who keeps 'the older ways, the older thought, the old wisdom, speech and humour' of the rural world alive.[92] This bucolic myth, then, is taken as reality, and the turbulent, divided, urban and industrial society – as, indeed, the actual conditions in rural Dorset – of the early twentieth century can be dismissed as 'artificial'. 'Mr Hardy's rural sketches', remarked Charles Whibley in 1913, 'are touched with an eternal truth . . . we are in a world unaffected by the thing called education, inspired by the follies of politicians, a world which is and will be always what it was. The fashions of the city may shift as they will.'[93] Such pastoralism was, in fact, a constant feature of literature and criticism in the period, which was attempting to 'discover', but in fact created, an 'essential England'. In relation to Hardy's work at least, however, its force as a myth is by no means terminated with the First World War; indeed, it is reproduced in subtly adapted forms even into the 1980s, as the following quotation from an advertisement for a course on Hardy's novels in the Adult Education department of a 'new' university indicates:

> Today our lives are so rushed and hectic and noisy. It is refreshing to escape into the old, traditional, rural world with the peace and calm that Hardy depicts so beautifully in his novels. His love of nature and folk-lore recreate an almost timeless world which unfortunately, even as he wrote, he saw fast disappearing. . . . Although these novels are a form of escape for us from modern, urban living they still remain distinctly modern in their outlook.[94]

Perhaps even more telling is a recent article in an Australian education journal describing a continuing education course – 'A weekend in the country with Thomas Hardy' – run by Sydney University at the Victoria and Albert Guesthouse, Mt Victoria:

> The whole idea behind the weekend was to try to recreate the world of Thomas Hardy and his mythical county of Wessex. We ate hearty food true to the period, made feeble attempts to speak with Wessex accents and wore Victorian costumes to our Wessex Public Dinner and Concert on the Saturday night. We even tried the appropriate country dancing.

'Cultural cringe' is what Australians – with fine double-edged irony
– call their relationship with the old world, and there is something
specially appealing about a 'guided bus tour where we crossed space
and time to visit Wessex, thinly disguised as a popular Blue Moun-
tains beauty spot'.[95]

The process of reproducing Hardy as the 'poet of Wessex', then,
has a number of characteristic features: most obviously, the reduc-
tion of his fictional *oeuvre* to a few key novels which focus on the
rural world; the acceptance of the 'character and environment'
criterion that his true forte is the depiction of nature and its human
fauna; the notion of 'timeless' universality in the 'elemental' human
drama played out in the rustic idyll of nineteenth-century Dorset; and
the sense of Hardy's nostalgia for a passing rural world, a world
more 'real' than the sophisticated urban culture which is superseding
it. His fiction thus comes to represent a mode of what we might call
'humanist-realist pastoral'.

Hardy's work, I want to suggest, is constituted in the terms outlined
above because, at roughly the point at which he is switching from
fiction to poetry (the years immediately prior to World War I), there
is an attempt in England to establish a cohesive national consciousness in a period deeply riven by domestic and international tensions.
There is a perceived need for a national culture to oppose social
anarchy. Crucial to this is a literary culture in which there is a
complex relationship between forms of romanticism and patriotism,
and the formation of a pastoral myth of rural England – often recall-
ing a past, more glorious heritage – which is the true 'essential
England' of national identity.[96] Evidence for this can be adduced in
a variety of forms: for instance, in the patriotic verse of the late
Victorian 'bardic' poets (William Watson, Alfred Austen, W. E.
Henley, Rudyard Kipling, Henry Newbolt, Alfred Noyes); in the
mystical nature poetry of G. K. Chesterton, John Masefield, and
A. E. Housman; in the volumes of *Georgian Poetry*; in the fiction
of John Galsworthy and E. M. Forster; in the founding of the
English Association in 1906; in the production of poetry anthologies
like Quiller-Couch's *The Oxford Book of English Verse* (1900); in
the increasing pressure for 'English' – both the national language
and the national literature – to become the central subject in the
school curriculum, a pressure which emerges in its most explicitly
ideological form with the Newbolt Report on *The Teaching of
English in England* in 1921; in the coterminous take-off of 'English
studies' in the universities, and the rapid and related development of
a professional literary criticism itself concerned to discriminate
'value' and to discern an 'English tradition' of 'great works' and

'great writers'; and, finally but centrally, in the canonization, in the Newbolt Report and elsewhere, of Shakespeare as the keystone of the national culture, as national genius and national poet *par excellence*: 'Shakespeare', said Newbolt, 'is an inevitable and necessary part of school activity because he is . . . our greatest English writer.'[97] This process involved a shaping of the past in which the 'real' England is an organic rural culture of national values and national pride, and the construction of a literary tradition which emphasized the 'Englishness' of the rich national heritage and which could be recuperated for a present bedevilled by urbanization, industrialism, and the 'alienations' of such a culture. What is really at issue, although generally unspoken, is the sense of division – especially class division – as the contradictions of a developing capitalist society emerge. (The Newbolt Report sees literature as a spiritual bulwark against 'the morbid condition of the body politic', against the 'lamentable consequences' which might derive from 'the social problem', and as, potentially, a great 'bond of national unity'.)[98] Fear of 'two nations' which had exercised intellectuals in the 1840s, is, by the first two decades of the new century, a fear of several nations in conflict, and the threat of social breakdown is insistent. Whither is fled, the cultural ideologues cried, that dynamic unity of national consciousness which had so clearly inspired the world of Shakespeare, Raleigh, and Drake? It is a mythical and partial history, but still a potent one, and in the Edwardian period especially (although later, too) there is a continual invocation of that earlier Elizabethan period in which a rich national culture flourished alongside other feats of national achievement. It is not without point that Sir Henry Newbolt both wrote poems like 'Drake's Drum' and chaired the Board of Education commission; nor that Quiller-Couch was a prominent member of the Newbolt Committee, edited the *Oxford Book of English Verse*, was King Edward VII Professor of English at Cambridge from 1912, and co-edited the Cambridge 'New Shakespeare' during the 1920s.

It is within this context that Hardy the poet of Wessex and the English landscape is shaped: his fictional *oeuvre* selectively trimmed to the six or so 'major' novels; the 'faults' and 'flaws' of late books like *Tess* and *Jude* disparaged; 'Merrie England' and 'the true romance of country life' discerned in the 'characteristic' works; and his poetry, as it gradually appears in volume after volume through the first thirty years of the century, recognized as central to an indelibly English tradition. Hardy is very much a writer that the national culture required to be a 'great writer'. As Martin J. Weiner notes in his chapter 'The "English Way of Life"?' in *English Culture and the Decline of the Industrial Spirit, 1850–1980*:

The 'Wessex Worshippers' . . . shaped their own version of
Wessex and made it into a mythic image for England itself. . . .
In such ways, Hardy's complex and realistic fiction was reduced
to a one-dimensional, repetitious chronicle of an appealingly
timeless and nonmaterial way of life under siege.

Indeed, Weiner's remarks on Hardy generally, and his whole
concern in this chapter with 'pastoral retreatism', 'old England', and
the burgeoning myth of the rural 'national past', confirm much of
what I am saying here about the appropriation of Hardy (amongst
many others in the period) by an ideology 'drenched in anxiety about
change', which desperately requires an 'essential' national identity:
that is, one which is beyond the depredations of historical
process.[99] From early in his career Hardy is 'the man who could
put before us the life of the English peasants', a man who 'belongs
by birth and temperament to the soil of England',[100] but he is also
rapidly presented (significantly by Charles Whibley, one of W. E.
Henley's protégés) as the Shakespeare of his generation – 'a
Shakespeare in his keen perception of human nature, a Shakespeare,
also, in the singing of his "native wood-notes wild"', and whose
peasants are 'the true heirs of Shakespeare's age'.[101] Another
contemporary finds that in Hardy's 'peasant characters we are made
to feel that life on the English soil has not changed essentially since
Shakespeare peopled his plays with country folk of his own day'.[102]
Hardy is here, of course, being critically placed and reproduced to
establish both the unity and longevity of English culture, and the
bond of genius at the heart of the national literature. In addition, in
this period, his closeness to 'the soil of England' underpins the pure
patriotism of the Georgian poets (for whom he was something of a
mentor), and his supposed 'nostalgia' for the rural past could be
represented, like theirs, as a corrective to the disharmonious modern
world. Equally significant, perhaps, is that in 1909 Sir Henry
Newbolt reviewed Hardy's epic poetic drama *The Dynasts* when it
was finally completed. Seeing is as 'the forerunner . . . of many
great days in the poetical life of the English-speaking race', he says
of the work's inception:

A strong bent of patriotism, traditional, local, personal, had long
interested [Hardy] in the 'vast international tragedy' of Napoleon's
career. . . . He determined accordingly to set out the story of this
'Clash of Peoples' in a poem of gigantic scale, and with the
British nation for hero.

And Newbolt ends that he does not 'care to imagine a time when
Englishmen will not read this poem with delight, and value it among

their great possessions'.[103] *The Dynasts* has not fulfilled Newbolt's hopes, but the 'Wessex Hardy' surely has.

For this process of nationalizing a great writer did not stop with the First World War, but is part of a continuing cultural politics most active at times of crisis when the national identity is most in need of sustenance. For Edmund Blunden, in the dark days of the Second World War in 1942, he is, predictably, the true 'poet' of rural England: 'so long as human beings are moved by the quality of the life of tree and wood . . . they will not be forgetful of Hardy', and 'as an artist of country life and occasion he has not many superiors among English poets'.[104] A year later in a war-time book which, as we have seen, still remains deeply influential in reproducing the rural-humanist tragedian of the universal struggle between Man and Fate, Lord David Cecil established firmly that Hardy's description of nature is his primary virtue, and, pre-empting the blurb writer with whom I started, states: 'Hardy's picture of Wessex is the most elaborate study of landscape in English letters.' Cecil, indeed, places him foursquare in the English tradition: 'he is very English. The English literary genius is, most characteristically, a poetic genius'; and, in a classic formulation, he later adds: 'The only tradition Hardy thoroughly assimilated was the ancient Shakespearian tradition, which is the heritage of all Englishmen.' One could hardly ask for it clearer than that. Hardy, we learn – born when 'rural Wessex was still feudal pre-industrial Wessex, with its villages clustering round the great houses and church, with its long-established families and time-hallowed customs', a world indeed 'responsive . . . to the love of home, to the beauty of spring and sunshine, the charm of innocence . . . the grandeur of heroism; to the horror of death . . .' (we must remember the war-time context, these were the Clark lectures in Cambridge, 1942) – is 'the last representative of the tradition and spirit of the Elizabethan drama'. Through him we catch a late glimpse of that 'old England': 'We take our farewell gaze at the England of Shakespeare through the eyes of one who, in spite of all his imperfections, is the last English writer to be built on the grand Shakespearian scale'; and it is thus also a feature of Hardy's vision that 'that rural England, which was hallowed for him by every tie of childish sentiment, was beginning to crumble before his eyes'.[105]

It is this aspect which dominates another extensively influential monograph, Douglas Brown's *Thomas Hardy* (1954). Hardy's work here is centrally concerned with his regret at the decline of the rural community in the face of urban culture, and we may hear very precise echoes, in the following quotation, of those early twentieth-century critics like Wright, Williams, and Whibley (see pp. 59–60 above) who also mobilized Hardy's 'Wessex' to oppose 'modern life':

> His protagonists are strong-natured countrymen, disciplined by the necessities of agricultural life. He brings into relation with them men and women from outside the rural world, better educated, superior in status, yet inferior in human worth. The contact occasions a sense of invasion, of disturbance . . . and the theme of urban invasion declares itself more clearly as the country, its labour, its people and its past consolidate their presence. . . . This pattern records Hardy's dismay at the . . . precarious hold of the agricultural way of life. It records . . . a deep-seated allegiance of the writer's personality, a degree of dependence upon an identified and reliable past.

This notion of Hardy's 'dismay' at rural decline enables Brown to read the novels (or rather, those he chooses to deal with) as an expression of it, so that *Tess*, for example, is 'not merely the tragedy of a heroic girl, but the tragedy of a proud community baffled and defeated by processes beyond its understanding or control'; and *The Mayor of Casterbridge* 'acknowledges the bitter situation of agriculture in contemporary England. Henchard suffers defeat, and passes, and the village rites pass with him.' All this is achieved, in true 'character and environment' terms, by 'the vivid sense of the meaning of the scenery, the human and the natural involving one another'.[106] In 1968 (another 'crisis' year), Irving Howe, in an also widely recommended book, continues to lend currency to the 'characteristic' features of Hardy's work: 'With the major exception of *Jude* . . . the Wessex novels form a prolonged celebration . . . of the English countryside' – or at least those novels 'which explore the life of Wessex'. For we learn that 'unfortunately the received opinion of Hardy's minor fiction is largely correct'; so out, as usual, go those novels which disturb the dominant rural-humanist image of Hardy. This is the Hardy who 'would always know and love the world of Wessex as nothing else: it represented for him the seemliness of an ordered existence, of all that is natural, rooted and tried'; this is a Wessex where 'there survives the memory of a life in which nature and society are at peace', where 'the past can be seen as embodying the sameness and continuity, the unifying rhythms, of a human existence that extends beneath or beyond the agitation of the historical process'; and where 'Nature' is not just background but a 'character', an 'animated presence', 'the source and repository of all the energies that control human existence. Like Wordsworth, Hardy instinctively unites nature and man, making the external setting a kind of sharer in the human fate.'[107] Well, we've heard it all before (especially at moments of 'agitation' in 'the historical process', like 1968) and no doubt will again. One has only to think of the mocked-up 'character and environment' photographs on the covers of the 'New Wessex' paperback edition of the novels (plate 1); or the nineteenth-century English landscapes on the Penguin (plate 2) and 'World's Classics' editions; let alone the tours round 'Hardy's Wessex' (plate 3), the books of 'Hardy Country' photographs, or the educational sound filmstrip (1987) which 'explores . . . Hardy's love and understanding of the countryside and the traditions of its people, his mental affinity with the aspirations of the Impressionists and his sensuous pleasure in nature'.[108] There are also countless books which have traced the exact contours of 'Wessex' in Dorset, notably by Hermann Lea and Clive Holland[109] but culminating with Andrew Enstice's *Thomas Hardy: Landscapes of the Mind* (1979) which, as far as I understand its point at all, wishes to compare Hardy's 'Wessex' in very great detail with nineteenth-century southern England in order 'to discover what he achieves by the changes in his own attitude to basically similar settings'.[110] Such topographical and antiquarian scholarship only serves to reinforce notions of the 'reality' of Wessex, and Hardy's circumscription by them.

Even more convincing proof of the depth of penetration of these constitutive critical discourses of Hardy is their emergence, differently inflected, in a 'social' critic like Merryn Williams whose whole enterprise in *Thomas Hardy and Rural England* (1972) is to demystify the 'Wessex Hardy' of popular imagination, but who can offer only a simple reflectionist reading of Hardy based on the notion that he does write a 'real' history of a 'real' place, and that he is 'the first writer to achieve the necessary range and realism of the novel of English country life'.[111] Equally to the point is the fact that a sophisticated quasi-structuralist like David Lodge cannot break with conventional responses: 'it is his ability to make concrete the relationship between character and environment in a way that is both sensuously particular and symbolically suggestive that makes him such a powerful and original novelist'; and he writes of *The Return of the Native*: 'subtract all description of the heath from the novel, and you would be left with a rather contrived melodrama of unhappy love, relieved by some amusing comic dialogue from the rustics.'[112] The lines of Hardy criticism were drawn early, but they survive remarkably well; and it is worth remembering here that critics like Cecil, Brown, and Howe at least, are the source of many of the A level examination questions discussed in the following chapter, as well as being the commonest 'further reading' texts in contemporary 'study guides' on Hardy.

Plate 1 Macmillan 'New Wessex' edition covers

Plate 2 Penguin 'English Library' edition covers

Plate 3 A tourist guide

Finally, in this critiography of Hardy as poet of an English national culture, a rather different and more recent recuperation, but one again in a period of social crisis for the ruling ideology: Donald Davie's *Thomas Hardy and British Poetry*, written soon after *'les événements'* of 1968 and published in 1973. It, too, has been a very influential book in its marking out, in modern poetry, of an English counter-tradition to that of modernism and its largely American successors; and it has an equivalent in the fiction and criticism of Malcolm Bradbury and David Lodge which has consistently recuperated an English liberal-realist tradition in the novel from the dominant discourses of modernism and postmodernism.[113] Davie's book is 'political' at that level, but also explicitly so at other levels too. It is a good example of the presence, within the theoretically 'disinterested' field of culture, literary studies, and English, of an active liberal politics. His 'foreword', while retaining a social dimension in the discussion of literature, nevertheless expressly detaches itself from 'accepting Marxist projections into a Messianic future, and hence [from] leftist programs in the politics of today'.[114] Within this general frame, Davie wants to claim the influence of Hardy as the most far-reaching for British poetry in the last fifty years, and, *contra* the 'reactionary' tendencies of the 'great modernists', as 'the one poetic imagination of the first magnitude in the present century who writes out of, and embodies in his poems, political and social attitudes which a social democrat recognizes as "liberal"' (6). What these attitudes are, Davie identifies as 'a margin for human choice but the slimmest margin imaginable, motivated in Hardy's words, by "loving-kindness, operating through scientific knowledge"'. This, Davie calls 'scientific humanism' (7). In Hardy, this is a tiny final hope for humanity based upon science and industrial technology, held against all the harrowing knowledge of what such developments have already 'inflicted on the fabric of social and interpersonal relationships in the England that he knew' (10–11). It is a diffident attitude, and its effect on later poets (primarily Philip Larkin, but others, too, in and around 'The Movement') has meant 'an apparent meanness of spirit, a painful modesty of intention, extremely limited objectives' (11). But it is poetry, nevertheless, which is responsible and challenging, compared to American (and other) modernists and apocalyptic excess. In the period after 1968, Hardy's 'engaging modesty and his decent liberalism' may seem, Davie says, like a 'cop-out' on the poetic vocation, which is 'to be radical, to go to the roots'. But Hardy, indeed, does achieve this, if only as a modest but *expert* workman 'in a corporate enterprise which from time to time publishes a balance-sheet called *The Golden Treasury* or *The Oxford Book of*

English Verse' (40). Davie's choice of anthologies is significant in my context here because it indicates once again an 'essentially English' construction of Hardy, albeit differently inflected.

Thomas Hardy and British Poetry is a wayward, although finally predictable book in that it purports to be celebrating Hardy's liberal lack of certainty against the proto-fascist tendencies of the reactionary modernists, but is in fact firmly pointed against the left who, as Davie sees it, have dominated the British intelligentsia roughly since Hardy's death. Presumably this is an instance of that old liberal slippage which can only perceive the politics of both the right and of the left as the same: totalitarian. For example:

> No one who has been involved in recent disturbances on British campuses – for instance at the University of Essex in 1968 . . . can doubt that we already have in England a politically conscious intellectual class in principled opposition to the national society, and ready on that principle to purvey 'distortions and special pleadings' to the nation's student youth. (91)

Notice, here, 'the national society' and 'the nation's student youth'. For beneath the liberal tolerance is an unquestioned assumption that 'the nation' is an ideologically innocent formulation, not one which is constructed by the ruling ideology – often in the form of a national culture (and thus incorporating an 'English' Thomas Hardy) – to neutralize the class divisions of a capitalist society. But in the end the contradictions of Davie's position overwhelm his argument; for although he abhors the left intelligentsia's totalitarianism, what he dislikes even more is its tendency to be in 'perpetual opposition [which] cannot be other than irresponsible' (91) – in other words, its refusal to be contaminated or incorporated by taking power. That seems to me to be an odd form of totalitarianism. Indeed it might just be that, paradoxically, it is Davie's inert liberalism which dominates 'the national society' and has manipulated the 'nation's student youth' for many years, obscuring in and by its 'openness' and its 'pluralism' the deep inequalities and injustices, the 'distortions and special pleadings', of a capitalist nation state. What Davie objects to – and objected to at Essex in 1968 – is having his own authority and liberalism (and they are not contradictory) revealed to be authoritarian, and to having them challenged. After all, liberal hegemony only survives by failing to acknowledge that pluralistic consensus is in itself an ideology. But an ideology cannot, of course, function effectively when it recognizes itself to be such. So liberalism, for Davie, remains ideologically innocent, and it is Thomas Hardy therefore – a Hardy who says, as quoted by Davie, 'I find that my politics really are neither Tory or radical'[115] – who is once more wheeled out as the 'national poet'. He is a writer who many years ago had faced similar problems – of a landscape destroyed, of a culture in ruins, of uncertain belief and weak commitment – to those which Larkin and Davie face today, and which Hardy bravely and modestly confronted (as they do) in technically expert verse. Well, it isn't the poet of 'Merrie England' and pastoral 'Wessex', nor of 'the English landscape' in any conventionally recognizable form. But it is, nevertheless, a good example of Hardy incorporated by criticism: himself shaped and positioned by the 'English tradition' he is purported to instigate; his poetry 'rewritten' by its association with Larkin's, so that Hardy's work is retroactively 'read off' from Larkin's – reproduced, in other words, as an ironic late twentieth-century liberal quietism on behalf of a national 'landscape' and culture ravaged by industrialism, urbanization, and totalitarian or doctrinaire politics. Perhaps, after all, it is not so very different to that Edwardian criticism which constructed Hardy's Wessex as a retreat from the 'desolating influences' of the 'artificial world of modern civilization'.

'Hardy' is constructed as 'the poet of Wessex' within the discourses in which he is reproduced, and this modelling and framing is not just a matter of literary criticism wishing to hold his work within a conception of humanist realism – although this is itself ideologically significant as we shall see in a moment – but involves a larger enterprise to do with the formation of an English national culture. In the final section of this chapter and in Part II, I want to disturb this process by hailing into view another 'landscape', another 'Wessex', another 'Hardy' – not so much because I think they are more correct, more 'real', closer to the dark heart of Hardy's secret meaning, but because they expose those ideological processes which inform the 'making' of 'the supreme poet of the English landscape', and which also manipulate and position us as the quiescent subjects ideology requires us to be. A very different landscape emerges when we change the frame: one which offers – for criticism, teaching, and private reading – a radical prospect.

A disruptive 'Thomas Hardy'

Why, then, should 'Thomas Hardy' have been constituted in the dominant forms demonstrated in the previous sections? Why has he been made to fit uneasily into the critical discourse of liberal-humanist realism; why has his 'improbablism' been criticized away, his 'faults' and 'flaws' acknowledged but dismissed, his 'minor' 'Novels of Ingenuity' excised, his work (suitably doctored) pulled into the national canon, his fiction either 'rewritten' by devoted

critics or virtually ignored by F. R. Leavis (even though his novels
were compared to George Eliot's, avatar of humanist realism and the
ideological centre of Leavis's socio-critical enterprise)? The answer,
I think, is that – at whatever level of consciousness – there is a
recognition of just how radically Hardy's fiction challenges and
refutes humanist realism and the whole cultural ideology which
informs and sustains it – not only in the 'minor novels', although
more explicitly there, but in all the novels. Terry Eagleton has noted
one point on which bourgeois criticism is virtually unanimous: 'that
Hardy, regrettably, was really unable to *write*', and that it has,
therefore, repressed the fact that 'the significance of Hardy's writing
lies precisely in the *contradictory* constitution of his linguistic practice' in order to confound 'the ideological disarray that his fictions,
consciously or not, are bound to produce within a criticism implac-
ably committed to the "literary" as yardstick of maturely civilized
consciousness'. Hence,

> criticism remains worried by the precise status of Hardy's
> 'realism'; and it is not difficult to see why. For the contradictory
> nature of his textual practice cannot but throw into embarrassing
> relief those ideologically diverse constituents of fiction that it is
> precisely fiction's task to conceal; it is by 'not writing properly'
> that he lays bare the device.[116]

We have seen that throughout the history of Hardy criticism his
'improbablism', 'pedantic' style, 'sensationalism', and other elements of his 'anti-realism', combined with his 'gloom', 'pessimism',
'ideas', and 'fatalism', have given the critics difficulties, and that
they have been 'dealt with' in different ways. In other words, the
fictional modality of Hardy's work seems itself to challenge or
unnerve not just literary-critical 'taste', but a whole world view.

But all the elements which are criticized in Hardy are, of course,
always present in all fiction – albeit to a greater or lesser extent
disguised. And in realism they are especially disguised, in so far as
the predominant fictional strategy here is the purporting to tell a true
story, a 'history' which is absolutely convincing in its verisimilitude.
This is certainly the case, for example, with George Eliot whose
work is itself full of non-realistic elements, but which the novels'
ideological and formal conviction and 'veracity' suppress. When
their presence does momentarily rupture the enclosing membrane
(realism), they are signs and symptoms of a contradiction, tension,
or strain within the world view they are articulating.[117] The
impossibility of realizing the latter in real terms (the gradual
humanistic reform of society, say, within industrial capitalism),
means the impossibility of 'telling things as they really are' except

in terms of fictive contrivance. The crucial formal difference between Hardy and George Eliot is that where Eliot is at immense pains to disguise fictive contrivance, to paper over the cracks in the realist project, Hardy often seems to parade them, to draw attention to artifice and the fictionality of fiction (his 'intrusive' style is a case in point). This process of demystifying the practices and deceits of realist narrative, destabilizes the realist myth as a whole: for how far is Eliot 'probable' and 'plausible' if Hardy, operating ostensibly within a realist paradigm ('Wessex'), flaunts its very speciousness? (The critics' answer, of course, is that Hardy has 'flaws' in his technique, is a 'faulty' realist.) But in addition, his contrivances – artifice, coincidence, or melodrama, for example – articulate a world in which individual men and women are the 'sport' of malevolent, or at least indifferent, forces which finally destroy their happiness, defeat their aspirations, and make a mockery of their life. Now, this can be regarded as a metaphysical 'pessimism' which, although unbalanced, results in a 'tragic vision' where fine but flawed individuals are destroyed in a duel with Fate: indeed this is how much criticism has and does perceive Hardy. But the 'victimization' of the individuals – and this is the aspect of Hardy which has been most emphatically ignored – is not by any means presented as 'metaphysical', but rather as a concrete, material, social process. Education, farming, lease and copy holding, marriage, railway journeys, and so on are material matters, and they represent the fundamental texture of Hardy's fictional world, whatever criticism has said and whatever his 'intentions' might have been. The point to notice here is that these processes of mundane victimization, these social 'tragedies' – so very radical, as a number of contemporary critics half-perceived, compared to George Eliot's humanist world view – are articulated in the demystifying anti-realistic modes noted above. Hardy's work, in other words, may be seen to propose the limits of fictional realism for depicting the real social forces, pressures, contradictions, and exploitations within which individuals actually live out their lives. Or, to put it still more provocatively, Hardy's work may even question the concept of the individual human subject altogether: 'character' becoming no more than the nexus of conflicting social and psychological determinants, and 'characters' no more than 'images' or representations of those determinants or their effects (hence, say, the stagey 'melodrama' of Alec d'Urberville, the *nouveau-riche* villain).

Such a version of 'Hardy', of course, calls in question the myths of bourgeois realism and liberal humanism in a very radical way; and it becomes a direct challenge to and rebuttal of George Eliot's classic humanist realism. It is here that we may perceive why F. R.

Leavis had to reject Hardy (and why so many other critics treat him in the way they do). For 'Literature', in order to affirm the values of 'Life' against the deadly pressures of a technologico-Benthamite mass civilization, has to show in its concrete experiential 'reality' how human beings can transcend their social environment and fulfil themselves as free individual subjects. By this process, 'society' can itself be redeemed. The emphasis on the empirically experiential is, of course, central to the notion of realism in George Eliot in both the literary and the philosophical (ideological) senses: realism helps people to understand and sympathize with their fellow beings in order to improve their own moral altruism and hence the condition of life generally; realism, therefore, must be grounded in the truth of experience in order to teach people about reality. Kate Belsey has pointed out that the 'Leavisian reading' 'manifests a prior commitment in its reproduction of the values and strategies of the text it undertakes to judge'; that it either selects texts with which it is ideologically in accord (and thus discards others), or that it 'finds' in the texts it chooses values which echo its own premises and practices. And as Belsey says, it is based on the notion of

> a universe whose sole inhabitant is [Barthes's] 'Eternal Man', a subjectivity which precedes all discourse, and whose silent presence both determines and transcends history. This 'human essence', the rightful heritage of individuals, can float free of the destructive forces of a mass society by re-establishing a connection with the 'essential life' inscribed in the great tradition of English literature.[118]

But Hardy's fiction, as I have suggested, rejects this: his 'improbablism' and anti-realism, his melodramatic, 'senseless', and contingent world, in which individual human beings are the victims of social processes they do not control, call the whole humanist myth in question. And so, for Leavis, Hardy has to go. Belsey has also pointed out that Leavisian criticism itself constitutes the object of its scrutiny, either by cutting away 'bad' parts of a text (half of *Daniel Deronda*, for example, is removed and the novel renamed 'Gwendoline Harleth' in order to fit Leavis's critical presuppositions), or by 'limit[ing] the possible readings of those texts, confin[ing] their meaning within the conventional, the acceptable, the authoritatively "obvious"'.[119] At the macro level, it is this process which constructs 'The Great Tradition', and Hardy's anti-realism makes his work not 'acceptable' for it.

And not just for Leavis, as we have seen. Many critics – less ideological, or less clear about their aims, than Leavis – have had to make Hardy's fiction 'acceptable', to recuperate it for realism.

For realism is not just a matter of literary form, it is the 'common sense' expression in aesthetic terms of an ideology in which the unified individual human subject 'makes sense' of her or his world by negotiation with external forces (society, Nature, and so on). S/he may win or lose (comedy or tragedy), but the conception of the unified human subject always potentially self-determining is not affected. And this presupposes a sensible universe – one which can be made sense of. One form of 'making sense' of the world is by way of the 'probablist' discourses of realism, in which 'plausible' characters are 'convincingly' deployed in relation to the 'credible' processes of the 'real' natural and social world. Realism, in effect, is the writing of the unified human subject onto the immensities of time, process, and history, and as such is a crucial instrument in liberal-humanist ideology's naturalizing function. It confirms that the world is anthropocentric, that the individual is free, and that society comes second. It is for this reason, primarily, that non- or anti-realist forms (gothic, melodrama, etc.) have been regarded as seditious and inimical by the dominant literary culture (they are, indeed, often deployed by those opposed to its informing ideology), and have been marginalized by the construction of 'canons' and 'great traditions' which exclude them. And it is for the same reason that potentially disruptive discourses like those of Hardy's fiction must be made to fit. Because they fundamentally challenge the authority of the individual human subject as the source of social efficacy – indeed, deconstruct the individual 'character' as unified being ('Jude' is merely the riven locus of social determinations; 'Tess' a collage of social images of her) – and because they imply an implacable social formation out of the control of individual voli-tion, they call in question the veracity of a realism which suppresses these perceptions. The essential fiction of bourgeois realism, as novelists since Defoe, Fielding, and Sterne have known, is the illu-sion of truth. When this comes to be believed as literal truth ('conviction'), then fiction and ideology are working very closely together, and the deception of 'telling things as they really are' has to be sustained at all costs. Hardy's fiction, in foregrounding the deception, jeopardizes the whole construct, and so has to be neutralized or reconstituted.

In the following two chapters, I will suggest how social discourses other than literary criticism participate in this process of reproducing 'good little Thomas Hardy'.[120]

2

'Thomas Hardy' in education

In an article entitled 'Hardy Rules OK' in the *Times Educational Supplement* (2 January 1981), Antonia Byatt indicated that of all the writers mentioned by prospective candidates to University College, London in 1980 as amongst their favourite novelists, Thomas Hardy was 'overwhelmingly' first. He received 194 mentions out of the 520 or so applications Ms Byatt saw (about half the year's total), with Jane Austen next at 165 and D. H. Lawrence third with 158. (As a poet, interestingly, Hardy only ranked twentieth, with 24 mentions – T. S. Eliot coming first with 104.) Confirming this impression of Hardy's contemporary importance at the advanced end of secondary education, is an article in the *Literature Teaching Politics* journal of 1982 which tabulates the number of 'mentions' authors receive in O and A level examination papers from the eleven examining boards over the period 1974–84. Hardy is third with 54 'mentions', only following Shakespeare with 190 and Chaucer with 56 (Dickens with 48, and Jane Austen with 46, come next).[1]

Ms Byatt admits that her figures 'are not statistically significant', and the ranking game is only partly serious, but she makes a couple of comments about her findings which are useful starting points for me here. First, she notes that although 'A level set texts clearly influenced the students' reading preferences', she has not included in her count any book only mentioned as an A level text unless the applicant also claimed to have read more by the same author out of interest. Second, she suggests that Hardy's popularity as novelist is even greater than the figures suggest because of 'the warmth and real enthusiasm of the praise afforded to him'. Third, she 'suspects, though of course . . . cannot prove', that D. H. Lawrence would have been ahead of Hardy five years ago and level pegging two years ago, and she goes on to ask:

Do we now have a generation of teachers who were taught by a generation who were preached Lawrence by Leavis, and discovered Hardy for themselves? Or does the rural nostalgia ally itself to the more simple, back-to-the-earth emotions that led to the passion for Tolkein?

A number of points arise from this which are relevant to debates about 'literary value'; the constitution of the 'canon' of great writers and their masterworks; the processes of cultural reproduction; and about the role of 'English' or 'Literary Studies' in education. First, we perceive that a lot of young people in the early 1980s are reading Hardy – a late nineteenth-century novelist – with some enthusiasm. Conversely, only one applicant had mentioned the 'Rothman's Football Year Book'; Ms Byatt is wry about this (was the applicant successful I wonder?), although she chooses to use a common contemporary football slogan for her own title. Hardy, that title claims, is very much a part of contemporary culture. Second, we see that it is only Hardy the novelist who is important, not Hardy the poet or Hardy the poet–dramatist of *The Dynasts*; although we don't know from Ms Byatt's article which novels of Hardy's constitute the favourite reading (I will return to this in more detail later). But certainly, only a part of Hardy's written *oeuvre* comprises his importance as a contemporary cultural figure. Third, we gather that Hardy has not had a stable position at the top of the list; that he is somehow in fashion now; that D. H. Lawrence held that position a few years ago; and that this had to do with the teachers' own education and with F. R. Leavis's messianic role in relation to him. Fourth, we may notice Ms Byatt's unquestioning assumptions that students 'discover Hardy for themselves' and that what constitutes Hardy's popularity is 'the rural nostalgia'.

The immediate questions within education which these issues raise are: why is Hardy being read so enthusiastically now; what Hardy is being read and in what ways; what is the relationship of academic criticism to education, and how does it manifest itself; and where, in this context, do Ms Byatt's assumptions stand? These are all questions, of course, to do with the 'making' of a 'classic author', and the answers to them show how heavily predetermined – in this instance by the institutions of education – the 'popularity' of Hardy's fiction is. But this crucial factor in a student's understanding of the nature and purpose of his or her education is withheld from the students themselves: the 'set texts' simply appear as objects worthy of study, as 'great novels' within the 'English' syllabus. How they got there and why they are these ones and not others, what the parameters of their 'readability' are and why they should be 'valuable' or 'important' (to an eighteen-year-old football fan in the 1980s, say), are questions not raised. And if they were, they would be answered from within the discourse which controls the notion of 'English' in education: that great novels are naturally here because they are inherently valuable, and that that is what they are here to teach you to be able to perceive. But in fact, the unspoken answers to those questions go a long way to explaining what 'Hardy', and why this particular 'Hardy', rules OK among young people in the 1980s.

What follows, in an attempt to provide those unspoken answers, is an interpretative analysis of the place of Hardy in school examinations since the early decades of this century. It is, of course, only a very partial sample: I was not able to study complete runs of papers for any of the examination boards (except, with a few gaps, the Joint Matriculation Board (JMB));[2] neither have I looked at both major 'levels' of examination papers consistently; and an accurate and comprehensive account is also complicated both by the change from 'Matriculation' to 'School Certificate' to 'General Certificate of Education' over the period, and by the different styles of papers and sets of 'alternatives' which the various boards employ. My research for this part of the book, and hence the sample, ended in 1981–2 (although because the Boards must publish their syllabuses at least two years ahead, my sample effectively runs up to 1983–4). I am aware, therefore, that in the past few years there may have been changes which would affect the profile to some small extent. Nevertheless, it is comprehensive enough to tell us when Hardy arrived on the syllabus; what Hardy texts students study; what kinds of questions are asked about him – hence what critical assumptions lie behind the teaching and examining of his work; and therefore to perceive that artificial construction, the 'great writer' Thomas Hardy, as constituted for the school student. Any reading of any of his texts will, of course, be constrained by the parameters of intelligibility set up by this figure, and what becomes immediately apparent, not surprisingly, is the consonance of it with the 'Thomas Hardy' of academic criticism. I should make absolutely clear before I begin, however, that I am dealing here with the dominant and determining structures and institutions within which a student taking an O or A level examination in English Literature may study Hardy. It has been pointed out to me that 'Hardy is less importantly constituted by critics and examiners than he is by readers', and that in the post-war period 'he is bound to appeal to an audience which – no matter how implicitly – sees itself as somehow dispossessed, curious about a lost past, urbanized, and strongly attracted to the idea that life is a series of fateful tricks'.[3] This may well be true, although it is still a largely conventional critical 'Hardy' who is held to appeal to the *mentalité* of the post-war generations. Equally, it has been quite properly explained to me on a number of occasions by practising teachers that what actually happens in the classroom may bear no resemblance to the Hardy figure set up by the examination papers. Hardy's presentation of gender, class, the rural economy, religion, the railways, and so on may all be treated as focal issues, and his works may be used for all sorts of purposes and in all sorts of contexts. This I quite accept; but one cannot but recognize, also, the profound pressure exerted by the ruling ideology of 'English' by way of its syllabus and its assessment. No teacher and no student within the system can fail to be shaped by it; and it is this informing structural formation which I am concerned to identify. Let me add that in what follows I am also sharply conscious of the difficulties and constraints experienced by teachers in secondary schools: that set books have to remain unchanged for several years because of the cost of replacing them; that what publishers make available delimits 'the syllabus'; that for public examinations there must be common syllabuses and standard expectations of assessment, so that students know what is required of them and there is parity across the system. Nevertheless, we must again recognize that these factors themselves work to reinforce the dominant critico-pedagogic ideology of 'English' or 'Literary Studies'; and it is this which I now wish to track.

Hardy's work seems to enter the school curriculum, by way of the examination boards, in the late 1920s. The first appearance I have found is of *The Mayor of Casterbridge* on the JMB Higher School Certificate paper in 1926; it was 'prescribed reading', and was followed in 1928 by *Under the Greenwood Tree*. (Hardy emerges on the Lower/Junior School Certificate syllabus a few years later, with generally similar texts: *Under the Greenwood Tree*, for example, first appeared for the JMB in 1931.) The Cambridge Local Examinations Syndicate introduced *Far From the Madding Crowd* in their Senior (Higher) School Certificate 'General English Literature' paper as one title in a catch-all question (which had been employed since 1921 at least): 'Name the authors of six of the following, and give a short account of any one of the works.' (It would also have been possible, in the Cambridge Local 1927 paper, to answer on a few of Hardy's poems from the set book, Methuen's *An Anthology of Modern Verse*.) Hardy does not reappear for either board until 1932, when the JMB have selections from *The Dynasts*, and Cambridge set *Under the Greenwood Tree*. Thereafter, through the 1930s and 1940s, both boards set Hardy fairly regularly, although not every year: the JMB set *The Dynasts* three more times, *The Trumpet-Major*, *Far From the Madding Crowd*, and *The Mayor of Casterbridge* once each and *The Woodlanders* five times; Cambridge set *The Return of the Native* once, and then seem to have concentrated on *Far From the Madding Crowd* and *The Mayor of Casterbridge* for the 'Prescribed Texts' paper, although on the 'Victorian Novel' it was always possible to answer on Hardy in more general terms. By the end of the 1950s Hardy is being set almost every year, often at both O and A levels in the GCE (from 1951), and from the 1960s through to 1981 Hardy is set every year at one or other level by most of the boards I inspected. (From 1976, in addition to JMB and Cambridge, I looked at the Associated Examinations Board (AEB) and the University of London, as well as making random checks on the Oxford Local and the Oxford and Cambridge Schools examination boards.)

A number of points may be made from this data. First, that from shortly before his death, when he first enters the syllabus, Hardy has become increasingly present on school English Literature syllabuses, until, in 1981, *Far From the Madding Crowd* was on the O level syllabus of both JMB and Cambridge, *Tess of the d'Urbervilles* on both the Oxford Local and the JMB A level, *Selected Poems* was on Cambridge A level, *The Mayor of Casterbridge* on AEB O level, *The Return of the Native* on both AEB A level papers, and *The Mayor of Casterbridge* on London A level. In other words, at the point when Antonia Byatt did her survey, Hardy is at his most emphatically present on the GCE syllabuses. It is also worth noting in passing, to be returned to in the following chapter, that three of the four fiction texts exist at this time in the form of film or television versions: Schlesinger's film of *Far From the Madding Crowd* (made in 1967, and released on EMI video in 1980), Polanski's film of *Tess of the d'Urbervilles* (made in 1979); and Giles and Potter's television version of *The Mayor of Casterbridge* (first shown in 1978 and repeated in 1979). None of the GCE examination questions, however, make any reference to the fact that the 'text' may be most immediately accessible to students studying these 'set' works of Hardy in visual, rather than the originally written, form.

Second, it is apparent that for much of the period covered, Hardy is presented as a novelist of note, but by no means so extensively as a poet. In the earlier part of the period, the JMB had occasionally set selections from *The Dynasts* (the last two occasions were in the 1958 and 1963 A level papers) but none of Hardy's other poetry until 1967, and then only a few poems in an anthology called *Ten Modern Poets* for O level. He reappears in this form in 1971–2 and 1979–80, but seems never to have been set as poet at A level. Cambridge first set Hardy as poet in 1963 (till 1965) when he moved from the 'Fiction' section of Paper VI to the 'Poetry' section. He reappears in an anthology, *A Choice of Poets* (ed. Hewett), for O level in 1972–3, and finally makes it to A level in his own right in 1981. Given the pre-eminence of T. S. Eliot in Antonia Byatt's sample, Hardy would seem to be affected by a critical orthodoxy which continues to boost the modernist movement, although the growing presence of Hardy as poet in the late 1970s may indicate the influence of Donald Davie's reassessment of the 'English' tradition in 1973 in *Thomas Hardy and British Poetry* (see pp. 70–2). In addition, in 1974 Macmillan published T. R. M. Creighton's new selection, *Poems of Thomas Hardy*, and in 1975 a revised edition of John Wain's *Selected Shorter Poems of Thomas Hardy* (almost an adjunct to both the 'New Wessex' edition of Hardy's works, which started to appear in 1974–5, and to the 'Students' Hardy', published in 1976) which was at the point immediately prior to Macmillan losing exclusive rights to Hardy's works (see pp. 45–6). Again, what determines 'Hardy's' accessibility, and his composition as 'great writer' for students, is by no means accidental or accounted for simply by a metaphysics of 'taste'.

Third, bringing the question of which texts constitute 'Hardy' in school education into sharper focus, it is apparent that a fairly narrow range of Hardy's novels are set by the examination boards. The three commonest and most regular are undoubtedly *Far From the Madding Crowd*, *The Return of the Native*, and *The Mayor of Casterbridge* both at O and A level. *The Woodlanders*, *The Trumpet-Major*, and *Under the Greenwood Tree* have been set in the past – the last two more commonly at O level (Cambridge set *The Woodlanders* in 1983, but that, in my sample, seems to be the first time it has been a 'prescribed text' since 1950 (JMB)); in recent years, however, they appear much less often than might be expected. *Tess* is not set before 1961 (for many years the novel was proscribed by the Vatican *Index* – which may help to account for its only recent provenance as an 'acceptable' text in schools), and then intermittently up till about 1979. *Jude* appears to have been set for the first time in 1977 by the AEB, the sole board to use the novel up to that point (Cambridge set it on an alternative O level paper in 1983). Of Hardy's other six novels, plus the shorter fiction (surprisingly), none has ever been on the syllabus of any board. Overwhelmingly, then, the novels which constitute 'Hardy' in school education are *The Mayor of Casterbridge, Far From the Madding Crowd*, and *The Return of the Native*. We shall see in a moment, from the kinds of questions asked, the main reason why this should be so: a self-fulfilling process in which critical (and social) assumptions select the works most appropriate for the realization of those assumptions in the critical discourse of the examination questions and answers. But it is worth remembering, also, how exactly this phenomenon locks into other elements of the critiography outlined in the previous chapter. The central 'set texts' are, of course, the 'novels of character and environment' of Hardy's own General Preface, which late nineteenth- and twentieth-century criticism has exclusively confirmed as the acme of Hardy's achievement in fiction. (As we have seen on pages 45–6, the Macmillan 'Students' edition of 1975 prints none of the 'minor novels' – despite their presence in the simultaneous 'New Wessex' edition – although it does include *Chosen Poems* and *Chosen Short Stories*. The 'Students' Hardy', it goes without saying, is the novelist of 'character and environment'.) Indeed, it is hardly an exaggeration to suggest that the school 'Hardy' is still in many respects the 'Hardy' of Lord David Cecil – a critic whose ghostly presence (see pp. 25–6) haunts the 'suggested reading' sections of contemporary student 'study guides' and which we will meet again in the examination papers.

Given the delimitation of the 'Hardy' who is on the study agenda, it is not surprising to find that the questions asked about him are both extremely similar across boards and over time, and that they operate for the most part within a restricted field of critical and ideological discourse – that identified earlier as humanist realism, including (when formally 'critical') the consequent obsession with the 'faults' and 'flaws' in Hardy's art. At O level, the questions almost invariably ask either for an account of some episode or feature in the book: 'By specific reference to incidents in the novel examine the part played by weather in *The Mayor of Casterbridge*' (AEB, 1979); or for some form of character analysis often requiring ethical judgements as though the characters are real people: '"Gabriel Oak, unlike Boldwood or Troy, loves Bathsheba unselfishly." Discuss this statement referring in your answer to Gabriel and *either* Boldwood *or* Troy' (AEB, 1976); '"His was not an ordinary nature." Bearing this quotation in mind, describe the character of Farmer Boldwood. Illustrate your answer by close reference to episodes in the novel' (JMB, 1981). In 1965, a JMB O level question asked whether students thought that Fancy Day in *Under the Greenwood Tree* was 'a normal young woman, or a weak and silly one'!

At A level the questions are rather more complex in form, although the focus is much the same. Nature and environment are emphasized: '"Egdon Heath, with all its sights and sounds so vividly and inescapably imagined, presides over the story, a vast, careless oppression" (Lascelles Abercrombie). Discuss this judgement' (Cambridge, 1934); 'How far would you agree that "Egdon Heath is felt to be formidably antagonistic to human society"? Give reasons and illustrations' (JMB, 1960); '"The true subject of the novel is Egdon Heath; the principal characters are much too vaguely drawn." Discuss' (London, 1977); '"The function of the heath is to describe the real circumstances in which man lives." Discuss' (AEB, 1980). And, cultural imperialism being what it is, here are two examples from the New South Wales Department of Education HSC papers: '"A novel in which the setting is never *merely* background." What is the contribution of the setting of *Tess* to the novel as a whole?' (1967); '"In *Tess* there is a close relationship between natural settings and characters." Do you agree?' (1980). Even more persistent are questions on 'character', which often involve concepts of tragedy. The *hamartia*: 'To what extent do the seeds of Michael Henchard's downfall lie within his own character?' (AEB, 1956); 'How far is Michael Henchard a truly tragic figure?' (London, 1980); 'Self-destruction has been said to be characteristic of many of Hardy's major characters. To whom could it apply in *The Return of the Native*, and how effectively does Hardy portray the process?' (London, January 1979). In June of the same year, with reference to the new set book *The Mayor of Casterbridge*, the same Board asked: 'The self destructiveness of Hardy's characters has often been commented upon. To what extent is Michael Henchard cast in this mould?' *Fate*: '"Hardy is driven by some sense that human beings are the sport of forces outside themselves." Discuss and illustrate, *and add a note to show how this attitude affects his greatness as a novelist*' (Cambridge, 1939, my italics); '"Hardy depicts a malign Fate functioning in men's lives, corrupting their possibilities of happiness and beckoning them towards tragedy." How far do you think this judgement true of this novel?' (JMB, 1957); '"Hardy's characters are in the grip of a single desire. The tragedy results from a fundamental struggle of wills." How far do you agree with this comment on *The Return of the Native*?' (JMB, 1975); 'How far do you agree that the attributes of the main characters bring about an inevitable catastrophe in *The Return of the Native*?' (AEB, 1981). *Universality*: '"Hardy's characters act consistently within the plot, but at the same time embody universal emotions." Discuss this statement in relation to two or three characters in *The Mayor of Casterbridge*' (London, January 1981). In June of the same year this symptomatically confused question was reformulated as: '"Hardy's characters may seem simple and rustic, but they embody universal human emotions." Discuss, etc.' Thus, at exactly the point when Byatt's Hardy 'rules OK', he rules in identical terms to those proposed by late nineteenth-century critics and their twentieth-century avatar, David Cecil.

A similar consanguinity and continuity, over time and between Boards, is apparent in the questions which proffer a 'critical' perspective on Hardy: a tendency to 'melodrama'; creaking plots; over-insistence on 'chance' and 'coincidence'; restricted 'character-ization' because of these elements; and 'pessimism' all appear. But what is noteworthy here is that, although the 'discuss' rubric always theoretically 'allows' the student to write against the drift of the question, the questions are invariably negatively framed so that the student is persuaded, in the first instance, to think in those terms. The underlying burden of all such questions is 'literary value', and an assumed agreement between critic–examiner and critic–student about a hypothetical model of the 'ideal' fictional masterpiece or, more precisely, of the ultimately 'probable' novel. Hardy is normally found wanting, of course; but what I want to pinpoint here is the closure this introduces on the possible ways of reading Hardy, or indeed any other writer: hold in view a notional model of a universally accepted, perfectly realistic novel, and any deviations from it instantly become negative 'faults' which cannot then be perceived as potentially positive experiments or even merely as interesting variations. (On a larger scale, the same effect is achieved by 'writing out' Hardy's 'minor' fiction; and, beyond that, by dismissing all fiction which is not 'great' enough to be included in the literary canon.) The following is a representative sample of such questions: ' "In *The Mayor of Casterbridge* Hardy has sacrificed his characters to the mechanism of the plot." What justice is there in this charge?' (Cambridge, 1943); ' "Although the setting of *The Mayor of Casterbridge* is realistic, the plot lacks conviction." Do you agree?' (London, June 1980); ' "The main weakness of the novel [*The Return of the Native*] is its plot." Do you agree?' (London, June 1976); 'Hardy's excessive use of coincidence has been criticised as a grave defect in his novels. What part does coin-cidence play in *Far From the Madding Crowd*, and with what effect?' (Cambridge, 1941); ' "One of the criticisms of Hardy's craftsmanship is that too much appears to depend upon coincidences and odd chances." To what extent could you apply this criticism to *The Mayor of Casterbridge*?' (AEB, 1955–6 'Specimen Question'); ' "Clym, the returned native, is too vague to carry much of the book's significance; Eustacia is merely melodramatic; Venn is, for all the world, like the typical cowboy-hero, always turning up just when he is wanted." How far, if at all, do you agree with this quotation?' (JMB, 1976); 'How convincing and effective do you find the conflict between Eustacia and Mrs Yeobright?' (London, January 1978); ' "Hardy's pessimism is so unmitigated as to be ludicrous." Consider this statement' (Cambridge, 1945); ' "In *The Mayor of*

Casterbridge, Hardy's vision is overwhelmingly pessimistic." Do you agree?' (London, January 1981).

The case I particularly wish to point to in this context is that of *Tess of the d'Urbervilles*. I mentioned above that *Tess* had been very rarely set until recently, and we have also seen that the early critical reaction to the novel was markedly ambivalent. It is symptomatic of the way school examination boards mediate literature that *Tess* has been continually represented in the same ambivalent terms. As one might expect, there are a number of 'character' questions, each of which, however, focuses on the moral ambiguity (primarily sexual) of Tess's personality (an issue which had exercised late Victorian critics, with Mrs Oliphant and Mrs Grundy over their shoulders): '"A pure woman." How far do you think Hardy was justified in describing Tess in this way in the sub-title to the novel? Give reasons and illustrations in support of your view' (JMB, 1961); '"Tess is a passive victim and at the same time a creature of self-will." How does Hardy bring out the paradoxical nature of her character?' (JMB, 1971); '"Tess is a murderess: and any assessment of her must take this into account." Discuss' (Oxford Local, 1980); 'Critics disagree as to whether Tess is completely blameless or at least partially responsible for her own ultimate disaster. Make clear your own view of this matter, referring in detail to the novel' (JMB, 1981). Far more persistent, however – indeed almost without exception whenever the novel is set – are questions which seek to circumscribe Hardy's 'artistic achievement'. In 1962, only the second time *Tess* was set in my sample, both the alternative questions on the JMB A level paper were of this kind: '*Either*: "Tess is the only character who is allowed to develop. The rest are static and unchanging." Discuss this statement as it relates to Tess and one other character. *Or*: "Melodramatic rather than tragic." How apt is this phrase as a description of *Tess*?' In the same year (1962), the Oxford and Cambridge question was: 'Consider the judgement of *Tess* as "full of faults, but a very great novel".' When it was set again by the same board in 1968, the question was: '"A coherent and convincing novel despite its obvious faults." Examine *Tess* with reference to this view of it.' In 1976 the AEB asked: 'Do you consider the element of melodrama in *Tess* spoils the novel?' And in 1980, when the Oxford Local required students to discuss the proposition: 'Despite the element of sheer bad luck, *Tess* has a tragic inevitability', the JMB set the classic formulation: '"*Tess* is a triumph despite its faults." Show to what extent you agree with this assessment of the novel.' How far this startling conformity of perspective is the result of subliminal anxieties about examining a novel which is so sharply conscious of the sexual and social exploitation of women, or of unthinking acceptance of a long-standing critical orthodoxy, or of a residual fear that Leavis was, after all, right to dismiss Hardy from the 'great tradition', it is difficult to say. What is certain, however, is that any student who does not find 'melodrama' amiss, or does not recognize the 'faults' as faults (one is expected to know what they are: are they self-evident, therefore, or scientifically classified?), or who thinks more in terms of social and sexual repression than of classical tragedy, will nevertheless be constrained to 'read' *Tess* in those vague, alien, and unexamined terms.

What we can deduce from all this is how restricted and predetermined 'Hardy' is as an educational discourse; how little of his work is on the syllabus (the 'minor novels' would, as for literary criticism, challenge and confuse its presuppositions); and how this 'primary material' is reproduced within very limited parameters of intelligibility: 'Hardy', once more, as the (waywardly) great tragic-humanist novelist of 'Character' struggling heroically with Fate, Nature, or other, pre-eminently non-social, forces. Only 'waywardly great' because, even in his greatest ('most characteristic') works, there are contradictory elements ('flaws') which intrude and disrupt. 'Hardy', then, must only be seen as problematical in these 'aesthetic' terms, not as a set of discourses so riven with contradictions that it challenges most of the preconceptions out of which the literary 'A level Hardy' is constructed in the first place. Quite clearly, the Hardy who rules OK is, in school examinations at least, 'primary material' in no more than a very dubious sense.

Finally, there are two striking absences in the examination papers I surveyed, right up to the present. First, and given that Hardy from the beginning has been admired for his female characters, there are remarkably few questions on women (or, more generally, on issues of gender) beyond a few 'character' questions on the lines of: 'Discuss Hardy's portrayal of women'; 'Is Eustacia an idealized heroine?'; and ' "Hardy's women characters are more convincingly real than his men." Discuss.' The questions on Tess, mentioned above, were on her character and its ambiguities, rather than on her gender or her sexuality, and the same is true of the few questions I have seen on *Jude*. This relates to the second absence: of questions, more generally, on 'social issues'. Throughout the whole run of A level questions I looked at, I could only find two which suggested that Hardy might have been a 'social novelist' of some kind, and both of these (on *Tess*, JMB 1961, 1971) ask for 'an account' of 'the conventions of society' or 'the influence of social pressures' in catch-all questions which include, as their other alternatives, 'chance', 'the nature of innocence', and 'tragic destiny'. In other words, students are not directed to any specific material issues which Hardy's fiction may raise, and given the *succès de scandale* which greeted two of his last novels in the 1890s, this is a striking (but by no means inexplicable) omission. But the Boards would claim, no doubt, that questions on the life of country people, on 'the past', on the significance of inns, or on the skimmington-ride in *The Mayor of Casterbridge*, are 'social' matters. There is one question on marriage as an issue in *Jude*, and that is hung on the quotation from Milton at the beginning of Part Fourth of the novel (AEB, 1980), and one (at O level, AEB, 1979) on the importance of 'the theme of religion'.

What becomes clear, I think, is the extent to which a particular literary ideology dominates GCE 'English' – one which has particular notions of taste, of value, of fictional mode, and of what constitutes 'the literary'. By way of a restriction of possible texts and, within that, of the possible ways of perceiving those texts, this ideology constructs a 'great writer' who conforms to and confirms that dominant ideology. This, if I can belatedly return to it, is the explanation for Antonia Byatt's unquestioning assumption about Hardy's 'rural nostalgia' which I noted at the beginning of this chapter. She draws attention to one element of the critical mythology which constitutes 'Hardy' by her naturalized acceptance that 'rural nostalgia' is inscribed *in* Hardy, not constructed *as* 'Hardy'. In this sense, the absence in the early 1980s of any address to questions of class and social mobility, of education, of the 'woman question', of work, of a rapidly changing rural social formation, of philosophical and religious controversy, is both reprehensible and entirely comprehensible. Whether it is comprehensible to the students, however, locked within the institutional apparatus of the education system and voting passionately for Hardy (which Hardy?), is another matter.

As a coda to this chapter, and to reassure readers that this is not a supercilious tertiary sector simply mocking its 'junior' partner, I will glance briefly at the 'Thomas Hardy' of higher education. There is no doubt that in the 1970s and 1980s at least, Hardy has reached his majority on 'English' syllabuses in polytechnics, colleges, and universities. In many cases he is a 'single' or 'special' author, and otherwise, of course, unfailingly appears on 'Period' and 'Genre' papers. There is no doubt, either, that he is extremely popular with many students – often, but by no means exclusively, by way of their exposure to his work at A level. The reasons given for this popularity are various – although it remains the 'major' Hardy of the 'novels of character and environment' – but the commonest are: his evocation of the rural past in 'Wessex'; his characters, and especially his female protagonists; his 'comic', 'peasant' scenes; his powerful story line; more occasionally, his 'themes' or 'issues' – fate, marriage and divorce, education, religious doubt; and, generally, a mysterious and inarticulate sense that somehow Hardy is 'modern', that the world view informing his fiction tunes in with the students' own consciousness (of 'loss', of *anomie*, of the 'satire' of life, of existential absurdity, of the 'victimization' of individual human beings – of the 'ache of modernism' perhaps). Conversely, what is disliked about Hardy, and it is interesting that this is a negative replica, the exact other side of the coin, are: his overlong and over-written 'descriptions of Nature'; his 'flat' and 'unconvincing' characters; his clumsy and improbable plots – too reliant on chance and coincidence; his 'depressing' themes and general atmosphere. It is apparent that – good or bad, liked or disliked – this is much the same 'Thomas Hardy' as before, still held within a humanist-realist frame of reference, and in which his virtues and his vices are inter-changeable – depending only on how one 'reads' him. But the problematic itself of this uncertainty or ambivalence is seldom directly addressed or engaged with as part of the course of study, despite the fact that the uncertainty about Hardy is reinforced struc-turally by the syllabus. Sometimes he is on a 'nineteenth-century novel' paper, sometimes on a 'Hardy to Conrad' paper, sometimes treated as a proto-modernist; most often, of course, he is presented as a 'transitional' novelist, somehow 'linking' George Eliot and D. H. Lawrence. He never quite fits: neither of period (Victorian or modern?) nor of genre (poet or novelist? his work is often studied separately), and he is never indisputably 'great' (unlike Dickens and George Eliot, or James and Joyce). But by and large, these problems are 'solved' by individual preference: his works are placed somewhere and treated accordingly. Thus, again, the problematic is not taken as the primary constitutive discourse of studying Hardy's work.

If we turn, once more, to examination papers as a form of access to the contemporary reproduction of 'Thomas Hardy' in higher education, we find ourselves in both familiar and unfamiliar territory. What is immediately clear, however, is that the absence of the controlling ideology of the secondary-level Examination Boards releases a much more varied and sophisticated Hardy. The individual predilections of the relatively autonomous examiners are clear and diverse (though they, too, in the authoritative/authoritarian discourse of finals papers achieve *ex cathedra* status); students are expected to have read more widely in Hardy's work; a more extensive and contemporary criticism informs the questions and the assumed answers; and the kinds of questions asked theoretically allow for diverse and independent student opinion to be expressed. Nevertheless, there is still a largely restricted and repeated range of topics, approaches, and texts perceptible in the following sample.[4]

A collection of specimen 'Hardy questions' set by members of the audience, at my request, *before* a lecture on the present subject at a Higher Education Teachers of English conference in the early 1980s produced some significant results. Off the top of their head, and on slips of paper unseen by others, my fellow academics came up with such questions as: 'Why is Thomas Hardy a great novelist?'; '"Hardy's work glorifies the force of nature and laments the weakness of man." Evaluate'; '"Hardy's view of life is essentially pessimistic." Discuss'; '"Character is Fate", said Novalis. To what extent can this be applied to the protagonist of *The Mayor of Casterbridge*?'; '"Hardy sees man as the helpless victim of a fate he cannot control; his picture of human existence is a pessimistic one." Discuss'; '"Like flies to wanton boys are we to the gods – they kill us for their sport." Discuss tragic fatalism in Hardy's novels'; 'Consider the view that Tess Durbeyfield's tragedy represents the tragedy of the English peasantry'; 'Discuss the role of minor or rustic characters in two of Hardy's novels'; '"*Tess of the d'Urbervilles*: A Pure Woman." In what ways does Hardy present Tess as such?'; 'Taking into account contemporary attitudes, to what extent is Angel Clare reprehensible in his behaviour towards Tess?' What is interesting about the results of this 'game', given the circumstances (unexpected and unprepared), is that these instant reflex versions of Hardy reproduce so many of the characteristics of conventional Hardy criticism and of the school Hardy we saw above: fate, tragedy, nature, character, ruralism, pessimism, and so on. To be fair to my colleagues, I am sure that in the quiet of their study, in the annual pursuit of 'something different to ask about Hardy', they would produce a less well-worn stereotype, and indeed the following sample of genuine questions suggests as much. But nevertheless, when caught off guard, experienced readers and teachers will still first identify the stock Hardy of stock criticism.

There are, of course, many conventional questions on finals papers focusing on notions of realism and tragedy, and on the nature of Hardy's 'achievement'. For example: 'Judging from *Jude the Obscure*, what would you say was the nature of Hardy's "sense of the tragic"?' (Newcastle Polytechnic, 1982); (under three quotations from *The Life*) 'Discuss notions of Tragedy in relation to Hardy's work' (Thames Polytechnic, 1983); 'Compare George Eliot's and Hardy's sense of human tragedy and loss in *The Mill on the Floss* and *Jude the Obscure*' (Dundee, Part III, MA, 1976); 'To which, if any, of Hardy's novels do you find the words "tragedy" or "tragic" most appropriate, and why?' (Cambridge Tripos, Part II, Special Subject, 1978); 'Discuss the relationship between "character" and "environment" in *one* or *two* novels' (ibid.); 'What have you found of permanent quality in EITHER Hardy's poetry OR *Jude the Obscure*?' (Newcastle Polytechnic, 1982); ' "In Hardy's novels, Fate takes sides with the disruptive tendencies of modern life: hence the tragedy." Discuss' (Thames Polytechnic, 1973). It is interesting to note, too, that in Indian institutions, for example, the same literary ideology transcends cultural difference: 'Discuss Tess as a tragic heroine who is a victim of fate, chance and circumstances. How can she be called a pure woman?' (Guru Nanak Dev University, Punjab, 1978); 'Comment on Hardy's use of rustic characters (in *Tess*)' (Kashmir University, 1972); ' "Hardy's background is the eternal framework of the hills and the moors." How is this related to the tragic spectacle of human relationships in his major novels?' (Indian Administrative Service); 'Examine the role of chance in *Tess*. Does it detract from the greatness of the novel?' (Kashmir University, 1972).

But the main distinguishing features of questions at this level are: first, a greater concern with Hardy's ideas or philosophy (for example, after 'quoting' Angel Clare, 'Is there a consistent morality in *Tess of the d'Urbervilles*?' (Glasgow, MA Hons, 'Special Author, Hardy', 1973); or ' "Hardy showed us that we do not have to choose between the simple general attitudes called 'optimism' and 'pessimism'." Discuss' (Cambridge Tripos, 1981). Second, a concern with social issues: women, education, social and economic change, religion, class (although this last, on occasions, is significantly negatively framed: 'A "I don't think Hardy was as interested in class as you suggest." B "He didn't need to be 'interested'. He had an instinctive perception of class differences and relations." A "What divides people and brings them together in Hardy is a good deal more profound than class" ' (Cambridge Tripos, 1979)). And third, a concern with aesthetic and formal matters: style, structure, irony, imagery, symbolism, satire, realism (the 'series of seemings or personal impressions' quotation from the Preface to *Jude* turns up on several papers). But again, it is instructive to notice how often the questions are negatively angled – even though the 'discuss' convention invites disagreement: 'Hardy makes the best use of his general knowledge of literature when that knowledge is least in evidence' (Cambridge Tripos, 1979); ' "The worst thing about Hardy was that he thought of himself as a writer." Do you have in mind a worse thing than this? Discuss the matter generally' (ibid.). And on a Glasgow University MA 'Special Author' paper (1973), four of the thirteen questions were cast in this way: two use quotations from Leavis and Morton D. Zabel on the 'straining', 'pretentious', 'stilted', or 'prosaic' style of Hardy's poetry and/or fiction; the other two, on single texts, read: '"the mechanical simulation of heat and depth and wisdom that are absent . . . Everything in the book strikes us as factitious and insubstantial" (Henry James). Discuss this criticism of *Far From the Madding Crowd*'; and 'Might one say of *The Return of the Native*, as T. S. Eliot wrote of Hardy's style, that is "touches sublimity without ever having passed through the stage of being good"?' I would merely point, here, to the continuing presence of the James/Leavis axis within Hardy criticism, and to the silent assumption that the student is already interpellated within an esoteric and naturalized discourse of aesthetic evaluation. Finally, and in all justice, I must acknowledge that I have found one question – on the Cambridge Tripos 'Special Subject' paper of 1978 – which introduces the 'minor novels' explicitly onto the higher education syllabus: '"Readers are right to concentrate on the six major novels but almost all of the lesser novels and short stories contribute to our deeper understanding of Hardy's art." Discuss the significance of *at least two* of Hardy's "lesser" fictional works.' This is a major breakthrough in some respects; but, nevertheless, to understand the full implication of the question's assumptions, one has to imagine a reckless candidate answering it by reference to *The Return of the Native* and *The Mayor of Casterbridge*!

'Thomas Hardy' at tertiary level, then, is a bulkier and more diverse figure than in secondary education, but he is still constituted by the ceaseless forming and reforming processes of the major discourses in which he remains actively present in history. It is to the forms of his reproduction in another public set of discourses, crucial to the popular dissemination of 'great literature' in the second half of the twentieth century, that I now turn: radio, television, and film.

3

'Tragedies of modern life'?
'Thomas Hardy' on radio, TV, and film

A recent 'study guide'[1] tells us that of the six best-selling novels on the list of 'one of the largest publishing houses' in 1983, two were by Hardy; they were: *Far From the Madding Crowd* and *Tess of the d'Urbervilles*. It is not without point that this study guide itself is on *Tess* and that the only other one about Hardy to date in that series is on *Far From the Madding Crowd*; nor, as we have seen in the previous chapter, that these novels, together with two or three others, are at the centre of the Hardy syllabus in secondary education. But it is even more to the point of the present chapter that these two books are the only ones, as yet, to have been turned into large-scale (and highly successful) modern films. There can be little doubt that for a very large number of people now, Bathsheba Everdene and Tess Durbeyfield are Julie Christie and Nastassia Kinski lookalikes, and that these heroines occupy a very different public space to Eustacia Vye, say, or Grace Melbury, who have not been so privileged. 'Bathsheba' (alias Julie Christie), for example, received a ten-photograph review feature in *Mayfair*, the 'men's magazine', when Schlesinger's film of *Far From the Madding Crowd* was released in 1967, in which we learn that after the death of the 'dashing wastrel Sergeant Troy (Terence Stamp)', 'Now Bathsheba must face the future alone; if a woman like Bathsheba is ever alone. And there is always the faithful Gabriel.'[2] Sadly, the only thing missing is a full-colour centrefold of Bathsheba lying on a haystack and telling us that she comes from Weatherby in Wessex, loves fast horses and sheep-farming, likes her men to shoot each other, but plans to marry 'soon'. Again, in an article in the *Guardian* in 1982[3] – one of a series on 'leading ladies in popular fiction' – in which Terry Coleman 'keeps company with the tragic maidens of Thomas Hardy', he tells us: 'it is probably true at the moment, thanks to the Polanski film, that the best-known heroine of any English novel is Tess.' (The article then goes on, disconcertingly, to deal with the least known of Hardy's heroines, Geraldine Altenville, who 'appears' in the first, lost, novel *The Poor Man and the Lady*!) Both these films are now also widely available on video (*Far From the Madding Crowd* on EMI in 1980 and *Tess* on Thorn/EMI in 1982). In addition, *The Mayor of Casterbridge* was made into a widely-viewed and much acclaimed BBC TV serial in 1978, although this is, of course, no longer publicly available. By 1980, then, there were modern media reproductions of three of Hardy's most 'characteristic' works, and it is the principal purpose of this chapter to offer some analysis of them and of their relationship both to their period culture and to the constitution of 'Thomas Hardy' as a contemporary cultural figure.

The history of the reproduction of Hardy in other media is less simple, however, than the existence of these three versions suggests, and it is perhaps worth offering a preliminary sketch of his presence on film, TV, and radio. It is surprising how few films of Hardy's work have been made given the strong romantic/tragic story lines, the well-defined 'big' characters, the 'picturesque' settings, and his own proto-filmic narrative techniques.[4] There are early American versions of *Tess* (1913, 1924) and of *Far From the Madding Crowd* (1911; there is also a silent English film produced by Larry Trimble in 1915), and early English versions of *Under the Greenwood Tree* (Harry Lachman, 1929) and *The Mayor of Casterbridge* (Sidney Morgan, 1921). A planned film of the latter was abandoned in the early 1950s because it became too expensive.[5] Apart from this, according to Johan Daisne's *Filmographic Dictionary of World Literature* (1971) and the BFI Index, there is scarcely anything else until John Schlesinger's *Far From the Madding Crowd* in 1967, and nothing thereafter until Polanski's *Tess* in 1979. Perhaps the oddest absence is any version from the inter-war period and the 1940s when many of the literary 'classics' were made into major romantic films, and one might have expected such a treatment of, say, *The Return of the Native*. Is it a measure of the insecurity of Hardy's 'greatness', and of the problematical nature of his narratives, that Vivien Leigh never played Eustacia Vye?

Hardy has fared a little better on TV, although not much. The BBC Programme Index[6] reveals that there were occasional readings from his work, or programmes about him, from the early 1950s to the early 1960s, but from 1964 to 1969 there appears to have been no Hardy on BBC television at all. In December of 1969, however, John Hale's dramatization of the short story 'The Distracted Preacher' went out, and this seems to have started a minor Hardy trend for a while. There followed a four-part serial on BBC 2 of *The Woodlanders* (dramatized by Harry Green) in February–March 1970 (repeated, June–July 1971); a six-part serial of *Jude the Obscure* (again by Harry Green) in February–March 1971, also on BBC 2; and a six-part series, 'Wessex Tales', in November–December 1973 on BBC 2 (repeated in May and June 1975).[7] In addition, an extract from *The Mayor of Casterbridge*, dramatized by Peter Prince, was included as a play insert in the Arts Feature programme 'Second House' in April 1975 (repeated, June 1976); and there was a 25 foot extract of the *Jude* serial put out by the Open University in June 1976. (Sadly, it is now almost impossible to view these programmes, and they are unlikely to be repeated again in the near future: Harry Green's versions of the two 'outsider' major novels, *Jude* and *The Woodlanders*, would have been especially interesting to assess in my context here.) Hardy's next major moment, as far as my sampling of the BBC Programme Index goes (up to 1980–1), was just before and after Giles and Potter's *The Mayor of Casterbridge*, when poems by him make repeated appearances on the 'Closedown' programme: in March, August, and October 1977; March, April, and May 1978; May, October, and November 1979; and March 1980. The seven-part serial version of *The Mayor of Casterbridge* (dramatized by Dennis Potter and directed by David Giles) was televised from 22 January 1978 on BBC 2 and repeated from 26 June 1979.

On the radio, Hardy has had a longer and more extensive career. From 1945, in the BBC Programme Index, he appears regularly – although usually on the Home Service, the Third Programme, and their later equivalents – as a contributor to 'interlude' or 'interval' programmes, more often as poet, but also as novelist; his prose works have been regularly read or dramatized; and programmes about him, as man of letters or man of 'Wessex', have been frequently broadcast. It is difficult to deduce very much about the production of 'Hardy' from the information on the BBC Index, but it is apparent, first, that although a fair number of Hardy's poems have been read, certain 'favourite' ones are continually repeated (these are echoed on the TV 'Closedown' slots): 'The Oxen' (usually at Christmas), 'The Darkling Thrush', 'Throwing a Tree', 'The Ruined Maid', 'At Castle Boterel', 'Channel Firing', 'In Time of "The Breaking of Nations"', and 'The Convergence of the Twain'. These are all, of course, well-known 'anthology' pieces,[8] and all of them represent Hardy to the listening public in 'characteristic' terms: the poet of Nature, of England, of personal loss and regret for the past, of astringent melancholy at the 'irony' and 'vanity' of human life and aspiration. The point surely must be that the public 'out there' does not itself demand the old favourites; rather, the radio producers – ignoring the many hundreds of Hardy's lyrics which the

95

public might respond to just as positively if ever they heard them read – are themselves constructing 'old favourites' by repetitious selection. They help to reproduce an image of 'Thomas Hardy' which represents a particular world view: one of ironic quietism and rural nostalgia in the 'madness' of the second half of the twentieth century, one in which 'culture' can only protect 'values' by disdainful retreat. It is not surprising in this respect, that Philip Larkin is so widely popular, nor, as we have seen earlier, that 'Thomas Hardy' has been cast as the progenitor of an essentially English twentieth-century poetic tradition of which Larkin is the contemporary incarnation.

Second, it is apparent in the pattern of radio broadcasting of Hardy that the majority of his novels have received some exposure. *Desperate Remedies* was read on 'Woman's Hour' in 1960; *A Pair of Blue Eyes* has been read twice (in 1964 and 1982); *Two on a Tower* was dramatized as a play, *Viviette*, by Frederick Bradwin, in 'Afternoon Theatre' in 1979; extracts from *The Dynasts* have appeared on occasions, as also readings of or from *The Return of the Native, Jude the Obscure*, and much of Hardy's short fiction. By some oversight, surely, even extracts from *The Hand of Ethelberta* were read as an 'interlude' at 9.45 p.m., 30 August 1947, on the Third Programme, and on 26 July 1948 at 10.07. No doubt most of the nation stayed up to avail themselves of these unique opportunities! I could find no trace, however, of *The Well-Beloved* or *A Laodicean*. But again each of the real favourites, significantly, has been dramatized, adapted, read, or used in 'interludes' several times since 1945: *Under the Greenwood Tree* (1948, 1950, 1951, 1956, 1962, 1965, 1966, 1969); *The Trumpet-Major* (1955, 1957, 1960, 1961, 1962, 1963, 1970, 1977, 1979, 1981); *Tess of the d'Urbervilles* (1947, 1951, 1954, 1964, 1965, 1967, 1971, 1975, 1978); *The Woodlanders* (1947, 1953, 1955, 1956–7, 1971, 1978, 1985); *The Mayor of Casterbridge* (1947, 1948, 1951, 1953, 1957, 1965, 1968–9, 1972, 1978); and *Far From the Madding Crowd* (1947, 1949, 1951, 1952, 1955, 1959, 1962, 1964, 1965, 1966, 1967, 1977). This, it goes without saying, is solidly the 'Wessex' Hardy of 'character and environment' – with two of the 'lighter' rural novels, *The Trumpet-Major* and *Far From the Madding Crowd*, appearing most regularly at full length.

Third, fairly obviously, we can see that Hardy is a pervasive and constant presence on radio since the Second World War, if only on the more 'highbrow' programmes, and that a large number of people, therefore, will have been exposed to a selection of his works in the context of, either, the 'school programmes' (and the tie-up here with O and A level set books is worth noting), or of the 'Book at Bedtime', 'Woman's Hour', 'Sunday Play', or 'Midday Serial' – all programmes of a 'relaxing', non-provocative variety. It is easy to see how the rural humanist-realist 'Thomas Hardy' fits the bill, and how the bill, in return, reinforces that constitution of him.

By far the greatest number of people in the contemporary period will have been exposed to Hardy in one or other of the visual media. A TV serial like *The Mayor of Casterbridge* may only go out on BBC 2, but its audience will include thousands of viewers who have hitherto never read a word of Hardy; and box-office successes like *Far From the Madding Crowd* and especially *Tess*, with their video back-up, will have audiences the majority of whom are not yet Hardy readers. As one reviewer of Schlesinger's *Far From the Madding Crowd* wrote in 1967: 'very few people among its potential audience – fans of Julie Christie and Terence Stamp – will have read the original anyway.'[9] In other words, thousands of people may well begin to read Hardy's novel (hence the 'best-selling' status of *Far From the Madding Crowd* and *Tess*) in the light of the film version, having been 'charmed by the considerable charisma of the actress', as James M. Welsh puts it in an essay on the same film, 'and will be responding as much to personality as to character – to star-acting, in other words'.[10]

What I intend to do here, therefore, is to offer an interpretation of these reproductions – not simply to compare written text and film or TV version, and certainly not to see whether Polanski 'caught the spirit' of Hardy or Schlesinger was 'faithful' to the novel – which is the fundamental error Neil Sinyard makes when discussing film versions of Hardy in his recent, slapdash book, *Filming Literature: The Art of Screen Adaptation* (1986) – but rather to expose what *kind* of Hardy these artefacts produce, how their own historical conjuncture determines their reproduction of Hardy, and what, therefore, is the discursive frame they set up for Hardy readers (both established and new) in the 1980s. I shall deal first with *The Mayor of Casterbridge* on TV, and then consider the two films.

Fortuitously, I was able to obtain a video recording of the BBC 2 serial *The Mayor of Casterbridge*.[11] Produced by Jonathan Powell, directed by David Giles and written by Dennis Potter, it starred Alan Bates (who, as we shall see, had already played Gabriel Oak in *Far From the Madding Crowd*) as Michael Henchard, Anne Stalleybrass as Susan, Jack Galloway as Farfrae, Janet Maw as Elizabeth-Jane, and Anna Massey as Lucetta. Significantly, it appeared as 'The Classic Serial' for the early part of 1978, and it is worth noting in passing the ambiguity of that title: at once the serialization of 'a Classic' (*The Mayor of Casterbridge*), and the serial itself as a 'classic' of its genre. Not surprisingly, therefore, it was a lavish and serious production taking fifteen months to film at a cost of £560,000, with an excellent cast, a highly respected writer/director team, filmed on location in the west country with authentic sets and settings for nineteenth-century Dorset and Dorchester (the village of Corfe Castle became 'Casterbridge'), and with 'most splendidly English music', as *Television Today* put it,[12] written and conducted by an American, Carl Davis. The week it started, the *Radio Times* had a still of Bates as Henchard on its front cover and a four-page photo-feature, with text by Claire Tomalin, on Hardy's life and 'one of [his] most popular books'. It was entitled: 'Hardy's perennial.'[13] The serial was also made in conjunction with Time Life Films, and was clearly aimed, therefore, at the American market – a factor which may well have influenced its particular style and presentation. As the *Sun* said (under the headline 'The man who sold his wife'): 'It cost £1,600 a minute to film. It stars film heart-throb Alan Bates in his first television series. And it will almost certainly be a world-wide hit.'[14]

In many respects, *The Mayor of Casterbridge* is a superb television 'period' serial. Over its six hours of total running time, it is pain-stakingly faithful to the novel in plot, dialogue, theme, character, and physical description – the only notable televisual rearrangement being in the opening and closing sequences when the novel's own time-sequence is disturbed by flashbacks and flashforwards (I will return to this). It is immaculately acted with great conviction by the cast, and it is beautifully set and photographed. But the questions arise: what exactly happens to Hardy here; what is the TV serial, as against the book, about; what is it for; and what is it offering – both in intention and in effect – to its audience? The answers are, I think, quite simple, and they are interrelated: not much else is happening here to the 'Thomas Hardy' we have already seen constructed over the last hundred years or so. This is the tragic humanist and rural annalist; the novelist of 'character and environ-ment'; the 'Wessex' realist *par excellence*. The crucial factor in the TV *The Mayor of Casterbridge* is its overriding concern with its own authenticity: true to the novel, true to history, true to its audience. Its 'meaning' is precisely its realism, its fidelity: the sense it gives, in its slow unfolding over six hours, of reproducing a reality. In no sense, however, is this a 'slice-of-life' serial, nor, unlike soap-operas, does it pretend a mundane verisimilitude: it is manifestly a staged and acted period drama about an unfamiliar community and set of characters and with a strikingly 'improbable' plot. What it is 'true to' is the historical myth of 'Wessex' and that is what it is offering its audience (particularly its transatlantic one, fascinated by the notion of their origins in 'old England'). It is the 'realization', with all the technical and professional expertise of TV realism, of a fiction of the past. *Television Today* commented: 'the physical setting was beautifully and accurately conceived – the agricultural implements and artefacts, the furniture, the vehicles . . . were perfect and a very real world was created.'[15] (See, in illustration, a still from the serial, plate 4.) As a minor but significant exemplum of my point here, there is, in the museum of Corfe Castle village (Casterbridge/Dorchester in the serial) a cart-sign bearing the name 'Henchard'. When I first saw it I thought: what an extraordinary (even Hardyan) coincidence – until I realized that it was in fact a 'prop', a sign-board from the TV production, now ensconced as part of Corfe Castle's 'real' history in the village's reliquary of its own past: the museum. The confusions and slippages here between history and fiction, the 'real' and the 'artificial', are salutary indices of the 'authenticity' attributed to the 'historical' or 'period' realism of both Hardy's fiction and the television reproduction of it. For, after all, there never was a 'real' Henchard sign-board to display in the museum – except in so far as the novel images one; so how, then, can the TV prop be a 'copy' of the real thing? In Corfe Castle's contemporary history the fake sign-board (representing the TV production) is as much a material reality as relics of its 'real' past as an agricultural village.

There are, it seems to me, a number of overlapping elements within the TV *Mayor of Casterbridge* which relate to this notion of what I might call 'thematic realism': 'character', 'environment', and 'Wessex'. First, one of the slight disappointments of the serial (especially from Giles and Potter) is that it raises expectations in its opening sequence that it may foreground 'social comment': Hardy as historian of the nineteenth-century rural economy (a reading, of course, which the novel will easily sustain without 'political' manipulation). Henchard, on the road, asks a man about work and if there are any new houses to let; the man replies that there is no work and that 'they' are pulling houses down rather than building new ones. We might expect from this some focus on migration from the land in Dorset, as a consequence of modern developments in the agricultural economy which accelerate the process. Further, the TV scene in the furmity-woman's tent at the fair, where Henchard finally sells his wife to a passing sailor, emphasizes throughout the oppression and degradation of women in this society. Are we not to expect, then, a version of that more contemporary 'Hardy' as proto-feminist, sympathetically portraying the iniquities of patriarchy by which 'the woman pays'? In neither instance, however, are these issues carried forward. Indeed, in the first case, it is surprising but

Plate 4 Still from the BBC production of *The Mayor of Casterbridge*: the market-place

indicative of the serial's orientation how little is made later of the clash between Henchard and Farfrae as representing the social conflict of 'old' and 'new' modes of thinking and business organization – which again the novel itself would clearly underwrite. The point is that the serial is primarily concerned with the personal drama of the two individuals ('characters'), rather than with the social drama which they allude to. Equally, in the second case, the oppression of women rapidly becomes no more than a reflex of Henchard's character – autocratic, self-willed, self-destructive – rather than an endemic feature of patriarchal society. So later episodes (Elizabeth-Jane's change of surname, Henchard's obsession with paternity, and his ferociously high-handed treatment of Lucetta) may indeed gesture – shocked – to the sensibilities of viewers in the late 1970s, but they are nevertheless held within the conception of an individual male's personality and behaviour. And this emphasis on 'character' and 'personal drama' – reinforced by Alan Bates's virtuoso performance as Henchard – is deepened as the serial increasingly focuses on the personal tragedy of Henchard and his relations with Farfrae, Lucetta, and Elizabeth-Jane. The casting of a star like Bates, of course, underpins this, and it is interesting to notice that the proclivities of the popular press further compound it. In an interview in the *Sun*, Bates's justification for taking a TV role was that 'Henchard is such a magnificent part . . . [he] suffers everything possible for a man to suffer in life. He is one of the great figures of world literature.' The *Daily Mail*, under the witty but significant headline 'Kismet, Hardy', claims that 'Henchard, perhaps the greatest of Thomas Hardy's literary heroes, has achieved the ultimate accolade of the 20th century – TV serialisation'; and Bates, interviewed once more, suggests that Hardy is 'so popular today' because 'he puts into words things we all feel taken to extreme'. Robert Gittings, in the *Radio Times*, draws extended and predictable comparisons between Henchard and Shakespeare's tragic heroes, in particular Othello (as does the *Daily Telegraph*), but finds the television character a 'pale shadow' of Hardy's own.[16] This emphasis on tragic character, of course, the novel itself colludes in; but the serial intensifies it by also detaching Henchard and the other main characters from their determining social environment. Equally, the 'themes' which underpin this personal drama, and which the serial gives prominence to, are: the 'flaws' in Henchard's otherwise noble character and the sense that he is fatally cursed by them ('Character as Destiny', 'How are the mighty fallen', and so on); his desperation to be a 'real father'; the inescapability of past wrong actions; and the 'irony' and 'fate' which govern the lives, especially, of great-spirited human beings. Indeed, the instances of televisual manipulation which I noted earlier in relation to the opening and closing sequences may simply be a 'hook' to catch the audience at the beginning and a closure 'recap' at the end, but they do also formally reinforce those themes: the cutting forward and back in time brings into high relief the ironic fate which is both a result, and in control, of Henchard's character. In particular, at the end when Henchard is out on the heath having left Elizabeth-Jane, he sees the original (now much aged) signpost of the opening sequence and is 'flashed-back' to the moment of the sale of his wife when he claims that he would be 'worth £1,000' were it not for her. Of course, by now, he has had his £1,000 and lost it again – his character and the whirligig of time having brought in their revenges. Again, it is worth noting in passing that the majority of reviewers were readily attuned to this trajectory of Fate, referring *passim* to Hardy's determinism; to his 'puppets working out a pre-ordained destiny'; to the 'archetypal forces' moving the characters; to Dennis Potter's own concern (expressed in his introduction to a Pan Books' paperback edition of *The Mayor of Casterbridge* published to coincide with the TV serial) with determinism: to the 'inexorable tide of fate', to Hardy's 'sense of the shape of our lives' and the inescapability of the consequences of our own actions.[17]

But this personal drama is played out against settings which, I have suggested, parade their authenticity and fidelity to the historical past – 'environments' which are as realistic as modern televisual art can achieve. As *The Listener* review put it: 'it looks as if the props department is going to steal the show', adding, significantly in my context here: 'take away Hardy's narrative long-windedness, and pictorialise it like this, and the nostalgia for Old England is as strong as a blow'[18] (the reviewer is by no means unequivocally sardonic). And this sense, too, of an English past is what the TV *Mayor of Casterbridge* is specifically about, what it is offering its audience. One of the most striking things about the serial is the solidity of the images of 'Wessex' which it provides. It is not unlike those local history museums which actually 'recreate' a room, a factory, a street, or an event, in all their palpable, experiential actuality: you sit on the labourer's stool, you touch the pistons of the steam-engine, you see the granary and the corn-carts: you are literally in touch with the past and with 'History'. But this dense facticity works to fetishize things, historical commodities; what is missing, in both museums and 'the classic serial', is any sense of the economy, of the social and political organization, of the mode of production, of the social relations, within which these 'things' and these 'facts' are comprehensible and have a meaning. So, in *The Mayor of Caster-bridge*, as I have noted earlier, there is no material analysis or presentation of the changing rural/urban economy of Dorset or Dorchester, and no material relationship between that environment and the personal drama played out against it. The characters, as it were, stand against a faithfully factual visual backdrop, but they are not located or determined by the history it attempts to recreate. Furthermore, it is Hardy's fictive 'Wessex' which is being given historical facticity in the realism of the serial – just as the 'Henchard' sign-board has now become a historical object in the village museum.

What *The Mayor of Casterbridge* production does, then, is, first, to reproduce the realist-humanist rural tragedian, 'Thomas Hardy', operating within the 'character and environment' conception of realism (see another still from the serial which, visually at least, is literal evidence of this: plate 5). Second, it effectively keeps separate those two terms, so that we have a personal drama of human character, which transcends the constrictions of a determinate history, set against a visually pleasing and authentic 'period' environment. Third, it simultaneously offers its audience, therefore, the human tragedy of Henchard's rise and fall (character being destiny) and a museum-like sense of directly experiencing 'our own' real past – which, in fact, is the fictive 'Wessex', itself a potent element, as we have seen, in the construction of the essential 'Old England' of the national culture and identity. Paradoxically, then, in its intensive and serious historical realism, the serial actually dehistoricizes Hardy. By fetishizing fact and a static relationship between characters and their environment, it perpetuates the myth of Wessex and displaces the history of Dorset. That displacement of history by myth, together with the asocial focusing on individual human subjects, is part of the whole ('English' and realist-humanist) cultural ideology in and for which 'Thomas Hardy' is constructed. The truly 'historical' achievement of the TV *Mayor of Casterbridge* is to carry that process forward in the technological discourses of contemporary culture.

Rather different ways of simultaneously de- and re-historicizing Hardy can be seen in the films of both *Far From the Madding Crowd* and *Tess*. John Schlesinger's *Far From the Madding Crowd*, the first major film version of Hardy's work to be made, was released in 1967 – a significant moment in terms of the way it represents Hardy. Running for two hours and forty-eight minutes, and filmed on location in Dorset and Wiltshire, it stars some already well-known 1960s actors and actresses: Bathsheba Everdene is played by Julie Christie, whom Schlesinger had already directed in his quintessentially 1960s films *Billy Liar* (1963) and *Darling* (1965),

Plate 5 Still from the BBC production of *The Mayor of Casterbridge*: Henchard and Susan

and who was at the height of her popularity (having also appeared in *The First Lady* (1963), *Young Cassidy* (1964), *Doctor Zhivago* (1965), and *Fahrenheit 451* (1966)). Sergeant Troy is played by Terence Stamp, succinctly described by Leslie Halliwell, in his *Filmgoer's Companion*, as 'British juvenile lead of the sixties', who was already famous for his performances in *Billy Budd* (1962), *Term of Trial* (1962), *The Collector* (1965), *Modesty Blaise* (1965), and *Poor Cow* (made in the same year as *Far From the Madding Crowd*), and for his off-screen, sixties lifestyle. Gabriel Oak was Alan Bates, whom Schlesinger had also directed in *A Kind of Loving* (1962), but who was already well known for his roles in *The Entertainer* (1959), *Whistle Down the Wind* (1962), *The Caretaker* (1963), *Zorba the Greek* (1965), *Georgy Girl* (1966), and *King of Hearts* (again made in the same year as *Far From the Madding Crowd*). Farmer Boldwood was played by the older, more established actor, Peter Finch, but he, too, had a string of earlier 1960s successes behind him: *The Trials of Oscar Wilde* (1960), *No Love for Johnnie* (1961), *The Girl with Green Eyes* (1964), and *The Pumpkin Eater* (1965). The screenplay, significantly, was by Frederick Raphael and the film produced by Joseph Janni – the same team as had worked with Schlesinger and Christie on *Darling*. Schlesinger himself, of course, was at the height of his success in the mid 1960s, having already made, in addition to *Darling*, *Terminus* (1960), *A Kind of Loving* (1962), and *Billy Liar* (1963). (He went on to make *Midnight Cowboy* in 1969 and *Sunday Bloody Sunday* in 1972.) *Far From the Madding Crowd* is itself lavishly produced (seven months to film on location; 64 featured players, 1,600 extras – all with costumes designed by Alan Barrett, scenic and costume designer for the Arts Council of Great Britain). It is beautifully (and tricksily) photographed, significantly again, by Nicholas Roeg; brightly acted and directed; and it bears, predictably, all the hallmarks of its moment of production. It is an indelibly 1960s 'Thomas Hardy' that results.

Clearly the film was launched as a potential box-office success – part of MGM's commercial enterprise – as well as being conceived as a 'serious', 'artistic' production: a duality well caught by the headlines of a release article in the American film-trade paper, *The Hollywood Reporter*: '"Far From the Madding Crowd" Film of Sweeping Beauty; Should Gross Well.'[19] Certainly it received all the razzmatazz of the big popular movie: from the poster advertising it (see plate 6) with its conventional 'romantic' images and style of drawing (what did the uninitiated think they were going to see – an up-date of *Beau Geste*?), through the Royal Premier at the Marble Arch Odeon with a swinging Princess Margaret present, to the

Plate 6 Advertisements for the films *Far From the Madding Crowd* and *Tess*

rapturous response of the reviewers. Perhaps the biggest piece of hype, which nevertheless suggests something of the cultural ideology in which the film is to be located, was the press junket organized by MGM for over 200 media people to visit what *The Film Daily* (an American trade paper) repeatedly calls 'the Hardy Country' in order to experience at first hand the 'natural settings untouched by time in the area of Dorsetshire, known as the "Hardy Country", many of them the actual sites of the novel', these 'natural settings' being 'not only highly photogenic but completely valid'.[20] During the week beginning Monday 18 September 1967, the week of the film's release, *The Film Daily* had continuous coverage of the tour: photographs of Julie Christie in mini-skirt and of producers and MGM magnates at functions; stills from the film (one of Stamp/Troy leading his cavalry troop is entitled 'There'll Always Be An England'); interviews with the actors and actresses (plus 'real' locals) who play the rustics and who 'lend such realism to the Dorset, England, peasants'; and an advert for a Bantam Books paperback edition of the novel to coincide with the 'roadshow release' of the film and 'featuring the cast on the cover'. Clearly, the late 1960s version of *Far From the Madding Crowd* is at once a piece of contemporary commercial culture – which must then be taken as an aspect of the film's 'meaning' – and in the long tradition of reproducing Hardy as the supreme annalist of Love, Life, and Death in rural England.

The press release for the film emphasizes these tendencies in its account of Hardy's 'classic novel of 1874': 'since that time this powerful story of love and turbulent relationships set amid the rolling countryside of the author's beloved "Wessex" has been a recurring best-seller through succeeding generations.' With Bathsheba, Hardy 'created one of the enduring heroines of literature', and his 'stock-in-trades' of 'wry humour, irony and a descriptive pen' produced 'a story destined at some time to be filmed'.[21] The trade reviewers, significantly, also latch onto the commercial force of the 'Wessex Hardy'. For the *Moving Picture Herald*, this is 'a love story of epic proportions' in which 'the English country-side plays a vital part' since 'Hardy's characters lived and loved in a very special part of England more than a century ago'; for *Kinematograph Weekly* it is a 'fine, British, prestige attraction', its 'points of appeal' being 'romantic drama', 'fine acting by well-known cast', 'familiar title', and 'lovely' photography; for *Variety*, it may even have a 'potential hold on the less sophisticated masses [on] a rainy after-noon' since it 'reeks with atmosphere', 'roam[s] splendidly throughout the "Hardy Country" in Britain's Southwest and thus capture[s] its richness and flavour frame by frame'; for *The*

Hollywood Reporter, as well as being 'a film of sweeping pastoral beauty and . . . romantic intensity', it is also 'one of the screen's most faithful adaptations of classic literature'; and for *The Daily Cinema*, its strength 'for the discriminating, lies in the remarkable re-creation of country life a hundred years ago, the fine photography . . . and the extra dimension given to reality by the fascinating faces of the extras hand-picked from the present-day inhabitants of Wiltshire and Dorset'.[22]

But this is not merely trade hype: the film itself very definitely works within the rural 'character and environment' conception, and it is also for the most part a faithful rendering of the novel. The main story line of events, characters, and their interrelations, circling round the magnetic figure of Bathsheba, is strictly kept to, and the rural environment lovingly presented as the backcloth for their activities. But it is worth remembering, here, that the novel which was Hardy's first major success (and which, as we have seen in a number of contexts, remains his most popular one; indeed, it is likely that this was why it was selected for filming in the first place), itself focuses strongly on the romantic story of Bathsheba and her lovers, and does not locate its main characters in their 'environment' nearly as determinately as do the later 'Wessex' novels. There are all the rural elements: the work folk, the sheep-shearing, the relief of the wind-swollen sheep, the harvest supper, the storm, the country fair, and so on, but in this novel they tend to be 'comic' or 'rustic' properties and settings rather than aspects of the matrix in which the protagonists' lives are formed. It is indeed, as the cover note on one paperback edition of *Far From the Madding Crowd* claims, 'a classic of pastoral fiction'.[23] The film, and this again may be why this novel was chosen, reproduces this with great fidelity. In fact, as a film is likely to do, it emphasizes the rural romance still further by way of its photography – aerial shots of the landscape, close-ups of rustic faces at the harvest supper, compression and sharpening of the story line (for example, it allows the audience to think that Troy has drowned himself until his reappearance, whereas the novel lets the reader know what has really happened), and constant foregrounding, in narrative and in filming, of the 'star' characters. But whatever its fidelity to the novel and its careful reproduction of 'Wessex', *Far From the Madding Crowd*, unlike the TV *Mayor of Casterbridge*, is in no way obsessed by its own 'authenticity' or by the relentless pursuit of a solid realism. Indeed formally, and despite its closeness to the novel as 'pastoral', it is happily 'inauthentic' throughout. Where *The Mayor of Casterbridge* seeks, in great density, to reproduce the 'real' past of nineteenth-century 'Wessex', *Far From the Madding Crowd* is constantly modern in attitude and appearance.

If it is a form of pastoral, it is 1960s pastoral: a bright, exuberant (despite its tragic elements and its moments of incipient hysteria), and colourful piece of filmic display, in which, as a friend commented to me, an emancipated 1960s young woman starts up her own business, has a series of difficult love-affairs, but settles down happily and prosperously in the end.

The most immediately striking aspect of the film is that despite its 'period' effects, it actually looks modern. This is partly because of the way it is filmed – a point I shall return to – but most obviously because the physiognomy of the actors is essentially modern – from the instantly recognizable 1960s film face of Christie with her Mick Jagger mouth to Stamp with his arrogant George Best features, right down to the gormless faces of the 'yokels'. A number of film reviewers, especially in the popular press, registered this at the time, in particular with regard to Julie Christie: 'she remains obstinately modern', remarked *Sight and Sound*.[24] Ann Pacey in the *Sun*, under a headline reading 'Alas Miss Christie, less than Victorian', thought that she 'may be as fashionable as a bell round the neck or a flower behind the ear', but that she was 'a mistake in a piece so deeply geared to the tempo and feeling of a fairly prosperous community in rural Victorian England'; and Alexander Walker in the *Evening Standard*, under his headline 'What's a swinging 1967 girl doing in Hardy's Dorset?', suggests that Schlesinger went wrong from the moment he cast Christie in the part: 'She keeps falling back on her old radiant mannerisms: she sings radiantly, pays her tenants radiantly, even milks a cow radiantly. But no amount of inner radiance can lift the curse of looking and sounding like a 1960s girl. It overlays her whole performance and gives it a jarring modern note.' The *Daily Mail* is more flattering – 'Darling Julie is sexy even in those Victorian skirts' – but in effect the message is the same: 'Who would have chosen Julie Christie, the embodiment of the Swinging Sixties, to play the proud, prim hapless heroine of this Victorian rustic melodrama?' The answer, a trifle unconvincingly, is: 'the sophisticated *Darling* team [who] have made such a good bucolic job' of the film.[25] This obstinate modernity of physiognomy is surprisingly also true of Boldwood and Oak – and it is instructive to compare Bates's face here with that of his Henchard in the BBC serial: in the one he looks like a modern man in costume, in the other a 'true' man of his period. Furthermore, the style and manner of the acting, of gesture and dialogue, reinforce this. For example, I was convinced that in an early scene in the film (when Oak proposes marriage to Bathsheba) the snappy courting dialogue and Bathsheba's repetition of the line 'I do not love you' to Oak (as later to Boldwood), sounded so modern and Frederick-Raphael-like that they could not be in the novel. In fact they are, almost verbatim; but they still do not read like they sound in the film's dialogue. Again, I decided that the scene in the film where Bathsheba's dress gets caught on Troy's spur and they thus meet for the first time, seemed so modern that it could not be such a large scene in the novel. But it is: and once more much of the dialogue is verbatim. Yet the effect in that Victorian literary work, though amusing and mildly erotic, is perfectly in keeping with its social and historical ambience. It is the discursive 'set' of the actors, one might say – styles of speaking, facial gestures (there are many close-ups), tones of voice – which give the film its bright, clean, vivacious, 1960s timbre.

We can see this insistent contemporariness again and most potently in the filmic presentation itself. The film is full of photographic effects, of tricks and whimsies, of set-pieces, of display, of the kind of bravura exhibitionism – of talent, of style, of technique, of exper-tise – which the sixties fostered. There are the aerial shots of Dorset; the brilliantly 'stagey' seaside scenes when Bathsheba goes to marry Troy (in the book they marry in Bath); the trick effect of the camera taking the place of the drunken Joseph Poorgrass driving Fanny's coffin home; the symbolic juxtapositioning of a shot of caged birds and of Julie Christie through the bannisters waiting for Troy to return; the two 'echoing' scenes when Julie Christie is revitalized by watching a little boy walking through a field; the stan-dard sixties shot of Julie Christie kicking autumn leaves; the loving focus of the camera on the mocking gargoyle which washes the grave away (not just after Fanny's burial, as in the novel, but again after Troy's death at the end of the film). There are little 'jokes': the appearance, for example, in an entirely invented and redundant scene, of a reddleman and of a 'Thomas Hardy' lookalike guest at Boldwood's Christmas party. Further, there are the echoes of Fellini – both in the photography and in the images the camera selects – which are most clearly seen in the big set-pieces: the seaside scenes mentioned above, with their washed-out images of a punch-and-judy show, of bathing-machines, and so on; the scene at the fair in which Troy does his 'Dick Turpin's ride to York' act, with clowns and other fairground business – a filmic *tour de force* which is hugely elaborated from the scene in the novel; and the final wedding-party scene with its dancing, its band, and its close-ups of the rustics' faces, which shifts, for the film's close, onto the musical carousel clock which – in the film, but not in the book – had been Troy's wedding present to Bathsheba.

In style, imagery, and manner, then, the film of *Far From the Madding Crowd* transmutes its otherwise 'faithful' rendering of Hardy's nineteenth-century novel into an exuberant display of 1960s *élan* and *joie de vivre*. In this respect its historical sense is not that of the past at all but of the present, and 'Thomas Hardy' is reproduced as a participant in the swinging decade. One noteworthy instance of this – although finally unconvincing in terms of the film itself – is the way the four stars talked about their respective roles in a series of interviews for *ABC Film Review* in the summer of 1967. Each of them stresses the 'complexity' or 'modernity' of the character they play, attempting, it would seem, to bring out for the 1960s a 'difficult', introspective, psychological realism. Bates, with disarming ingenuousness, given both the character of Gabriel Oak in the novel and his own performance in the film, emphasizes how 'complex' a character and how 'emotional and volatile' Oak potentially is, and remarks that 'it's what goes on in his mind that interested me and I had to convey'. Finch feels that Boldwood is a 'difficult, complex' character who has 'an obsession which I feel could occur in any period of history'. For Stamp, Troy 'isn't a typical Victorian villain' any more than Bathsheba is 'a typical Victorian girl', but is 'essentially a man who lives for the present. To him, the past is yesterday, and the future is tomorrow. He lives for the day and suffers from neither hope nor nostalgia.' (Troy as existential hero is a remote possibility, but in the film he is straight off the King's Road!) Appropriately Stamp adds: 'I have drawn absolute comparisons to the character from personal experience and people I am quite close to.' Finally, Julie Christie, in her comments on Bathsheba, tellingly but unselfconsciously reveals her own incipient but insecure feminism (1967 is towards the end of a period of 'liberation', but just before the new wave of the women's movement proper):

> Looking at [her] from a modern point of view and not from a Victorian way – which makes a lot of difference . . . I see her as instinctive rather than intellectual; spirited but never petulant. She's afraid of losing her independence in a man's world. . . . If I were a Victorian girl looking at her . . . I'd probably admire her imperiousness because I'd be a bit in awe of her unconventional attitude as a woman of those days.[26]

What is apparent here is the way each of the actors superimposes modern attitudes on to the character they play, rather than reinterpreting the characters as modern beings. It is this which gives the film its contemporary patina, without in any sense recasting the novel in late twentieth-century terms: Bathsheba is not a proto-feminist, Troy is not an existentialist, and Boldwood is not a neurotic capitalist, just as Oak is not a working-class hero; they are merely 'characters' played in a thoroughly modern manner. One reviewer was both witty and perceptive when he titled his piece 'The Wessex set'.[27]

In this way, of course, Hardy's novel is kept 'popular' by being made to seem contemporary, and it is a clear example of the process by which a 'great writer' is reproduced and reconstituted by the period in which s/he is being consumed. But we may ask: what messages are being conveyed by this modern film which are different to those of Hardy's novel? One answer, again, might be: not many. As I have suggested, the film follows the book closely, and it is also a version of pastoral, presenting a romantic story against a picturesque setting. Neither does it exploit the modernity of Julie Christie's playing of Bathsheba, or Terence Stamp's of Troy, by creating a radically 'modern' reworking of the original: the modernity, as we have seen, is more a matter of tone and manner. Nevertheless, in the brooding obsessiveness of Boldwood who thinks he can buy Bathsheba's love; in the fun-loving irresponsibility of Troy; in the film's suggestion (*contra* the novel, see below) of the limits of Bathsheba's self-control and independence; in the bright febrile world of the film's images and its hints (*à la* Fellini) of the grotesque underbelly of its own tinselly and exuberant glitter; in its loving regard for the rural (however pastoralized) – in all this it does, perhaps, have messages for the 1960s which, ironically, may not after all be so different from Hardy's. Gabriel Oak does not go to California (in the film or in the book – and in 1967 the significance of not stepping westward is sharper); he stays and makes himself and Bathsheba happy in the rustic idyll of Dorset – far from the madding crowd. Does the film's pastoral, in fact, offer a warning and an alternative to the sixties: forget the razzmatazz and seek out real human values? Or is it pastoral in the other sense, one which Hardy's work has so often sustained: an escape into that 'real' organic world of pre-industrial, precivilized rural England where men with hearts of Oak – superior to the trendy Troys – rescue uppity young women from the perils of their own independence? In this context, let me adduce one of the few occasions when the film substantially deviates from the novel: the scene when Boldwood shoots Troy. In the film, Julie Christie, frantic, lays her face on Troy's wound and is thus besmeared with his blood, where the novel very precisely says she pillowed his head in her lap, 'held her handkerchief to his breast and covered the wound, though scarcely a single drop of blood had flowed'. And the film scene's dying fall is of Christie shrieking 'Frank, Frank, Frank', ignoring the fact that the novel presents Bathsheba as preternaturally calm; describes her as 'the stuff of which great men's mothers are made . . . loved at crises';[28] and allows her to remove Troy's body to her own house, wash it and prepare it for burial before silently collapsing from strain and shock. Clearly the film scene is more dramatic, but its effect is also to repossess the 'independent' Bathsheba as, essentially, a romantic and emotional woman.

As far as the evidence of the director and of some contemporary reviewing is concerned, the film's message lies in a combination of both the versions of pastoral mentioned above. Significantly, the Press Release blurb simultaneously drew attention to the reappearance of the producer/director/scriptwriter trio of *Darling* – 'that internationally-acclaimed study of the emptiness of life at the "jet-set" level' – and *Far From the Madding Crowd*'s theme of 'the timelessness and endurance of the people and the land'.[29] Schlesinger himself is quoted as saying – ironically, given so much of what we have heard above – that:

> we wanted audiences to feel that they were seeing something that was not totally foreign to their own experience. We didn't want them to feel they were looking at a lot of fictitious people played by well-known actors dressed up in period clothes. Our approach was to give the film epic proportions in terms of what Hardy's novel deals with, that is, man pitting his strength against the elements and the capriciousness of fate which underlies the everyday occurrences in people's lives.[30]

Elsewhere he comments: 'I think Hardy's novel has some relevance to our own time in which people are seen pursuing some ideal, failing to reach it and falling back on a compromise.'[31] Is Schlesinger here sounding the knell of the 1960s? Is *Far From the Madding Crowd* the *riposte* to *Darling*? Is this an early warning of the dream that failed? Certainly Julie Christie's comments in the interview quoted earlier bear out these nascent notes of compromise, passivity, and quietism – of late twentieth-century pastoral retreat after the *éclat* of the post-war boom: 'I think, as in parallel cases in modern times, she settles for [Gabriel] when all else goes up in flames and tragedy. . . . I don't think she even knows she loves him even at the time of their marriage. I think she just finds he's right for her and they'll settle down and live a placid, hard-working life at the farm together as if all the terrible tragedy and drama with Troy and Boldwood has all been a bad dream.'[32]

Equally, there is little doubt that reviewers at the time perceived, under all the 1960s glitter, this pastoral of human values, endurance, and retreat as the positive, fundamental burden of the film. Some simply admired the beauty of the cinematic representation of the 'open English countryside'; the 'misty loveliness' of Roeg's photography; 'the freshness of English scenery 100 years ago – like

Paradise after the expulsion of the pylons'; or the 'series of sometimes breathtakingly evocative pictures of man and beast in their natural and unquestioning setting of downs and seascapes and comfortable farms'.[33] Others, even when critical, perceive the pastoral impulse more explicitly: *The Hollywood Reporter* – in a significant, ideological correlation of profit and pastoral – rejoices that 'the picture's romantic and human reaffirmation, in the midst of a glut of films suffering from blind pessimism and brutalization, ensures popular appeal and outstanding grosses';[34] and *The Daily Cinema*, despite its back-hander – 'Forget that "classic" tag. Shorn of Hardy's comments and his detailed reporting of farming methods and rural life, this is lush all's-well-that-end's-well hokum – and none the worse for that' – nevertheless comes up with a significant 'rating' for the film: 'Bound to evoke the nostalgia for the simple life of the countryside which nestles in the hearts of the most unlikely of city-dwellers.'[35] Finally, in a serious and perceptive review in *Sight and Sound*, James Price, recognizing that 'the Hardy country is the real subject here' (just as the desert is in the first part of David Lean's *Lawrence of Arabia*), points to the 'painterliness' of the film and to

> the images of sowing, sheep-dipping and harvesting, emphasising as they do the Arcadian character of the story, creat[ing] feelings both of timelessness and of a time from which an urban audience is totally cut off. It is here, it seems to me, that the specific appeal of the film lies. . . . Pastoral myth for the smokebound consumer is as potent as it was in the time of Beaumont and Fletcher.

Price also feels that the film moves in its conclusion to: 'an ideal state of equilibrium . . . in which time ceases to exist, of two people in a room beside a fire'; he continues:

> As Gabriel says, 'Whenever I look up, there you will be; and whenever you look up, there will I be.' By repeating this line from the first reel in the last script seems to make this classical statement of pastoral quietude even more emphatically than Hardy does.[36]

(Do we hear echoes in this of the Beatles' contemporary hit, 'When I'm 64'?) What Price sharply perceives is how the film of *Far From the Madding Crowd*, despite all its 1960s verve and its modernity of manner, reproduces that potent myth of timeless rural idyll, away from the 'desolating influences' of civilization, which has been at the centre of the 'essentially English' Thomas Hardy for so long.

Roman Polanski's *Tess*, made some twelve years after *Far From the Madding Crowd* and almost simultaneously with the TV *Mayor of Casterbridge*, has similarities to both in their different ways; but it is markedly dissimilar in its historical reproduction of Hardy by offering, unlike them, a modern re-interpretation – of the main character especially. Released in France in 1979 and elsewhere in 1981, it was produced by Claude Berri and Timothy Burrill, with screenplay by Gerard Brach, Polanski, and John Brownjohn, and it stars Nastassia Kinski as Tess, Peter Firth as Angel Clare, and Leigh Lawson as Alec d'Urberville. What is immediately apparent, then, is that Polanski not only directs the film but also has a hand in the screenplay, and that the main actress and actors are relatively unknown. In other words, Polanski's interpretative mark is very much on the film, and the faces of the protagonists, unlike those in *Far From the Madding Crowd*, are unfamiliar: invoking neither a 'period' physiognomy nor other roles in which they have starred. Polanski can thus construct his own 'private' representation of Hardy's novel; and, not surprisingly, a recurrent message in interviews with him is that *Tess* is *his* film: 'All my films have been the result of an inner necessity and yet, until *Tess*, I've never had the impression of making a film that *exactly* matched my deepest feeling. *Tess* is that film. *My* film. Certainly the film of my maturity.'[37] (The force of this is emphasized, perhaps, by the dedication 'to Sharon' on an otherwise blank screen at the end of the credits (a point I shall return to) – Polanski again repeatedly claiming in interviews that it was Sharon Tate, his murdered first wife, who had introduced him to the novel, which he became very excited by, offering her the part of Tess, although that film of course was never made.) Polanski was already, by the time of *Tess*, a well-established and highly-regarded director, albeit with a controversial private and public life, who had made such films as *Knife in the Water* (1962), *Repulsion* (1965), *Cul de Sac* (1966), *Dance of the Vampires* (1967), *Rosemary's Baby* (1968), *Macbeth* (1971), *What?* (1972), *Chinatown* (1974), and *The Tenant* (1976), in many of which his fascination with psychological disturbance, violence, and destructive sexuality had appeared as motifs. *Tess* was therefore something of a surprise, being restrained in all those areas which had been most characteristic of Polanski's previous work – although, as we shall see, it still evinces strong elements of his world view. The film was widely, but by no means unproblematically, acclaimed by the critics; was nominated for many awards (although those it won were mainly for its 'craft' – cinematography, costume design, and art direction); and it was hugely successful with the public.

For an independent production, *Tess* was a large-scale and lavish affair (it cost just under £5,000,000 – at the time, the most expensive film ever made in France). It started shooting in July 1978 (the year the copyright on *Tess of the d'Urbervilles* ran out), Polanski having bought the film rights from the estate of David Selznick whose greatest dream – apart from making *Gone With the Wind* – was to film *Tess*. The film was stricken with disaster: the shooting took over eight months, using forty different locations in Brittany and Normandy (many of which had to be returned to at different seasons of the year) and involving the reconstruction of Stonehenge (in France) as it would have been in the nineteenth century. It was filmed by Geoffrey Unsworth (who died while it was being made) and then by Ghislain Cloquet. The result is beautiful to look at and very long: its running time is three hours.

The film was conceived, in Polanski's own phrase, as 'a great love story' and as a faithful, artistic reproduction of Hardy's novel: his 'masterpiece', the Press Release says, 'and the most emotionally powerful of all his novels', which also 'paints a vast canvas of rural life in 19th-century England and contains some brilliantly perceptive comments on human nature – then and now'.[38] The brooding romanticism of *Tess*, both in cinematic and thematic terms, is inescapably confronted in the symptomatic features of Nastassia Kinski, looking out from the advertising poster (see plate 6) and from the innumerable publicity stills which focus on her face. (The trailer – 'a lyrical series of dissolving shots . . . set to Sarde's haunting music',[39] or, more cruelly, 'a sticky confection of scenic schmaltz and apparently risible acting'[40] – also promotes this aspect of it.) This is, of course, the 'general public' presentation of the film, and although it is highly influential in the reproduction of 'Hardy' in the 1980s – 'required viewing', as one critic symptomatically put it, 'for girls [sic] with *Tess* on their "O" Level syllabus'[41] – it is not, as we shall see, an entirely accurate representation either of Polanski's intentions or of the effect of the film itself. The trade papers, by no means uncompromisingly positive, nevertheless emphasize these aspects of *Tess*: 'physically handsome in the sumptuous manner of those adaptations of classic novels to be found in the "Masterpiece Theatre" series on Public Broadcasting Service'; 'sensitive, intelligent screen treatment of a literary masterwork', 'lambent color photography', 'superb production design'; 'exquisitely beautiful to look at', 'very good in selected up-market popular cinemas and art houses'.[42] Even so, they are worried by the length of the film, by Polanski's 'slavish' faithfulness to the novel, Nastassia Kinski's emotional range, and the film's apparent failure to achieve the 'accumulative emotional power'[43] of the book.

Much of the reviewing of the film also focuses on similar points.

The 'positive' critics admire Polanski's faithfulness to the novel: 'the result is pure Hardy' (which means, 'its pure romanticism, its scale, passion, grandeur, drama'); *Tess*'s cinematic beauty – a 'ravishing spectacle', 'it glows with brilliant "optical effects"'; and its historical accuracy – 'it looks, to my eyes, convincingly Wessex', 'the camera captures much of the spirit of Wessex: the innocent gaiety of the dancers in their white frocks, the wrinkled pathos of the aged instrumentalists, the languorous beauty of the countryside at dusk'.[44] Paradoxically, many of the 'negative' critics focus on the same features but from the opposite point of view: it is a 'sluggish film of ponderous beauty'; 'little more than a mountingly tedious sequence of pretty picture postcards'; 'a collation of second-hand picturesque effects . . . [of which] probably the most offensive . . . is the ubiquitous gold light that shimmers around and about almost everything on the screen, as if this were a Biblical movie and we were awaiting the Incarnation'.[45] Partly because of this, but also because of its reverential yet simplistic adaptation of the novel, it fails to evoke the reality of the world of the book: 'what is lacking . . . is the pervasive sense of poverty and drudgery that the novel abounds with . . . a certain grimness of life. . . . The Durbeyfield family's poverty, and the village's poverty, is obscured in *Tess* by the magnificent photography and landscapes, and Tess's beauty, rather than a contrast to the hardship and poverty the family is mired in, is, instead, an extension of the beauty of the land'; 'the image of Wessex that Polanski has conjured up . . . is the kind traditionally used on television to extol the wholesome, back-to-nature properties of sliced bread or dairy butter'; 'shorn of its extraordinarily complex ramifications, this allegory [of theological dispute] is reduced in the film to piddling proportions, with Angel playing rustic shepherd to Tess' shepherdess in a coy homage to pagan bliss'; 'there is none of Hardy's attack on industrialization, nor his portraits of the brutalized and degraded workers, no sense of people working and feeling the work in their bodies'.[46] At best, for such hostile critics, the film is 'a lethargic form of realism . . . a realistic presentation of romantic sentiments'; a good attempt which misses 'an all-important beat, a heart-beat'; at worst, it has 'the air of an expensive classy/commercial product, the result more of market research than intimate inspiration'.[47]

Much of this criticism contains some truth, particularly given the way the film was received by the public and its consequent contribution, therefore, to the reproduction of 'Thomas Hardy' in conventional terms. But ironically, much of it also rests on the reviewers' own reading of the novel itself, and hence on preconceived expectations of Polanski's film version. If one reads the novel as social drama and then finds the film failing, or if one perceives the film as a factitious cinematic extravaganza, slavishly faithful to the novel but essentially lacking its passionate romantic force, then one is reading the film as though one were reading the novel. But film and novel are not the same thing: the film remakes the novel as a late twentieth-century cultural product; as, in a sense, an autonomous artefact. Neil Sinyard offers a classic example of what we might call the 'originalist fallacy' when he remarks of the film: 'there is nothing very Hardyesque about it. It is a subdued and sober film, Hardy without the glaring faults, but without the sublimity as well.'[48] To be 'Hardyesque' – at least within the conventional critical paradigm – there have to be 'faults' of course. Would the film have been more 'Hardyesque' if it had retained them? What we must 'read', in fact, as late twentieth-century cultural critics, is the film, and then see how, why, and to what effect it recasts the novel. In this context, but without falling into intentionalism, and before I offer my own reading of the film (which, in any event, was made quite independently), I want to look at some of Polanski's public statements about the film he was making. In the light of this we can see how beside the point is much of the criticism noted above, and also how accurate it is, at times, in its unwitting perception of the film's ideological trajectory.

In interviews, Polanski is quite emphatic that the film of *Tess* is a 'modern tragedy' and that it relates to his other earlier works (which, as one critic has put it, 'depict the claustrophobic lives of ordinary individuals caught in an ever-tightening web, a web that seems to be spun from their own emotional entanglements and yet bears the external shape of destiny').[49] In an interview in *Screen International*, while shooting the film, Polanski said: 'I hope there is something that remains, some sort of line that goes through all the films, that makes it possible to say "That is a picture made by that director."' Unwilling to be drawn on the 'connecting line' to Hardy's novel – which, the interviewer proposes, is 'the darker aspects of Victorian society – poverty, ignorance, its unforgiving religion and rigid class system – that are largely the cause of Tess' suffering' – Polanski merely replies: 'I just do what I feel at a given moment of time.'[50] But in a later interview with *Continental Film Review*, he says: 'Actually *Tess* should be a film about intolerance, a very romantic, very topical story. This modern aspect was already in Hardy, all we did was focus on it.'[51] And in October the same year (1979), in *American Film*, he observes that although he has been 'influenced a great deal by surrealism and the theatre of the absurd . . . the world itself has become absurd and almost surreal', and so now he wants 'to go back to the simplicity and essence of human relationships'. Hardy, he notes, 'links the girl to the rhythm of nature, within a Victorian society at odds with everything spontaneous and natural', and adds emphatically: 'Tess belongs to the present, to the modern age, to you and me. She is the first truly modern heroine.'[52] Whether or not Polanski had read John Fowles's novel *The French Lieutenant's Woman* (1967; the film version appeared in 1981 – the year *Tess* was released in the USA and Britain, and with strikingly similar poster advertisements), the coincidence of Fowles's Hardy-influenced presentation of Sarah Woodruff as early existentialist woman, and Polanski's conception of Tess as 'the first truly modern heroine' is striking. For what we undoubtedly have in Polanski's Tess is a late twentieth-century existential heroine: 'Maybe if Tess were less noble in the mind, if she lied, if she accepted certain things that she finds instinctively repulsive, she could have lived a happier life than she did. But then she wouldn't be Tess of the d'Urbervilles, and we wouldn't be here talking about her.' And Polanski concludes his interview by saying: 'Tess, you must remember, was a pure woman . . . She broke Victorian moral codes, but she responded to natural law, to nature, her nature. That's what the whole book is about. The film is an accusation of the hypocrisy and injustice of that rigid society – and by extension of any rigid and repressive society.' Such a world view – of a society's 'rules and mores . . . based on irrational prejudices and superstitions' and of a 'hypocrisy' opposed to the spontaneous natural self[53] – governs Polanski's film and explains, if not justifies, its particular articulation. Andrew Rissik, in a venomously hostile review, sees the film's central failure as the mismatch between the schmaltzy romanticism of the film's visual style and the 'resolutely anti-romantic' sensibility which directs it as a 'modernist novel' in an 'existential universe'.[54] Rissik may have a point about the general effect (although my feeling is that he enjoyed hating the film so much that he misrepresents it), but he is quite wrong to see Polanski's existential sensibility as 'anti-romantic'; indeed, one could say that an uncompromising focus on the 'natural' individual in a hypocritical world, on personal freedom and 'good-faith', is the late twentieth century's own (pessimistic) form of romanticism. Rissik sees the film as only a 'bloodless and anaemic' sequence of inauthentic pretty pictures; Polanski conversely believed that *Tess* is 'such strong material that we mustn't be worried about beautiful pictures', that 'people don't go to the cinema to see a collection of beautiful photographs. They go to experience something. The *emotion* is the thing. . . . Emotion is the main thing in all art.'[55] It all depends, I suppose, on what one conceives of as 'the emotion': the 'passion' Rissik finds in the novel and misses in the film, or the deep existential despair belied by the visual beauty of Polanski's *Tess*.

But let me turn for a moment – before returning to its 'cultural meaning' – to some consideration of the film itself. Sensitively acted and beautifully set and photographed, its leisurely, even self-indulgent pace allows the film to establish its environments in great depth and solidity, to juxtapose, for instance, the sense of unchanging antiquity in the dirt and poverty of the agricultural labourers' lives with the almost modern environs of Alec d'Urberville's house or the seaside town of Sandbourne. There are also superb individual scenes: for example, the deadly Victorian 'interior' of Angel and Tess's first breakfast together after their wedding-night confessions, or the turnip-grubbing at Flintcomb Ash. The film thus attains the sense of solid historical realism which I noted as a feature of the BBC *Mayor of Casterbridge*, although it does not fetishize it as the serial did. *Tess* is not interested in the past as a museum-piece (neither, as we shall see later, as a dynamic set of social relations), rather as an appropriate 'period' environment for its story. But in this, therefore, it also avoids the modern pastoral images of *Far From the Madding Crowd*. The characters are convincingly located in this physical setting, although the film's predictable focus on Tess's tragic love-story and her personal relations with Alec and Angel once more detaches them from the 'environment' in a larger sense, so that the film can in no way be seen as a social drama. Indeed, while the blurb on the video tape of *Tess* gets it wrong in almost every way – 'Today, he would be tried for rape. In her day, she was accused of seduction. What she did shattered her world for ever. "Tess" – Roman Polanski's brilliant evocation of a woman's struggle against the hypocrisy of her age'[56] (the film is by no means clear that Alec actually rapes Tess (nor is the novel), nor is she ever 'accused of seduction') – it is most emphatically wrong in that final suggestion (perhaps with the 1981 film of Fowles's *The French Lieutenant's Woman* in mind) that Tess is locked in conflict with the social ethics of her time. Although this may be the major thrust of Hardy's novel (but even there the character herself is not conscious of her 'struggle'), it is only implicit in the film because it is played down in Polanski's fascination with the romantic tragedy, the embryonic existentialism of Tess, and with the very modern sense of her *anomie*. The film of *Tess* effectively dehistoricizes the nineteenth-century novel, and rehistoricizes it by its interpretative frame, as did the other film and serial in their different ways. If, as critics suggest,[57] one of the problems with film in general, and *Tess* in particular, is its 'literalness', its non-figurative presentation of 'the actual', then it can be seen here as the 'modern' existential heroine detached from the 'real' historical determinations which should account for her. Certainly Tess is superimposed on a realistic 'period' background, but she is not organically related to it. This may reinforce the sense of her 'alienation' from her society, but it is a characteristically ahistorical existential alienation in which the particular and specific historical conjuncture is finally immaterial.

Nevertheless, the film is, in many respects, again closely faithful to the book: most of the main scenes are present in the correct order, large amounts of the dialogue are reproduced *verbatim*, and there are only a few added or extended scenes. But it is, of course, in some of the more significant changes that we can see the existentializing 'interpretative frame' at work. For example, the early scene is cut in which Tess has to drive the cart to Casterbridge because her father gets drunk after hearing of his noble heredity, and Prince the horse is impaled on the mail-cart's shaft, splashing blood on Tess's dress. In its place is merely a reference to the family 'needing a new horse'. The scene's loss reduces the sense of Tess caught in the toils of economic and historical process: doomed by the potent power of the past (heredity), caught in the social and economic relations of her present class (family), and subject to the potentially destructive forces of modern change (the mail-cart) – all factors which the novel's discourses emphasize. In this respect, Tess is very exactly determined by her environment, which the film, as I have suggested, detaches her from. (A number of reviewers noted how this absence of the 'connections' which Hardy insists on causes an otherwise 'faithful' reproduction to become a *reductio ad absurdum*; how Tess is meaningless as a character unless she is seen as 'a victim of class'; how the film's 'absent' violence (unusual in Polanski's work) is 'the brutality of poverty'; and how, 'for all its superb emphasis on landscape and the rhythms of rural life, Polanski's film fails to establish the ties which root Hardy's Tess so firmly in the earth'.[58]) This lack of social determinants is reinforced by the film's underplaying of the corruptive influence of the *nouveau-riche* Alec on the community of Trantridge around his house, The Slopes (there is no suggestion, either, that Alec's money derives from money-lending in the north); and later, when she and Angel arrive at their honeymoon house, by the surprising (because very filmic) omission of the sinister d'Urberville portraits on the landing in which Tess's features are discernible. Polanski, after all, makes quite a lot of the heredity issue – although mainly, in effect, to highlight, on the one hand, the superstition which the film (rightly) presents as endemic to Tess's 'old' rural society; and on the other, Angel Clare's half-baked socialism (in the novel he is only a half-baked 'free-thinker'), represented by his repeated hostility to 'old, worm-eaten families' and – in one of the film's few obvious anachronisms – by the presence of a copy of Marx's *Capital and Capitalist Production* as Clare's bedside reading. A great deal of the sense of

121

Tess as a victim of history is dispelled by playing down the 'old' d'Urberville connection. For Tess, at least as the novel presents her, and despite her 'ache of modernism', is not a proto-'French Lieutenant's Woman', the existentialist 'free woman' cutting her way out of the stifling thickets of Victorian society; she is very precisely a figure imprisoned by history, beset by the moribund past and the entrepreneurial present and future, whose tragedy is that she is dimly conscious of her plight.

But to be fair to the film, it does attempt to show the social and sexual exploitation of Tess, while not factitiously trying to make her an embryonic feminist. Indeed, one reviewer of *Tess*, Jane Marcus in *Jump Cut*, under the title 'A Tess for child molesters', furiously belabours Polanski for 'raping' Hardy's text; for failing to see that Tess is 'the great Unwed Mother' who causes women to 'weep for joy' when she kills Alec; for showing Tess as meek and passive rather than enraged and powerful; and for being 'a voyeur of victimization who infantilizes *our Tess*' (my italics). That last phrase is, I think, significant: for Tess in this guise may be a strategically feminist reconstruction, but she is in no sense the quiescent and historically-disabled country girl of the novel. What Jane Marcus wants is what she says Polanski fails to give us: 'a Teresa of the lettuce fields of the Southwest among similar migrant workers as deeply attached to the earth as Tess is to her Dorset fields.' Marcus would be quite justified in criticizing the film's persistent voyeuristic delight in Kinski's face (although the novel does it, too, in presenting Tess as an innocent *femme fatale*), but to criticize it for not being faithful to a notion of '*our Tess*' is beside the point. A modern female director might properly do it, but to 'expect' it of Polanski is politically naïve. Nevertheless, it is in its treatment of the heroine and her relations with her two lovers that we find the film's most noteworthy contemporary 'reinterpretation' of *Tess*.

Tess is played as naturally beautiful and sensuous (the close-ups of Kinski's mouth echo the novel's obsession with it), and hence as artlessly but fatally attractive to men. She is also played, for the most part, as in a passive, dreamy, almost trance-like state. The most obvious examples are the scenes (not in the novel) after her seduction by Alec, when she has become his mistress and he rows her on the river and entertains her in the garden marquee; the romantic idyll, immediately before the wedding (and again not in the novel), when she and Angel run through the countryside and she adorns his room with wild flowers; and the scene when Angel rediscovers her in the boarding house at Sandbourne, where she is Alec's kept woman, dolled up in whorish style, who acts and speaks like a zombie. The effect of this is to reinforce the sense of her estrangement from her society and her 'Age'. The novel implies it; the film brings it into bold relief. Nastassia Kinski's own comments on her role are illuminating here: she found herself 'taking on [Tess's] patience and strength and courage'; and adds: 'I've always dreamed of being a person like her. She's not spoiled by the society she moves through. She stays untouched. She goes through everything for love.'[59] Polanski's Tess is someone trying to be her own woman, adrift in a world whose values she cannot relate to, who wants to love and be loved as an existential human subject in a society of exploitation and sham. She is doomed, not so much by history, but by her difference. She is, in late twentieth-century terms, *l'étranger*: the authentic individual whom the world must destroy. Polanski's comments in the interviews cited earlier underwrite this interpretation, as does his statement in the Press Release:

> I had always wanted to film a great love story, but what also fascinated me about this novel was its preoccupation with the vicissitudes of fate. The heroine has every attribute that should make for happiness – personal beauty, an engaging personality and a spirited approach to life – yet the social climate in which she lives and the inexorable pressure it exerts upon her gradually entrap her in a chain of circumstances that culminates in tragedy.[60]

(Is this where the dedication to Sharon Tate, pregnant and ritualistically murdered by the 'Manson family' in 1969, finds its relevance?) It is an inflexion of late twentieth-century liberal tragedy, in which individual good faith is held to be the only true political action: 'a pure woman faithfully presented by Roman Polanski' – for Tess's existential being is what the film really portrays.

It is implied, paradoxically, even in the famous scene in The Chase, when Tess is seduced by Alec. There is no hint of rape; the novel is by no means explicit, but the film is deeply ambiguous as to what happens here. Tess, mesmerized, relieved, grateful, first of all lets Alec kiss her; it is unclear whether Kinski's face at this point registers passivity or pleasure. As Alec becomes more ardent, the film slides into fuzzy soft-focus which makes it difficult to see the sexual act unambiguously: is Kinski/Tess struggling with Alec, or writhing with pleasure; does she fight, or does she succumb to the release of sex, of being 'loved', at that overwrought moment? The film, of course, does not say. (Polanski in an interview, however, implies a rather more dubious ambiguity: asked the usual question about rape/seduction, coercion/consent, he replies: 'it's both, actually, or neither . . . It's half-and-half. It happens by insistence, and by using physical strength in certain ways. But physical strength was almost inevitable in those days; it was part of Victorian courtship. Even on her wedding night a woman might be expected to resist.'[61] It is here that a feminist critic might properly challenge Polanski's implication: for it is strongly redolent of the 'woman-enjoys-it-really' explanation of rape.) If anything, this sense of Tess as emotionally adrift is reinforced by the fact that, immediately following her seduction, Polanski inserts the sequence of scenes in which the trance-like Tess has become Alec's mistress (later, confessing to Angel, she admits that she 'became Alec's mistress' – a loaded phrase absent from the novel, as indeed is her whole 'confession'). Only then does she realize that this is *mauvais foi* and she abruptly leaves, wishing she 'had never been born'. It is at this point that the film brings into high relief Tess's flash of spirit when she answers Alec's 'That's what every woman says' with: 'How can you dare to use such words! . . . Did it never strike your mind that what every woman says some women may feel?'[62] It is a moment which the film makes unforgettable in its presentation of Tess, just as later, when the vicar refuses to give 'Sorrow' Christian burial and she does it herself, the film emphasizes her defiant selfhood in opposition to the hypocrisies of social convention. Equally, in all her relations with Angel Clare it is her passionate commitment to him (hence the interpolated scene of her decorating his room with flowers), her trust, and her anxiety about her own 'bad faith', which are emphasized. And combined with all this, is the prominence given to Tess's obsession with death, her wish for the 'courage to die', and her final act of *l'étranger*'s expiation: the killing of Alec. The overtly sexual scene with Angel in their hideaway afterwards, which the novel, of course, cannot provide, intensifies this sense of existential being – as does our knowledge that she herself must 'pay' by dying. Significantly, the film ends with Tess's arrest at Stonehenge (the legend on the final screen stating that she was hanged at Wintoncester – 'aforetime capital of Wessex') and not with the novel's strange coda in which Angel and 'Liza-Lu (Tess's sister who has become her surrogate) watch her hanging from a hill above the town and then walk away hand in hand. Clearly, it would be difficult for the film to carry this off, but its absence also effectively leaves the focus on Tess's 'nobility' and individual tragedy, as Polanski's own comment again implies: 'Even in Hardy the hanging is almost an epilogue. I don't think it's essential. The story is clear enough and sad enough without it. You know Tess is doomed.'[63]

Polanski's film of *Tess*, then, is remarkably faithful to the novel, but in its emphasis and focus, in its selections and inclusions, in its casting and filming, in its interpretative frame, it reproduces a reading that the novel will sustain, but which is essentially late twentieth century in its ideological orientation. By freeing Tess from her historical determinants and by locating her in the film principally in her own emotional space, Polanski reproduces her as the existential heroine of his own time and tragic vision, as someone trying to live an authentic life in an inauthentic society. That this world view in fact represents despair at the claims of social being and political action, and can merely affirm the 'free' but doomed individual, may well account both for the film's popularity in the 1980s and for its whimsical anachronism of making Karl Marx the bedtime reading of 'inauthentic' Angel Clare.

I have attempted to show in this chapter some of the ways in which a 'classic writer' may be reproduced in the contemporary period, beyond criticism and education. What we see is the continual and inescapable process by which Hardy's work is variously dehistoricized and simultaneously rehistoricized in the ideological discourses of the present. *Far From the Madding Crowd* is an effervescent sixties pastoral which contains some salutary lessons about personal and social responsibility; *The Mayor of Casterbridge* offers us, in 1978, a museum of our national past, and a lesson on the importance of 'character'; and *Tess* is an existential pastoral in which personal integrity is the only lesson. Perhaps we should be able to see the ideological trajectory of the late 1960s to the early 1980s in these versions; perhaps not. One thing is certain, however, 'Thomas Hardy' remains a potent cultural figure in our own time, and a figure – despite his popularity in America and Japan, despite being filmed in France with a German actress by a Franco-Polish director, and despite contemporary interpretations of his 'relevance' – who remains essentially the 'Wessex Hardy' of 'character and environment'. In the still powerfully realist discourses of the visual media, those two terms retain their conventional separation: 'characters' in – but not of – an 'environment'. And in that separation lies the crucial displacement of history by pastoral – a crux in the ideology of any 'national culture'.

I hope to have shown throughout Part I the importance of a critiography within historical criticism: that studying the production and reproduction of literature in history denaturalizes the ostensibly unproblematical 'primary material' of the texts, indicating how they are historically produced for the present, how they are constructed and appropriated by the dominant ideological institutions, and how they are naturalized in hierarchies of 'value'. In this, it also serves to free writings from that incorporation, enabling other suppressed discourses (*Tess*'s 'faults', the 'minor novels') to emerge and take their place as constituent discourses of a different 'Hardy'. For the closures of the major/minor opposition do not simply exclude certain texts, they also limit the ways in which all may be read. This is where a critiography, as with historiography, consciously asserts its political function. If 'Hardy' is recognized as only constructed in discourse, then Hardy can be reconstructed just as properly on behalf of an alternative interest. As with the variable facticity of the fact in history, the newly visible discourses alter the perception, the 'meaning', of the whole set of discourses. It is to some indication of just such an effect that I address the second part of this book.

Part II

Remaking Thomas Hardy

4

Hardy and social class: reading *The Life*

Amongst Terry Eagleton's suggestive and tantalizingly brief comments on Hardy in *Criticism and Ideology* is the statement:

> Ambiguously placed within both his own declining rural enclave and the social formation at large . . . Hardy's situation as a literary producer was ridden with contradictions. They are contradictions inseparable from his fraught productive relation to the metropolitan audience whose spokesman rejected his first, abrasively radical work.

He goes on to comment on the clash of formal modes in Hardy's writing, and adds: 'The formal problem of how to reconcile these conflicting literary modes . . . is the product of Hardy's unusually complex mode of insertion into the dominant ideological formation and its span of possible literary forms'; and he also refers in passing to him as 'that later petty-bourgeois novelist of rural life'.[1] A number of interesting issues are raised by these comments which Eagleton never fully explains or develops. Leaving aside for the moment Eagleton's problematical reference to Hardy's 'first, abrasively radical work', *The Poor Man and the Lady* – which was never published, does not exist in manuscript and which is known about only from *The Life* and from the remnant published as *An Indiscretion in the Life of an Heiress*[2] – we may ask: what exactly was the 'ambiguity' of Hardy's insertion within the dominant ideological formation and within 'his own declining rural enclave'? what was his 'fraught productive relation' to the dominant literary world of his day? in what senses was Hardy 'petty-bourgeois'? and how can these factors be perceived as pervasively structuring and informing his writings?

Questions of social class as a major element in the study of Hardy's work are not, as we have seen in chapter 1, very prominent. Biographers like Gittings and Millgate, of course, deal with Hardy's class origins and their 'presence' in his work, but only *en route* to

129

other questions concerning the so-called 'major fiction'. Equally, many critics make passing reference to Hardy's class – especially, again, to that of his origin – but they are usually either historically imprecise, as Merryn Williams has indicated, or they dismiss the class elements in his work as errors, aberrations, or singularly less significant than other themes. Merryn Williams's own book, *Thomas Hardy and Rural England*, is one of the few notable examples of a thesis concerned with social class and with Hardy as social historian. But here, as in the essay written with Raymond Williams,[3] the emphasis is almost exclusively on the 'rural' Hardy – his class origins and his concern with movements and changes in the rural community – and not with what we might call Hardy's 'real' class position when he became a successful novelist and poet, i.e. that of 'professional writer', 'man of letters', and London socialite. The point is, and this is where Eagleton's remarks are corrective and helpful, that Hardy's class position and the social determinations which 'produce' him are shifting and complex; and this needs to be acknowledged if both his work as a whole, and the process of shaping and reproducing 'Hardy' as outlined in Part I, are to be accounted for and understood. For the pressure, and suppression, of acute class consciousness are intimately related in Hardy's work – both in its actual production, and in the way Hardy himself is complicit, as we have seen, in constructing a particular conception of it which is then widely reproduced in criticism, education, and elsewhere. Hardy's social origins in a specific class fraction in mid nineteenth-century Dorset are, of course, important, but only within the frame of the upwardly-mobile professional writer operating in a metropolitan, upper-class-dominated, social and literary culture. To put it crudely: it is *this* Hardy who wrote, and not the Ur-Hardy of Higher Bockhampton. The fact that so much criticism and other adulation has emphasized the Dorset Hardy – whose 'real' feelings and 'real' commitments are to his so-called 'peasant' roots, and whose work is at its best when closest to this milieu – is merely an instance of the process of reproduction noted above.

Hardy was born into what Merryn and Raymond Williams[4] call the 'intermediate' class – within the broad rural structure of landowners, tenants, and labourers: a fraction composed of lifeholders or copyholders who were sometimes family farmers but more usually part of the ancillary dimension of the rural economy: the craftsmen, artisans, and tradesmen who serviced its primary functions. This relatively independent group was put under intense pressure in the course of the nineteenth century in England by developments in monopoly capitalist farming and by urban manufacturing industry, and Hardy comments a number of times in his writing on their gradual dispossession. The nature of this class of Hardy's origin is itself complex, as the case of Hardy's own family indicates.[5] His father was from humble beginnings but became a relatively prosperous self-employed mason and subsequently a master-mason employing several men and owning property (a number of other Hardys were also masons), although his eldest brother John was an ordinary labourer who married a labourer's daughter and had seven children. His mother, herself the daughter of a servant, George Hand, had been a cook and lady's maid, and was one of seven pauper children brought up on parish relief – although her mother was the 'exceptionally well-read'[6] daughter of a yeoman farmer who had come down in the world by her misalliance with George Hand. Jemima, Hardy's mother, was herself a woman of great strength of character, passionately keen on reading and the owner of a small collection of books (including her favourite, Dante's *Divine Comedy*), who had powerful aspirations for the education and upward social mobility of her children (Hardy's sister went to a training college and became a teacher). One of the other Hand sisters, Martha, had married a man who became farm manager on the Marquis of Salisbury's estate at Hatfield, and whose brother had a medical practice in Welwyn; but the rest of the Hand children remained in Puddletown. The brothers were all bricklayers whose fortunes rose and fell – Christopher ultimately becoming a mason, too, although never so prosperous as Thomas Hardy senior because of bouts of heavy drinking (apparently he also beat his wife); and the two other Hand sisters married leaseholding craftsmen – Maria's husband, James Sparks, being a well-connected cabinet-maker. Of the Sparks' daughters, with whom Hardy was very friendly, Rebecca had done an apprenticeship and carried on a dressmaking business helped by two of her sisters as seamstresses (although they later went into domestic service, where Martha became pregnant by the butler of the house and was sacked), and Tryphenia went to Stockwell Training College in London and became a headmistress at the age of 21. Mary married John Antell, a cobbler and autodidact (often seen as 'partly' the model for Jude),[7] who had taught himself Latin but who, like his brother-in-law Christopher, was prone to heavy drinking (and also beat his wife). The sons, however, were carpenters. As Gittings points out, both the Antell and Sparks families, though in the craftsman class, were always very close to poverty.[8]

This rough sketch should indicate something of the complex and shifting composition of the class of Hardy's origins. He had strong

131

past and present connections with servants and labourers, with craftsmen more or less thriving, with other more upwardly-mobile relatives, with some of the brutalities and promiscuities of rural social life, with strong elements of autodidacticism, and with people – especially young women – who, by way of education in particular, moved into a different section of the *petit bourgeoisie*. The young Hardy is, then, already placed in a volatile class position: both of, and not of, a class fraction which is itself in a precarious position in the larger structure of the rural social economy. As the Williamses suggest,[9] it is precisely this uncertain, mobile, and complex situation for the 'intermediate' class which makes their class location such an issue, and Hardy so conscious of it. At its crudest, it was the question of whether one stayed within one's original social class and culture, or moved 'up' from it by way of those forms of aspiration which that culture itself sustained and encouraged. Hardy's education was one of those forms of aspiration (on his family's part) which predetermined his later class position. But even so, it is in the metropolitan profession of writing that Hardy's 'true' class position is ultimately to be located, not in the 'intermediate' rural class from which he derives. And it is a self-consciousness of the tension between that class position and the one of origin which marks all of Hardy's work.

One of the commonest perceived forms of upward social mobility in nineteenth-century England was through education. (Hardy's fiction continually introduces it as a motif, although never, significantly, as unproblematically beneficial; more often it is the cause of disruption, alienation, non-communication, frustration, and so on.) Hardy's own progress falls within this common pattern. Under his mother's influence, he apparently started to read very young. This was followed, when he was eight, with schooling at the new National School in Bockhampton, which was free, and in the following year at a British and Foreign Society school in Dorchester. The latter was run by Isaac Last who had a considerable academic reputation, which appealed to Hardy's mother, and who also taught Latin as an 'extra' which Hardy took – his father paying. In 1853, Last opened his own Academy in Dorchester, and Hardy went there with him as a fee-paying pupil, until he left in 1856 to be apprenticed to Hicks the Dorchester architect. Hardy, therefore, left school at 16, some three or four years later than if he had attended an ordinary school; but his education thereafter was mainly by personal reading, with assistance from better-educated friends like Horace Moule. His later prickliness about this lack of higher education (which gave rise to a dubious remark in *The Life* about the possibility of his going to Cambridge)[10] thus suggests Hardy's sense of being only partly educated in terms of conventional upper-class criteria. It is a reflex of Hardy's contradictory class insertion that he could, nevertheless, attack Oxford University so fiercely in *Jude the Obscure.*

From 1856 to the mid 1870s (when Hardy's career as a novelist began to take off), he worked for architects in Dorchester and London. But in addition to joining a profession, he mixed, especially at Blomfield's in London, with a wholly new class of people, the profession being dominated by 'public-school men from the upper classes',[11] and made the most of the cultural activities available in London – churches, theatres, concerts, art galleries, and so on. He was also reading widely throughout this period. Significantly, Hardy did well in his profession, winning a RIBA essay prize in 1863, but there is a sense in which, in that particular world, Hardy, like so many other lower-middle-class young men of the new meritocracy, could never have competed on the same terms as his more privileged colleagues: the sense of class inferiority would have been strong and continuous. Only within a field where the structure of pre-eminence was not already predetermined by class factors, was social success in terms of personal merit a real possibility. Literature was such a field. How far Hardy perceived his life in such a consciously preconceived fashion, and decided to become a writer for this reason, is impossible to know. Nevertheless, he did decide to become a writer, and he worked very hard at it. He was also relatively successful from quite an early stage, his second published novel, *Under the Greenwood Tree* (1872), being a minor success (and later growing in popularity), and his fourth, *Far From the Madding Crowd* (1874), a great popular success both in Britain and the United States.

However, the field of writing itself – of the 'Reviews', of *belles-lettres*, of the higher journalism – was by no means open, democratic, or meritocratic in the second half of the nineteenth century, and part of the hard work Hardy had to put in was to make himself acceptable in that world. John Gross, in *The Rise and Fall of the Man of Letters*, suggests that until the 1850s the profession of journalism was still of shaky social status, but by the late 1850s and early 1860s, with the appearance of the *Saturday Review* in 1855 (with which Horace Moule was connected, and which was to be Hardy's influential reading from 1857 onwards),[12] and with the advent of *Macmillan's* (1859) and the *Cornhill* (1860) – both of which were later to publish Hardy – this was rapidly changing, the *Saturday Review* itself employing mainly Oxford and Cambridge graduates and serving 'the interests of the most powerful section of the community'.[13] From the 1870s onwards the profession of letters was very much in the hands of the educated upper class, with Leslie Stephen and John Morley – two of Hardy's earliest advisors and editors – representing this interest. Gross, in commenting also on the absence of Victorian critics with a working-class background, writes: 'One reason for the broad similarities of outlook among Victorian men of letters was that most of them were children of the business or professional class, with little or any knowledge of working-class life or of the industrial regions.'[14] It was this social group which Hardy had to engage with and was later to enter, and it is significant that one of his closest friends thereafter was Sir Edmund Gosse, an assiduous professional man of letters and one of considerable social aspiration. Hardy entered it, however, as an imaginative writer, not as a critic or reviewer; and in this sense, again, on his own terms and not those of its class determinates.

I have suggested that Hardy worked hard at making himself a successful literary man, and indeed, as I shall indicate below, he contributes a great deal to the making of 'Thomas Hardy' by way of 'Florence Emily's' *The Life*, in which he literally 'writes himself' as he wished to be perceived. But the *actual* process of becoming a writer is significant too. Hardy had started writing poetry in 1860 or earlier, and it is reiterated time and again in *The Life* that poetry was more important to him than fiction (e.g. 'Hardy by this time had quite resigned himself to novel-writing as a trade, which he had never wanted to carry on as such' (see also pp. 152–4)).[15] How far one believes *The Life* is a problem, as we shall see, but what is certain is that, after *Jude* and *The Well-Beloved*, Hardy gave up fiction writing altogether and concentrated on *The Dynasts* and lyric poetry. Many suggestions have been made as to the reasons for this, but the simplest (whilst not being definitive) is that he was by then prosperous enough not to have to write for money as a priority. All I want to establish for the moment is that Hardy, in deciding to become a writer, had a careful eye on the market and its requirements. This is borne out by his response to the earliest criticisms (from publishers' readers, editors, and reviewers) of his first works. It is also, perhaps, a sign of the tense ambiguity of Hardy's social and professional location that his first (unpublished) novel, *The Poor Man and the Lady*, should have been, in the words of *The Life*, 'a striking socialistic novel' (56), offering 'a sweeping dramatic satire of the squirearchy and nobility, London society, the vulgarity of the middle class, modern Christianity, church-restoration, and political and domestic morals in general . . . the tendency of the writing being socialistic, not to say – revolutionary' (61); and that his last novel, *Jude*, seems as close to *The Poor Man and the Lady* in cast of mind as any of the others intervening.

However, what is clear from *The Life* and other evidence is that Hardy tried hard to get it published, but that Alexander Macmillan, John Morley, and George Meredith, Chapman and Hall's reader, felt that although it showed excellent qualities they would not recommend publication. Macmillan (following Morley's comments) said that the satire on the upper classes was overdone – 'your chastisement would fall harmless from its very excess' (58); that Hardy 'meant mischief' (62) by the book; that 'the thing hangs too loosely together' (59); and that it had 'a certain rawness of absurdity that is very displeasing, and makes it read like some clever lad's dream'.[16] But Meredith, speaking very much as the professional literary man, offered particularly interesting advice in my context here. *The Life*, in a characteristically ambiguous passage (Hardy sounds considerably more sophisticated, conscious of his intentions, and sympathetic to the forms and theme of that first novel than is explicitly claimed by his 'biographer'), notes that Meredith

> strongly advised its author 'not to nail his colours to the mast' so definitely in a first book, if he wished to do anything practical in literature; for if he printed so pronounced a thing he would be attacked on all sides by the conventional reviewers, and his future injured.

It repeats, a little later, that 'in genteel mid-Victorian 1869 it would no doubt have incurred, as Meredith judged, severe strictures which might have handicapped a young writer for a long time' (61–2). Meredith recommended rewriting the story, 'softening it down considerably', or better still, attempting 'a novel with a purely artistic purpose, giving it a more complicated ''plot'' than was attempted in *The Poor Man and the Lady*'. Hardy tried one more publisher, then gave it up and started writing *Desperate Remedies*, taking 'Meredith's advice too literally' in respect of its plot (62–3).

Morley, for Macmillan, rejected this second novel on the grounds that

> the story is ruined by the disgusting and absurd outrage which is the key to its mystery – The violation of a young lady at an evening party, and the subsequent birth of a child, is too abominable to be tolerated as a central incident from which the action of the story is to move.[17]

Hardy then offered the manuscript to Tinsley, who agreed to publish it, on Hardy's own advance of £75, if certain revisions were made. The novel duly appeared without the 'violation' scene – Hardy having agreed to all Tinsley's suggestions.[18] It is interesting to remember, too, that when the novel was reviewed by the *Spectator*[19] – quite

savagely in places, and with conventional Victorian moral outrage –
Hardy was shattered by it. This, Robert Gittings has suggested,[20]
was because Hardy was obsessed by the idea that the novel had to
be a financial success, and that such criticism would kill its sale. It
is also noteworthy that those qualities the *Spectator* (and other
reviews) praised – especially Hardy's handling of the 'rural' scenes
– are brought fully into the foreground in his next novel, *Under the
Greenwood Tree*. This was turned down once more by Macmillan
(via Morley) as 'slight', but was finally published by Tinsley –
Hardy again, according to Gittings, being desperate to make some
money from writing.[21] In this case, however, the reviews were
generally favourable, the *Athenaeum* praising it for doing what it had
pointed out Hardy did best in its review of his previous novel: 'we
especially commended [*Desperate Remedies*] for its graphic pictures
of rustic life somewhere in the West Country. Here [*Under the
Greenwood Tree*] the author is clearly on his own ground, and to
this he has confined himself in the book before us.'[22] It is a good
instance of the 'making' (in two senses of the word) of Hardy the
novelist. At this point, Tinsley proposed that Hardy should write a
serial for his popular monthly, *Tinsley's Magazine*; and so with *A
Pair of Blue Eyes* Hardy moved into the treacherous waters of
Victorian periodical publication where the pressures on a novelist to
conform to convention – both moral and aesthetic – were intense.
Perhaps the most striking contradiction in Hardy's novel-writing
career is his willingness to accommodate these pressures, to change,
revise, cut, suppress, to play the system for all its worth; and,
conversely, to produce novels which time and again reject fictional
stereotypes (even those of his own successfully established mode:
why follow *Far From the Madding Crowd* with *The Hand of
Ethelberta*, for example?) and which were bound to shock the
Victorian moral conscience.

At about this time, Hardy also became intensely professional in his
material dealings with publishers. Leaving aside the (apparently
fictive)[23] tale in *The Life* about his buying a book on copyright law
to deal with Tinsley, the early volumes of his *Letters*[24] and *The
Life* indicate how concerned Hardy was with copyright, publication
details, and proof-reading for example, and how keen he was to
accommodate demands for his work *and* the pressures of public taste
in the family magazines. This tendency is most apparent in his dealings with Leslie Stephen over the publication in the *Cornhill* of *Far
From the Madding Crowd*, his first really successful novel. Hardy
seems to have accepted almost all of Stephen's suggestions for revision and improvement of the serial: *The Life* focusing particularly on
Stephen's powerful sense of the prudery of the Victorian reading

public and of Hardy's need to take cognizance of it (98–9). Perhaps more significant in my context here, is the much-quoted passage from a letter to Stephen, printed in *The Life*, in which his desire for success is made quite explicit:

> 'The truth is that I am willing, and indeed anxious, to give up any points which may be desirable in a story when read as a whole, for the sake of others which shall please those who read it in numbers. Perhaps I may have higher aims some day, and be a great stickler for the proper artistic balance of the completed work, but for the present circumstances lead me to wish merely to be considered a good hand at a serial.'
> The fact was that at this date he was bent on carrying out later in the year an intention beside which a high repute as an artistic novelist loomed even less importantly than in ordinary – an intention to be presently mentioned. (100)

Robert Gittings has taken issue with the constant misrepresentation of this passage, but, in effect, he too can only finally confirm that Hardy wished for big sales in order to be able to marry.[25] The inference surely must be that, for whatever reason and despite disclaimers in *The Life*, Hardy wished to be a successful literary man and recognized that Stephen could help him to be one. In conjunction, we should notice that it is also by way of Stephen that Hardy was introduced into the upper-class and intellectual circles which were to be his dominant social milieu thereafter. And it is from this point on in *The Life*, as we shall see, that Hardy begins to present himself as literary-man-about-town and the familiar of noble people – again, despite disclaimers that he enjoyed socializing. It is at this time, indeed, that Hardy effectively joins that other class, the Victorian intelligentsia, and feels the need to disguise his social origins so carefully (Leslie Stephen and Lady Thackeray, for example, had no real sense of his class background). But it is also at this point, we should remember, that Hardy wrote *The Hand of Ethelberta*, a novel in which he checks and disrupts his publishers' and critics' expectations of him. This departure is presented in *The Life* and elsewhere as a refutation of his sole interest in 'rustic scenes' and to mark his independence from the shadow of George Eliot which had fallen over him with *Far From the Madding Crowd*. As we have seen in chapter 1, Hardy's own sense of his rejection of Eliot's humanist realism is significant, but more to my point here is that, just as he moves from one class group to another – precisely by way of the profession of writing – he produces a novel which is obsessively concerned with class relations, with class deception, and with his heroine's upward social mobility assisted by the composition of 'fictions'. It is also worth bearing in mind both Hardy's ambiguous comments on *Ethelberta* in *The Life* (he claims, amongst other things, that it was some thirty years ahead of its time and, in the same sentence, that his 'socialistic story', *The Poor Man and the Lady*, was similarly so),[26] and the fact that it has been the most disregarded and disliked of all Hardy's fiction, the one least 'characteristic' of his 'true genius'.

During the latter half of Hardy's fiction-writing career, the contradictory nature of his socio-professional insertion continues to be acute. As his letters reveal, he is exceptionally conscious of, and conscientious about, the business of being a professional literary man: money, publication arrangements, copyright, and so on are of first importance to him. He continues to write for magazines, making elaborate arrangements (especially with *Tess* and *Jude*) to accommodate public morality: in these cases in particular, he published heavily cut and adapted serial versions; printed the excised parts elsewhere as 'episodic adventures of anonymous personages';[27] and finally reassembled all of the original for book publication – even, in the case of *Jude the Obscure*, under a different title[28] (*The Return of the Native*, also, had its ending adapted under editorial pressure).[29] The central contradiction here, of course, is of Hardy continuing to produce novels which he well knew would be execrated, but nevertheless going to the immense labour of playing the system in this way. As an example of the 'alienation' consequent on this process, see the passage in *The Life* in which Hardy describes it in relation to *Tess*:

> Hardy carried out this unceremonious concession to
> conventionality with cynical amusement . . . But the work was
> sheer drudgery, the modified passages having to be written in
> coloured ink, that the originals might be easily restored . . .
> Hence the labour brought no profit. (222)

Hardy, in fact, lies athwart the whole system: the lower-class rural man who has entered the educated and privileged domain of a metropolitan cultural class, and cannot admit his origins; the poet who is forced to be a novelist in order to succeed, and who becomes popular and respected as the latter; the serious and radical writer of fiction who must accommodate his work to the commercial and ethical pressures of late Victorian serial publication: the entire fabric of his life is a mesh of fictions. The profound alienation which marks all Hardy's work – the clash of modes, the mannered style, the derisive irony, the 'satires of circumstance' – is determined by the *anomie* of his class and professional contradictions. And this alienation, stemming from the perceived 'unreality' of one's life

(Hardy repeats this notion continuously in his (auto)biography), is most exactly expressed in the paradox of Hardy's production of his own 'life': 'Florence Emily Hardy's' *The Life of Thomas Hardy* is itself a fiction, and many of the contradictions within which he lived coalesce there.

Hardy's last 'novel', then, was not, I suggest, *Jude the Obscure* or *The Well-Beloved*, but *The Life*, supposedly written by Florence Emily, actually written by Hardy himself, and passed off under her name after his death.[30] The fiction is a complex one: Hardy creates a third-person biographer who recounts the life story of a writer called Thomas Hardy. In this way, Hardy is quite literally 'writing himself' – his 'life' exists only as the written discourse in which it is articulated (as Tristram Shandy had understood 150 years before). But it is also, precisely, the practice of the novelist who establishes a narrative 'voice', who sustains the illusion of authenticity, and who creates a 'character' – a fictional other – who develops as the novelist directs him to and who 'turns out' correctly, as the novelist wishes him to be perceived. What distinguishes *The Life* from other third-person autobiographical fictions, however, is that Hardy also produces an autonomous *author*, to make the illusion of veracity even more complete.

The Life quotes Hardy's memorandum for 9 January 1889, which includes the comment: 'Art is the secret of how to produce by a false thing the effect of a true' (216). The irony of this is striking, once the nature of the deception is understood, and indeed it is clear that a great deal of 'art' went into creating the illusion of biography: from the 'Prefatory Note' under 'FEH's' initials but clearly in Hardy's style, to the 'few notes . . . made by his wife for the remaining weeks of 1927' (440) which end the book, and which, in being distinguished from Hardy's own notebooks (these having supplied the rest of the material for the biography), tend to confirm the integrity of the whole. Many such devices for greater verisimilitude are employed throughout. 'The author' does not 'know' something when it is obvious that Hardy himself would have known; for example 'It is not known whether the Italian Contessa in *A Group of Noble Dames* was suggested by her; but there are resemblances' (195); or 'Hardy's reply was written down but (it is believed), as in so many cases with him, never posted; though I am able to give it from the rough draft' (243–4). Notes about the 'world of fashion . . . which Hardy did not think worth recording' (see pp. 145–8 for more on this fiction) are said to come from 'diaries kept by the late Mrs. Hardy' (245). There are continual reminders that Hardy's notes were for 'private consideration, which he meant to

destroy, and not for publication' (201), and that he would have
nothing to do with publishing his 'recollections': 'an issue which has
come about by his having been asked when old if he would object
to their being printed, as there was no harm in them, and his saying
passively that he did not mind' (202). The irony here – given that
it is Hardy himself who is writing and selecting the material – is
sharp indeed. Again, on the meagreness of Hardy's later memoranda: 'But it accords with Hardy's frequent saying that he took little
interest in himself as a person, and his absolute refusal at all times
to write his reminiscences' (323); and '"it is absolutely unlikely that
I shall ever change my present intention not to produce my reminiscences to the world"' (350).[31] All of this, of course, is by a man
writing his own life as though it were someone else's biography of
him. Indeed, the sheer scale and elaborateness of the deception
makes it very difficult to know how to read *The Life* at all. When
is Hardy being ironic (if he does not know that the reader knows the
secret)? Do the 'notes' and 'memoranda' date from the dates they
are given? Does he still mean or believe the things he writes down
or 'quotes'? Is any part of it utilizable in illuminating Hardy's work?
If so much of it is provably misrepresentation, grossly selected and
partial, are the unprovable parts anymore to be trusted? Ironically,
Hardy's tactic for blocking later biographies by others produced a
work so devoid of trustworthy information that is completely blots
out any sense of the 'real' Thomas Hardy from our perception. But
perhaps that was his sole intention. *The Life*, then, is one immense
fiction in which Hardy presents himself as he wishes to be regarded.
But, precisely because of the self-conscious fictionality of the enterprise, questions of his 'intention' are beside the point. What we have
merely, as in his repeated definitions of his novels, is a 'series of
seemings', 'impressions' – the reality of which exists only in the
discourse itself and nowhere else. All we can really know is that,
for some reason, Hardy decided to represent himself in this guise.
But we can still ask: what, then, is the 'character' of Hardy which
The Life presents? For, as with any fiction, *The Life* can be read,
in this respect, on at least two levels: first, in terms of intention –
what Hardy may have intended to present his 'character' as; and
second, in terms of what the work may reveal about the 'character'
which is not consciously intended. These readings, for the most part,
will be undertaken simultaneously here.[32]

The most striking feature of *The Life* is that by page 35 of the
454-page Macmillan paperback edition (1975), Hardy's early life and
background have been dealt with: he is 22 and off to London. This
means that we are told very little indeed of Hardy's family or of his
class origins. As Robert Gittings has pointed out:

He omits almost totally all his other close relatives, uncles, aunts, and very numerous cousins. The touchstone throughout seems to have been social class. Labourers, cobblers, bricklayers, carpenters, farm servants, journeymen joiners, butlers have no place in Hardy's memoirs, though he was related to all of these; nor, among women, do cooks, house-servants, ladies' maids, or certificated teachers, regarded in the nineteenth century as little better than servants.

Gittings tentatively accounts for this by saying: 'probably the most powerful motive was some sort of snobbery', but he later adds:

Yet snobbery is too sweeping and easy a dismissal . . . In early life he had to fight the massive social stratification of the Victorian age. Finally he broke through from one class to another; but one can only guess what violence this did to his own nature. To shut the door on a social past from which he had escaped became a compulsion in his later life.

Gittings further notes that 'the gulf' between the educated

and one of his own background, who, however full of simple wisdom, could literally not speak the language which Hardy had acquired, haunted his mind. In novels, he might extol the instinctive rightness of the peasant; in life, he always sought the company of the educated. Again, one can only guess the conflicts this caused.[33]

What Gittings is indicating here – although his world view will not allow him to enunciate it – is the major fissure or 'fault' in Hardy's ideological construction. Certainly, it is not simply 'snobbery of some sort', but the irresistible result of class mobility: Hardy was *déclassé* by dint of his profession, and within that position, as a *petit-bourgeois arriviste*, he could not speak of his social origins. Certainly, we can 'only guess' at the 'violence [done] to his own nature'; but we can nevertheless perceive the degree of alienation it causes – in producing one's own 'life' the way Hardy did and in the traces which mark all his work. We can perceive it, however, only if we can get behind the literary-critical Hardy of tragic humanist realism and the 'novels of character and environment'. Certainly, within that perspective, Hardy may seem to 'extol . . . the peasant'; but beyond it, the emphasis of Hardy's work is fixedly on those for whom the 'language' of social, sexual, and intellectual 'conflict' is most insistent.

The Life presents a type of the literary man Hardy had become. Not only are much of his family and early social life left out, but when they are mentioned they are continually implied to be of a higher social class and educational achievement than they were. In the first three pages, Hardy heightens the impression of the Hardys as being of long-standing yeoman stock, although now in decline, but with excellent historical antecedents: 'it was a family whose diverse Dorset sections included the Elizabethan Thomas Hardy who endowed the Dorchester Grammar School, the Thomas Hardy captain of the *Victory* at Trafalgar, Thomas Hardy an influential burgess of Wareham, Thomas Hardy of Chaldon, and others of local note' (5). The Hardy house is presented as a large and prosperous dwelling with 'two gardens (one of them part orchard)'; the community as being 'lifeholders of substantial footing like the Hardys themselves' (3); and Hardy's father, at his death, as being 'the only landowner of the name in the country' (5). The same is done for his mother's side of the family: the long line of their ancestry is indicated, as are the noble connections and the relative prosperity and status of his maternal grandmother's family: she was

> the daughter of one of those Swetmans by his wife Maria Childs, sister of the Christopher Childs who married into the Cave family, became a mining engineer in Cornwall, and founded the *West Briton* newspaper, his portrait being painted when he was about eighty by Sir Charles Eastlake. The traditions about Betty, Maria's daughter, were that she was tall, handsome, had thirty gowns, was an omnivorous reader, and one who owned a stock of books of exceptional extent for a yeoman's daughter living in a remote place. (7)

What is remarkable here, as elsewhere, is not factual inaccuracy (Hardy never literally gives wrong information), but the selection of the detail: why is it necessary, for example, to hear so much about Hardy's maternal grandmother's brother-in-law – except that he is the one who can be deployed to establish family prestige? Conversely, when Hardy deals with his grandmother's fall from fortune because of her imprudent marriage, he mentions his grandfather only as a 'young man' and not as a servant; moves swiftly to an inconsequential anecdote about his maternal great-grandfather; passes inexplicitly over the family's poverty (they were, in fact, on Poor Relief); and sidesteps from his mother's painful memories of early exigence to her voracious appetite for reading.[34] He slips over his father's occupation in a sentence, and emphasizes their involvement with church music for the next five pages, noting in passing that the choir – 'being mainly poor men and hungry' – had large suppers at the Hardys' house (12). Apart from a brief reference to 'the Hardys being comparatively independent of the manor' (18), this accounts for all of Hardy's description, in *The Life*, of his family and class background, although there are passing mentions of his noble ancestry and connections throughout. In 1888, when thinking about *Tess* and visiting the valleys of the 'Great' and 'Little' Dairies, he significantly noted 'the decline and fall of the Hardys much in evidence hereabout'; and, remembering a man 'walking beside a horse and common spring trap' (John Durbeyfield?), who was pointed out to him as 'represent[ing] what was once the leading branch of the family', he comments: 'So we go down, down, down' (214–15). On his father's death in 1892, he notes that he was buried 'near the knights of various dates in the seventeenth and eighteenth centuries, with whom the Hardys had been connected' (248). And in 1927, six months or so before his own death and right at the end of *The Life*, Hardy extensively refers, in his address on laying the foundation stone for the new Dorchester Grammar School, to the Thomas Hardy 'whose namesake I have the honour to be', and who had founded the original school (428).[35] Certainly the impression *The Life* leaves is one of a poor-genteel scion of good family with an impeccable heredity; it writes Hardy's past as it 'should have been'. At another level, it suggests someone obsessed with class and social status.

A corollary to Hardy's deceptive presentation of his background, here, is his constant reiteration of the absence of any autobiographical elements in the novels – and especially those which might hint at his lowly origins. In the case of *A Pair of Blue Eyes*, he spends nearly a page 'proving' that Stephen Smith is not a self-portrait ('he having ever been shy of putting his personal characteristics into his novels'); claims that 'Smith's father was a mason in Hardy's father's employ'; and that Knight, the educated and well-connected reviewer, was 'really much more like Thomas Hardy'. He also denies that Elfride, except in minor physical details, is based on Emma Gifford (73–4). Some twenty pages later he states that Old Dewy in *Under the Greenwood Tree* was not a portrait of his grandfather, adding: 'there was, in fact, no family portrait in the tale' (93); on the publication of *Far From the Madding Crowd*, he notes with exclamatory surprise that its author had 'been discovered to be a house-decorator(!)' (102); and in the 1912 section of *The Life*, while correcting the proofs for the 'Wessex' edition of *The Return of the Native*, he reproduces a letter in which he notes that Clym 'is the nicest of all my heroes, and not a bit like me' (358). Furthermore, in an interesting passage on the inception of *Jude*, Hardy effectively denies his own father's (and uncle's) trade by remarking that 'it was possibly his contact with the stonemason [Hardy was making the designs for his father's tombstone] that made him think of that trade for his next hero', and continues disingenuously, 'though in designing church stonework as an architect's pupil he had of course met with many' (252). Later Hardy sternly denies that Christminster was Oxford – merely a fictive device for realizing the 'difficulty of a poor man's acquiring learning at that date'; and adds, in a sentence heavy with suppressed irony: 'It is hardly necessary to add that he had no feeling in the matter, and used Jude's difficulties of study as he would have used war, fire, or shipwreck for bringing about a catastrophe' (278–9). And in 1919 there is the well-known definitive rejection of anything autobiographical in Jude:

'To your inquiry if *Jude the Obscure* is autobiographical, I have to answer that there is not a scrap of personal detail in it – it having the least to do with his own life of all his books. The rumour, if it still persists, was started some years ago. Speaking generally, there is more autobiography in a hundred lines of Mr. Hardy's poetry than in all the novels.'
It is a tribute to Hardy's powers of presentation that readers would not for many years believe that such incidents as Jude's being smacked when bird-keeping, his driving a baker's cart, his working as a journeyman mason . . . were not actual transcripts from the writer's personal experience, although the briefest reference to biographical date-books would have shown the impossibility of anything of the sort. (392)

Finally, we should remember that Hardy reproduces the deeply contradictory 'memorandum' of 28 April 1888, in which he seems at once to admit and reject his personal connection with Jude: 'A short story of a young man – "who could not go to Oxford" – His struggles and ultimate failure. Suicide. [Probably the germ of *Jude the Obscure*.] There is something [in this] the world ought to be shown, and I am the one to show it to them – though I was not altogether hindered going, at least to Cambridge, and could have gone up easily at five-and-twenty' (207–8).[36] *The Life* undoubtedly protests too much.

An equally insistent note in relation to Hardy's strident class consciousness is heard in the way he presents his life after his recognition as a novelist. The younger Hardy is characterized as bookish – 'having every instinct of a scholar he might have ended his life as a Don' (34) – a theme related to the notion of his going up to Cambridge in the 1860s (whether or not this was within his father's financial competence is uncertain, but the reason Hardy gives for his failure to go there was Horace Moule's advice against it).[37] And as a young architect at Blomfield's in London, Hardy appears as an ordinary young man without much money, although little is said of his early life there. The 'biography' instead moves rapidly to the publishers' responses to *The Poor Man and the Lady* and to Hardy's manifest pride (some sixty years later) in the praise of men of letters:

Thus it happened that a first and probably very crude manuscript by an unknown young man, who had no connection with the press, or with literary circles, was read by a most experienced publisher, and by two authors among the most eminent in letters of their time. Also that they had been interested to more than an average degree in his work. (62)

The aspiration to succeed, to be accepted into the social world of men like Stephen and Morley, is realized with the success of *Far From the Madding Crowd*; and from then on *The Life* is heavily and tediously laden with references to Hardy's noble or famous acquaintances, and with the social doings of a well-known literary figure. The sheer preponderance of this kind of information reveals its very considerable importance to the writer and to his conception of the 'character' he is portraying; and it is germane to my point that much of it reads like an out-of-date 'Court and Social' column. Some scattered examples will suffice to give the tone:

In the early part of [1885] . . . Hardy accepted a long-standing invitation to Eggesford by his friend Lady Portsmouth . . . He found her there surrounded by her daughters, and their cousin Lady Winifred Herbert, afterwards Lady Burghclere. (170)

On a trip to Ireland in 1893:

'Met on board John Morley [Hardy's early critic and advisor], the Chief Secretary, and Sir John Pender. Were awaited at Dublin by conveyance from the Viceregal Lodge as promised, this invitation being one renewed from last year . . . We were received by Mrs. Arthur Henniker, the Lord-Lieutenant's sister. A charming *intuitive* woman apparently. Lord Houghton (the Lord-Lieutenant) came in shortly after.' (254)

(The whole episode, told in considerable detail, is an excellent example of the way in which Hardy wished to present his life as a successful literary man at this time.) And in 1896, during the furore over *Jude*:

he and his wife passed this season much as usual, going to Lady Malmesbury's wedding and also a little later to the wedding of Sir George Lewis's son at the Jewish Synagogue; renewing acquaintance with the beautiful Duchess of Montrose and Lady

Londonderry, also attending a most amusing masked ball at his friends Mr and Mrs Montague Crackanthorpe's, where he and Henry James were the only two not in dominoes, and were recklessly flirted with by the women in consequence. (276)

By the time Hardy stopped writing fiction, therefore, he was a fully established literary man whose acquaintance was almost exclusively among the aristocracy, gentry, and high intelligentsia of the period. It is no surprise that his later years are even more totally depicted in such terms – as befitting the 'greatest living English writer'. This, then, is the dominant picture as *The Life* presents it. It is peculiarly impersonal, giving little sense of the man who wrote the novels and poems beyond the desired image of successful man of letters. Hardy has simply become his own creation (like Ethelberta, as we shall see). But nevertheless there are elements in *The Life* which reveal tensions and contradictions in this creation, as well as even more sharply foregrounding Hardy's obsession with status and class. These may be defined as: his disclaimers about social ambition; his ambiguous political and social attitudes; his attitudes to women; and his presentation of himself as poet rather than novelist.

From the beginning, *The Life* emphasizes Hardy's disdain for social climbing. Indeed, this is reiterated so often – bearing in mind the suppression of his class origins and the cataloguing of his fashionable social life described above – that it draws attention to itself and implies either the opposite or a deeply divided consciousness. As early as page 15, in a passage on his childhood (which, significantly, is echoed very exactly in *Jude*), *The Life* notes 'that lack of social ambition which followed him through life'; and forty pages later, it says 'he constitutionally shrank from the business of social advancement, caring for life as an emotion rather than for life as a science of climbing' (53). Nevertheless, he did 'abandon verse as a waste of labour', and take up novel writing to 'achieve some tangible result from his desultory yet strenuous labours at literature during the previous four years' (56–7). As we have seen above, Hardy worked hard to be a success and achieved a very high degree of social and literary status. But *The Life* – written when all this is secure – claims that 'under the stress of necessity he had set about a kind of literature in which he had hitherto taken but little interest – prose fiction', and causes Hardy to remember announcing to his colleagues at Blomfield's 'an indifference to a popular novelist's fame' (57). This, of course, would have been just as he was commencing *The Poor Man and the Lady*! Equally, it is suggested that Hardy took little real account of the social functions *The Life* so assiduously records; for example:

he mostly was compelled to slip away as soon as he could from these gatherings, finding that they exhausted him both of strength and ideas, few of the latter being given him in return for his own, because the fashionable throng either would not part from those it possessed, or did not possess any. (266)

This is a classic symptom of an inferiority complex, in which a disdainful superiority protects Hardy from admitting the desired participation. But even more unconsciously ironic is the occasion when Hardy 'quotes' a memorandum of his attendance at the Royal Academy dinner of 1887 which reveals his acute sensitivity about social status: ' "I spoke to a good many; was apparently unknown to a good many more I knew. At these times men do not want to talk to their equals, but to their superiors" ' (199). Characteristically, the following two pages are packed with notes on social engagements and with the names of noble or famous acquaintances, although the passage ends: 'But Hardy does not comment much on these society-gatherings, his thoughts running upon other subjects' (201). It is the peculiarly un-ironic articulation of these contradictions in *The Life* which signifies the alienated class consciousness of its protagonist; an impression reinforced by the immediately subsequent and heavy-handed parenthesis (to establish the 'authenticity' of *The Life*) that these 'memoranda' were for 'private consideration' and that he had 'meant to destroy' them (201–2, see above pp. 139–40). Considering that Hardy is, in fact, writing this, and is himself selecting and including these 'memoranda' with a view to publication in *The Life*, there is a sense in which the whole passage displays a discourse so defensive that it can convey nothing of what Hardy might have meant, but only the contradictions which produce it. The same many-layered and schizophrenic deception is apparent in the following passage from 1892:

> *Tess of the d'Urbervilles* was also the cause of Hardy's meeting a good many people of every rank during that spring, summer, and onwards, and of opportunity for meeting a good many more if he had chosen to avail himself of it. Many of the details that follow concerning his adventures in the world of fashion at dinner-parties, crushes, and other social functions, which Hardy himself did not think worth recording, have been obtained from diaries kept by the late Mrs. Hardy.
> It must be repeated that his own notes on these meetings were set down by him as private memoranda only; and that they, or some of them, are reproduced here to illustrate what contrasting planes of existence he moved in – vibrating at a swing between the artificial gaieties of a London season and the quaintnesses of a primitive rustic life. (245)

147

Here again Hardy at once parades his social success as a writer, and denies his own regard for it, by way of the 'fiction' of *The Life*'s authorship. But it is he, after all, who is reproducing these 'notes', and not an objective biographer; and it is he, therefore, who introduces his social status in the first place, while simultaneously claiming no interest in it. Finally, we may note that the passage ends with a factitious juxtapositioning of the two 'planes' of Hardy's life (did he ever really live 'a primitive rustic life'?), pivoted on the suddenly arresting (and therefore authentically felt?) notion of 'vibrating at a swing'. It is from this contradictory but dynamic oscillation, I think, that Hardy's creative impulse derives.

A related sign of the tensions in Hardy's class location and ideological consciousness is *The Life*'s minimal presentation of his political attitudes. Indeed, after the early comments on the 'socialistic, not to say revolutionary' tenor of *The Poor Man and the Lady*, there is scant reference to politics at all – the 'biography' being at pains to characterize Hardy as almost totally apolitical: he is 'quite outside politics' (169) and 'not a bit of a politician' (268). This distancing from the political is, of course, a further reflex of his ambiguous class position as *arriviste* man of letters, of his suppressed origins and of his ambivalent desire/disdain for social status. And once again, the contradictions are perceptible in the discourses of *The Life*, as it works to construct the image of Thomas Hardy, writer. The case of *The Poor Man and the Lady* is itself interesting. It is difficult, of course, to know what the 'socialism' of that novel may have consisted of. Gittings believes that it probably derived from Hardy's reading of the *Saturday Review*, in which case it would have been a kind of radical conservatism.[38] But this does not square with the class attitudes in what we can deduce of that novel, nor with those of later novels in which oppression and exploitation by the socially superior, or by the dominant ideological institutions and conventions, is a central issue. *The Life*, however, states that 'portions of the book . . . had no foundation either in Hardy's beliefs or his experiences' (61), and that the manuscript was destroyed (43; we do not know why or when Hardy chose to destroy it – except that, late in life, he systematically destroyed everything which might controvert the representation of 'Hardy' in *The Life*). What the 'official' voice cannot suppress, however, is the sense of Hardy's residual sympathy for the novel;[39] nor the fact that more than thirty years later, in his last and most outspoken fiction, *Jude the Obscure*, he returned to a 'socialistic' hero. It seems likely, in other words, that in the struggle to succeed as man of letters a significant political stance had to be abandoned or suppressed – its vestiges visible only in the subversive forms and hypersensitive class consciousness of the novels.

Otherwise, *The Life* works hard to present Hardy as being somehow 'above' politics. The first reference is a 'memorandum' of February 1881 characteristic of an apolitical liberalism: '"Conservatism is not estimable in itself, nor is Change, or Radicalism. To conserve the existing good, to supplant the existing bad by good, is to act on a true political principle, which is neither Conservative nor Radical"' (148). But since it is unlikely that Hardy's memoranda would have contained only one isolated note of this kind – if he was keeping notes of his 'thoughts' at all – it is interesting to consider why he should 'select' this one when constructing *The Life* in the 1920s. Equally, he registers disdain for politicians themselves (most of whom, of course, were from the higher social groups Hardy was newly entering):

> 'Consider the evenings at Lord Carnarvon's, and the intensely average conversation on politics held there by average men who two or three weeks later were members of the Cabinet. A row of shopkeepers in Oxford Street taken just as they came would conduct the affairs of the nation as ably as these.' (172)

Together with the class hostility (although characteristically Hardy does not identify with the shopkeepers either), goes the superciliousness of the intellectual: '"Plenty of form in their handling of politics, but no matter, or originality"' (180). As we have seen in relation to Hardy's 'disdain' for the fashionable world, this inferiority/superiority ambiguity is very typical of the class consciousness of the *déclassé*. Here, it results either in a vague humanistic populism: political talk at a society gathering was on '"everything except the people for whose existence alone these politicians exist. Their welfare is never once thought of"' (238); or in a kind of anti-democratic Arnoldianism on behalf of 'culture': 'Democratic government may be justice to man, but it will probably merge in proletarian, and when these people are our masters it will lead to more of this contempt, and possibly be the utter ruin of art and literature!' (236); or in liberal-humanist despair at the political condition of the age: '"We call our age an age of Freedom . . . the human race is likely to be extinct before Freedom arrives at maturity"' (347). More generally, the contradictions of Hardy's position (not of the ruling class, but no longer, as man of letters, of the lower class and yet still enslaved by the market and conventional ethics) produce a passive, apolitical alternativism (characteristic of liberal humanism) which is also inscribed by the uncertainties of its class commitment. This is Hardy's version of it in 1888, as 'quoted' in *The Life*:

'I find that my politics really are neither Tory nor Radical. I may be called an Intrinsicalist. I am against privilege derived from accident of any kind, and am therefore equally opposed to aristocratic privilege and democratic privilege. (By the latter I mean the arrogant assumption that the only labour is hand-labour – a worse arrogance than that of the aristocrat, – the taxing of the worthy to help those masses of the population who will not help themselves when they might, etc.) Opportunity should be equal for all, but those who will not avail themselves of it should be cared for merely – not be a burden to, nor the rulers over, those who do avail themselves thereof.' (204)

The confusion in the very articulation of this passage is symptomatic of the confusion in Hardy's sense of his class allegiance, although it is interesting to perceive that 'meritocracy' is his real theme. Hardy's rejection of politics, however, results in the (self-confessedly) unsystematic conception of a neutral and unconscious power (the 'Immanent Will') governing the universe – a metaphysical displacement of his lack of a secure social and political philosophy. Falling between religion (a God-controlled universe) and materialism (a man-controlled history), what we may call his 'dynastic' thinking is witness to the contradictions and ambiguities in Hardy's late Victorian intellectual and class positions. Unable, on the one hand, to follow a 'socialistic' logic because of his newly-acquired social status, nor, on the other, to accept the conventional political, social, and religious orthodoxies of the ruling class, Hardy occupies an apolitical space as 'writer', bolstered by an eclectic and factitious metaphysical myth of 'History'. What may be perceived in his novels are the marks left by these contradictory pressures, which themselves tend to expose the literary and social ideologies (realism and humanism) within which Hardy is himself historically situated. These markings can only be perceived, however, once the constructions of the dominant critical tradition, which continually constitute 'Hardy' in discourses other than those of social class, have been cleared away. *The Life* has a particularly ambiguous role here since it is both one of Hardy's fictions and complicit in the construction of 'Hardy' as the essentially apolitical, 'disinterested', tragic poet and man of letters; in other words, as one of Arnold's 'class aliens'.[40]

Such tensions and contradictions, however, are especially perceptible in *The Life* in Hardy's attitudes to women. Questions of gender relations and sexual politics I will return to in a later chapter, since they relate centrally in Hardy's fiction to those of social class and the profession of writing; here, I merely want to indicate that *The*

Life's concern with class is perhaps most ambiguous in relation to women. Even a cursory reading of it will reveal Hardy's obsessive fascination with women of all classes[41] – dairymaids, prostitutes, music-hall dancers, society beauties, chance sightings on trains and in the street – although Hardy is presented, of course, as being on intimate terms for the most part only with upper-class women. It is quite clear that he enjoys their company and admires their lifestyle and physical beauty, and their names are paraded across the pages of the 'biography' as evidence of his success and social status. Yet the most insistent note, again, is one of disdain for the very qualities Hardy seems to admire, a note sounded regularly either in his unfavourable comparison of these upper-class women to women from a similar class to his own (on a visit to Whitelands Training College, he comments: 'How far nobler in its aspirations is the life here than the life of those I met at the crush two nights back' (235) – his sister Mary and Tryphenia Sparks had both gone to training college); or in his comparison of them to women of a lower and less 'respectable' kind (as when, after leaving a society party, he is effusively kissed and thanked by a girl he shares his umbrella with on a bus – 'An affectionate nature wasted on the streets! It was a strange contrast to the scene I had just left' (265)). Further, with the characteristic superciliousness of the socially-inferior intellectual that we have noted, he scorns their uselessness, noticing a woman in a Landau, for example, 'in violet velvet and silver trimming, slim, small; who could be easily carried under a man's arm, and also, if held up by her hair and slipped out of her clothes, carriage, etc. etc., aforesaid, would not be much larger than a skinned rabbit, and of less use' (237); and he stresses the underlying similarity of high- and low-born women when, listening to a lady reciting Gray's 'Elegy', he identifies her as

> the duplicate of the handsome dairymaid who had insisted on his listening to her rehearsal of the long and tedious gospels, when he taught in the Sunday school as a youth of fifteen. What a thin veneer is that of rank and education over the natural woman, he would remark. (304)

I will return in more detail to Hardy's perception of the artificial 'fiction' of class status in the following chapter on *Ethelberta*; and, in my final chapter, to his 'Poor Man and the Lady' complex in relation to his profession as writer, where an even more complex set of contradictory class and gender relations emerge (Hardy's own social and intellectual aspirations seem to be displaced onto his female characters, who are then held in check by the novels' deployment of patriarchal strategies). Here, however, I merely wish to establish that *The Life*, while attempting to display Hardy's nonchalance about his social inferiority, in effect reveals his domination by it, and that there is a strong gender dimension to the uneasy play of his class consciousness.

Finally, in this analysis of the fiction constituted by *The Life*, there is the matter of Hardy's presentation of himself as poet rather than novelist, and its relation to his class self-perception. Indeed, the most striking features of the book are the diffidence with which Hardy treats his novels and novel-writing career; the emphasis on the long period of planning for *The Dynasts*; and the insistence that he was primarily a poet. Writing *The Life* in the 1920s as a famous practising poet who had given up fiction nearly thirty years before, Hardy clearly wished to build his 'biographical' self in that image. He notes early on, for the years 1865–7 (i.e. immediately prior to writing *The Poor Man and the Lady*), that he read poetry almost exclusively and 'never ceased to regret' that Scott, the poet of *Marmion*, 'should later have declined on prose fiction' (48–9); and he insists that after *Desperate Remedies* had been published and *Under the Greenwood Tree* rejected by Macmillan, he would have 'thrown up authorship at last and for all' and concentrated on architecture so that he could marry Emma, but for a chance meeting with Tinsley who encouraged him to send in a manuscript – which he cavalierly did (87–8). Hardy's commitment to novel writing is invariably minimized, as though he first did it by chance and then purely as a money-making trade. After the success of *Far From the Madding Crowd*, *The Life* tells us 'that he did not care much for a reputation as a novelist in lieu of being able to follow the pursuit of poetry', which, it adds, 'becomes obvious' from the letter to Leslie Stephen on getting 'to be considered a good hand at a serial' (99–100, see above, p. 137). And in a startlingly disingenuous sentence just afterwards, he emphasizes the pecuniary basis of his work: 'For mere popularity he cared little, as little as he did for large payments; but having now to live by the pen . . . he had to consider popularity' (102; it was at this point that he wrote the deeply alienated fiction, *The Hand of Ethelberta*). After the publication of *The Mayor of Casterbridge*, having commented on the 'damage' he had done to it '*as an artistic whole*' (my italics) in the interest of newspaper serialization, *The Life* adds: 'However, as at this time he called his novel-writing "mere journeywork" he cared little about it as art' (179) – although it then reproduces an adulatory letter about the novel from R. L. Stevenson. Immediately afterwards, it is recorded that: 'Hardy by this time had quite resigned himself to novel-writing as a trade, which he had never wanted to carry on as such. He now went about the business mechanically' (182–3). On his visits to police courts while writing *Tess*, *The Life* disdainfully reflects on his 'being still compelled to get novel padding' (227); and on the publication of that novel it prophesies the coming end of Hardy's novel-writing career (240–6 *passim*). With the publication of *Jude* and *The Well-Beloved*, *The Life* neatly sums up its theme: 'and so ended his prose contributions to literature . . . his experiences of the few preceding years having killed all his interest in this form of imaginative work, which had ever been secondary to his interest in verse' (286). These disparaging remarks are reinforced by the 'biography's' cavalier disregard of the novels themselves, which are only briefly mentioned in passing and about which we learn scarcely anything as regards Hardy's intentions in them, their gestation, formal composition, and so on. He clearly decided to ignore them except as pot-boiling fictions written 'mechanically' for the commercial market. From here on, *The Life* emphasizes the continuity of Hardy's primary interest in poetry: 'many of the verses had been written before their author dreamt of novels' (299); 'the poetic tendency had been his from the earliest' (384); 'I wanted to write poetry in the beginning. Now I can' (401); and it devotes considerably more space to the formal craftsmanship of Hardy's lyric poetry and the themes of *The Dynasts* than it ever does to the novels.

Finally, one other passage is of particular interest. Having noted that in 1900 the Hardys stayed in a hotel in London rather than taking a flat or house, *The Life* comments:

> He possibly thought it advisable to economize, seeing that he had sacrificed the chance of making a much larger income by not producing more novels. When one considers that he might have made himself a man of affluence in a few years by taking the current of popularity as it served, writing 'best sellers', and ringing changes upon the novels he had already written, his bias towards poetry must have been instinctive and disinterested. (305)

This is a very peculiar argument. Why is Hardy so concerned to prove the 'instinctive and disinterested' nature of his commitment to poetry? Why is he so disparaging about novels which he actually took immense pains with, then and later, especially for their book publication (*vide* the 'Wessex' edition of 1912)? The answer, I think, must be that for the 'character' of Hardy which *The Life* wishes to present – well-born man of letters, familiar with the noble and famous, and above the pettiness of ambition, social climbing, and the market-place – the image of 'the poet' is more suitable than that of the toiling novelist sweating away in the commercial purlieus of the publishing trade. When Hardy could afford to stop writing fiction, he did; and *The Life*, in its incessant obsession with class and status, constructs an image of the true poet, 'instinctive and disinterested', freed now from even the taint of writing fiction (tainted, because it had been the escape route from his class origins). What *The Life* produces, in effect, is a piece of *petit-bourgeois* wish-fulfilment ('some clever lad's dream', John Morley had said of *The Poor Man and the Lady*):[42] an image of the pure literary man Hardy desired to be. By destroying all the evidence he could muster which might disprove *The Life*'s account, by attempting to pre-empt any other biographies (and the existence of *The Life* still makes it difficult to 'see' another Hardy), Hardy, in a very exact sense, wrote his own life.

However, by treating it as the last of Hardy's novels, I have attempted to bring into view, by way of its silences, its contradictions, and its very fictiveness, that other Hardy who is also part of its discourse: a writer obsessed by class to such a degree that he has to recast his life as a written fiction. In this way, *The Life* 'reveals' the informing ideology by which its author is so deeply alienated, just as the novels produced by this author can expose in their own discourses the alienating and destructive processes of a class society. For them to do this, however, requires the removal of those accretions of critical and educational practice which have sought (and Hardy himself was party to it) to obviate the marks of those processes and to constitute 'Thomas Hardy' as a body of work which colludes with the dominant social and cultural ideology. It is for this reason that I now turn to one of Hardy's most deprecated novels, *The Hand of Ethelberta*, and counterpose it with *The Life*, arguing that where one is fiction presented as fact, the other is fact presented as fiction. *The Hand of Ethelberta*, generally regarded as 'perverse', 'wrong-headed', 'artificial', and 'improbable' (a 'novel of ingenuity', as Hardy himself called it), is also the novel most overtly and uncompromisingly concerned with the perversions of social class; and for these (related) reasons it has been excluded from the canonic 'Hardy'. Replace it in the *oeuvre*, with its specific orientations of form and animus sharply exposed, and it effects a radical adjustment of perspective on the rest of Hardy's work.

5

Hardy and social class:
The Hand of Ethelberta

Towards the end of *The Hand of Ethelberta*, there is a scene in which the heroine narrates one of her 'fictions' to the guests at Lord Mountclere's house. It is, in fact, the strangest of her fictions – the true story of her life and origins up to the point at which she enters society as fashionable widow and writer of poems:

The narrative began by introducing to their notice a girl of the poorest and meanest parentage, the daughter of a serving-man, and the fifth of ten children. She graphically recounted, as if they were her own, the strange dreams and ambitious longings of this child when young, her attempts to acquire education, partial failures, partial successes, and constant struggles; instancing how, on one of these occasions, the girl concealed herself under a bookcase of the library belonging to the mansion in which her father served as footman, and having taken with her there, like a young Fawkes, matches and a halfpenny candle, was going to sit up all night reading when the family had retired, until her father discovered and prevented her scheme. Then followed her experiences as nursery-governess, her evening lessons under self-selected masters, and her ultimate rise to a higher grade among the teaching sisterhood. Next came another epoch. To the mansion in which she was engaged returned a truant son, between whom and the heroine an attachment sprang up. The master of the house was an ambitious gentleman just knighted, who, perceiving the state of their hearts, harshly dismissed the homeless governess, and rated the son, the consequence being that the youthful pair resolved to marry secretly, and carried their resolution into effect. The runaway journey came next, and then a moving description of the death of the young husband, and the terror of the bride.

The guests began to look perplexed, and one or two exchanged whispers. This was not at all the kind of story that they had expected; it was quite different from her usual utterances, the nature of which they knew by report. Ethelberta kept her eyes upon Lord Mountclere. Soon, to her amazement, there was that in his face which told her that he knew the story and its heroine quite well. When she delivered the sentence ending with the professedly fictitious words: 'I thus was reduced to great distress, and vainly cast about me for directions what to do,' Lord Mountclere's manner became so excited and anxious that it acted reciprocally upon Ethelberta; her voice trembled, she moved her lips but uttered nothing. To bring the story up to the date of that very evening had been her intent, but it was beyond her power. The spell was broken, she blushed with distress and turned away, for the folly of a disclosure here was but too apparent.

Though every one saw that she had broken down, none of them appeared to know the reason why, or to have the clue to her performance. Fortunately Lord Mountclere came to her aid.

'Let the first part end here,' he said, rising and approaching her, 'We have been well entertained so far. I could scarcely believe that the story I was listening to was utterly an invention, so vividly does Mrs Petherwin bring the scenes before our eyes. She must now be exhausted; we will have the remainder to-morrow.'

They all agreed that this was well, and soon after fell into groups, and dispersed about the rooms. When everybody's attention was thus occupied Lord Mountclere whispered to Ethelberta tremulously, 'Don't tell more: you think too much of them: they are no better than you!'[1]

There are a number of points to be made about this passage. First, it recounts Ethelberta's life up to the point of the ridiculously abbreviated account, delivered in a single sentence, on the first page of the novel. Second, it stops at exactly the point where the novel itself had begun, in taking up the story of her deception of society as a young widow of good family and of her career as poet and fictionist. The reader, therefore, now has both the novelist's and Ethelberta's accounts of the 'truth' (albeit in both cases presented as fictions). Third, it 'was not at all the kind of story that [her listeners] had expected; it was quite different from her usual utterances' – one, indeed, which tells the truth about her 'real' class background, although presented as a fiction and accepted as such by her audience (her earlier stories (see pp. 131–3) had been 'romances', although purporting to be the exact truth). We may recall here that Hardy shocked and disappointed his editor, Leslie Stephen, and the reviewers by producing *The Hand of Ethelberta* after *Far From the Madding Crowd*, and that *The Life* refers to his 'plunge in a new and untried direction' – much to 'the consternation of his editor and publishers' – which 'had nothing whatsoever in common with anything he had written before'.[2] Fourth, Lord Mountclere, the elderly aristocratic roué Ethelberta finally marries and dominates, who is himself no mean intriguer and illusionist – his house has a sham façade of stone over brick, of which the novel remarks 'as long as nobody knew the truth, pretence looked just as well' (305), and a staircase where 'the art which produced this illusion was questionable, but its success was undoubted' (304) – stops the story at the point at which the novel has begun its own narrative and advises Ethelberta about her audience: '"Don't tell more: you think too much of them: they are no better than you."' Mountclere thus implies at once the pervasive lie of a class society, Ethelberta's merit in rising in it, and the necessity of sustaining the deception. In this respect, what we have here is not dissimilar to what *The Life* was later to do for Hardy himself. Fifth, the passage draws our attention to an obsession, anything but unique in the novel, with social class, with the nature of fictions and story-telling, with deception and illusion, and with the connections between all of these issues. And sixth, it underwrites (although it does not say it) the correlation between the story the novel narrates and the ironic slant of the novel itself: the fiction of a young person who achieves social success by way of making fictions – class fictions and written fictions – but in which the truth is told only as a fiction – both within the novel and as the novel. *The Hand of Ethelberta* is, in other words, a self-reflexive novel of a highly complex order.

What I shall do here is bring into view some elements of this complexity which have been obscured by a critical orthodoxy that marginalizes *Ethelberta* in Hardy's *oeuvre*; at the same time suggesting why this orthodoxy has had to reject the novel if its conception of 'Hardy', and indeed of the 'great tradition' in fiction, are to be sustained. I shall consider the novel as a set of discourses freed of the conventional criteria of 'value' in fiction ('flat' characters, artificial plot, obtrusive style, and so on), and so hope to release potencies which those criteria make inaccessible. I shall show (while avoiding intentionalism) how *Ethelberta* self-consciously foregrounds issues of social class, gender relations, and the artifice of realist fiction writing. And I shall suggest that the exposure of the alienating lies produced by these systems is more readily perceptible in Hardy's other fiction once it has been identified in such uncompromising form in *The Hand of Ethelberta*. Just as *Ethelberta* may seem to be 'the joker in the pack'[3] of Hardy's novels, but can be recuperated by conceiving it positively as a complex set of anti-realist discourses and not as a failure of literary decorum, so Hardy's work as a whole (itself uneasily placed in the canon of

English literature) can only be comprehended if the interrelations between class, gender, and fictionality are regarded positively as constituting the fabric of his work. Indeed, any 'reading' which does not consider these factors positively can only proceed by way of omission, excision, and suppression; by stripping 'Hardy', in other words, of those subversive elements which are at play in his texts and which literary criticism cannot accommodate without endangering its own unspoken ideological presuppositions.

Hardy wrote *The Hand of Ethelberta* immediately after *Far From the Madding Crowd*, the novel which made him successful. Its very position in his career, then, especially as it is so apparently unlike the previous novel, suggests a conscious decision on Hardy's part to do something entirely different; and indeed, as we have seen, *The Life* seems to confirm this – Hardy, nearly fifty years later, writing that he took 'a plunge in a new and untried direction'. But *The Life* as usual is curiously ambiguous about the novel and its inception. It suggests, on the one hand, that Hardy took 'the unfortunate course' of rushing into another novel 'before he was aware of what there had been of value in his previous one: before learning, that is, not only what had attracted the public, but what was of true and genuine substance on which to build a career as a writer with a real literary message'; or again, that he did it for money and in response to gossip about his social origins. On the other hand, *The Life* implies a serious purpose: 'Yet he had not the slightest intention of writing forever about sheep farming, as the reading public was apparently expecting him to do, and as, in fact, they presently resented his not doing.' It further adds that he 'had at last the satisfaction of proving . . . that he did not mean to imitate anybody'; and that Hardy himself took the novel seriously: commenting (on the critics' 'chief objection . . . that it was "impossible"') that 'it was, in fact, thirty years too soon for a Comedy of Society of that kind – just as *The Poor Man and the Lady* had been too soon for a socialist story, and as other of his writings – in prose and verse – were too soon for their date'.[4] (We should register here Hardy's sympathetic correlation of *Ethelberta* and that earlier, 'lost', 'socialist story'.) But however ambiguous *The Life* may be, we can be certain that it was a strange and self-conscious novel to write at this stage of his career, if for no other reason than because of the amount of disguised autobiography it contains.

There is little question now about the similarities between the character of Ethelberta and Hardy himself. Robert Gittings has given a useful synopsis of them in *The Young Thomas Hardy* and in the Introduction to the 'New Wessex' edition of the novel, but it is

worth noting the main ones again here. There is the central structural irony of their both being lower-class people making their way
in society by the profession of writing and disguising their class
background; both are poets by inclination who have to turn to fiction
to make a living – Hardy calling Ethelberta's poems, in the serial
version of the novel, 'Metres by Me'[5] and which echo his own
early 'She to Him' sonnets; Hardy's class background and his
relatives' occupations and social status are reproduced for Ethelberta
– servants, carpenters, schoolmistresses, and so on; there is the
reference in the title to Hardy's mother's family name of 'Hand';
and in addition, there is the important point, not noted by Gittings,
that at the very end of the novel Ethelberta, in her security and
success, is 'writing an epic poem, and employs Emmeline as her
reader' (409). Leaving aside the no doubt fortuitous similarity of
name with Hardy's first wife Emma, it cannot be fortuitous that
Hardy was planning to write his own 'epic poem' *The Dynasts* when
he could afford to stop writing fiction, and that the first reference
to his earliest thoughts on this project occurs in *The Life* in the
middle of the pages on *The Hand of Ethelberta* and whilst he was
writing that novel: 'In this same month [May] of 1875, it may be
interesting to note, occurs the first mention in Hardy's memoranda
of the idea of an epic on the war with Napoleon – carried out so
many years later in *The Dynasts*.'[6] It seems likely, then, that Hardy
was self-consciously re-presenting himself as Ethelberta, and producing an immense irony which only he could savour: his most open
and accurate account of himself and his real social relations
presented as a fiction in which his heroine does the same, only for
both 'true stories' to be received as fictions and, in the case of the
novel itself, to be criticized for being 'impossible'.

What is equally clear is the similarity between Ethelberta and
Hardy in terms of their fictional theory and practice – which again
suggests a high degree of self-reflexivity. *The Hand of Ethelberta* is,
indeed, the only novel of Hardy's in which there is substantial and
explicit address to questions of fiction writing, since even *The Life*
contains only passing 'notes' on Hardy's views about fiction and, as
I have indicated in the preceding chapter, deals only cursorily with
the novels, the reader being left to make what s/he can of the
'memoranda' about them. Nevertheless, certain notions and terms
are reiterated throughout *The Life*, the 'literary notebooks', the few
essays on fiction,[7] and the (often opaque) 'Prefaces' which Hardy
at various times attaches to the front of his novels (including the
ones for *Ethelberta*, which I shall consider below). It is not, I think,
too self-fulfilling an argument to state that these circle around a
problematical relation to realism and a sharp consciousness of the

artifice of art, which leads Hardy at times to an embryonic conception of such modern critical notions as 'making strange'
('defamiliarization') and 'alienation' (*verfremdungseffekt*). My point
simply is that, in the part of *The Life* which deals with the period
from the late 1870s to the mid 1890s, when Hardy was at the height
of his novel-writing career, there is continual evidence of a
consciousness at work in which these issues were actively present.
Whatever our attitude to 'intention', then, we cannot properly ignore
the mindset of the novelist, nor can we disregard, excise, or explain
away fictional features in his novels which may themselves appear
problematical but which are also the articulation of that mindset.

Early in *The Life*, in a letter to Hardy's sister Mary shortly after
he had arrived in London, there is an equivocal comment about
Thackeray (the equivocation being compounded by finding a moral
tone proper for writing to a younger sister) which nevertheless
initiates an iterative theme of Hardy's: 'He is considered to be the
greatest novelist of the day – looking at novel writing of the highest
kind as a perfect and truthful representation of actual life – which
is no doubt the proper view to take.'[8] 'No doubt': but is that
Hardy's 'view'? Certainly many of his later comments would seem
to reject such a classic formal realism (whether it is true of
Thackeray or not). The earliest of these seems to be a memorandum
(3 June 1877) in which he says:

> 'So, then, if Nature's defects must be looked in the face and
> transcribed, whence arises the *art* in poetry and novel-writing?
> which must certainly show art, or it becomes merely mechanical
> reporting. I think the art lies in making these defects the basis of
> a hitherto unperceived beauty, by irradiating them with "the light
> that never was" on their surface, but is seen to be latent in them
> by the spiritual eye.' (114)

Art is not 'mechanical reporting', but an 'irradiation' of 'a hitherto
unperceived beauty'. A similar view is repeated in January 1881
when Hardy notes: 'This [perfect] reproduction is achieved by seeing
into the *heart of a thing* . . . and is realism, in fact, though through
being pursued by means of the imagination it is confounded with
invention' (147). Now it might properly be claimed here that there
is nothing original or unique in Hardy's thinking, that it is in line
with mainstream nineteenth-century romanticism. But my point is to
indicate the cast of Hardy's consciousness, and to notice how
increasingly sharply such commonplaces are inflected. Later the
same year (July 1881), *The Life* 'reproduces' some 'notes on fiction,
possibly for an article that was never written':

'The real, if unavowed, purpose of fiction is to give pleasure by gratifying the love of the uncommon in human experience, mental or corporeal.

'This is done all the more perfectly in proportion as the reader is illuded to believe the personages true and real like himself.

'Solely to this latter end a work of fiction should be a precise transcript of ordinary life: but,

'The uncommon would be absent and the interest lost. Hence,

'The writer's problem is, how to strike the balance between the uncommon and the ordinary so as on the one hand to give interest, on the other to give reality.

'In working out this problem, human nature must never be made abnormal which is introducing incredibility. The uncommonness must be in the events, not in the characters; and the writer's art lies in shaping that uncommonness while disguising its unlikelihood, if it be unlikely.' (150)

This passage is regularly quoted in Hardy criticism, most usually to reinforce notions of Hardy's fundamental realism and to 'explain' (away) the use of contingency and coincidence in his plots; but placed together with his other comments which tend towards 'defamiliarization' as a fictional principle, his sense here of 'shaping that uncommonness' takes on a potentially non-realist resonance. A further, and related, strand in Hardy's thinking is picked out in the following note (June 1882), when he reflects: 'so in life the seer should watch that pattern among general things which his idiosyncrasy moves him to observe, and describe that alone. This is, quite accurately, a going to Nature; yet the result is no mere photograph, but purely the product of the writer's own mind' (153). What we have here in embryo is Hardy's constant presentation of his fictions as 'impressions' or 'seemings', an idea more fully enunciated in a series of highly significant jottings from the spring of 1886: 'My art is to intensify the expression of things . . . so that the heart and inner meaning is made vividly visible' (3 January 1886; 177). This, of course, could equally be the claim of a realist, but the phrasing ('intensify the expression', 'vividly visible') suggests an aesthetic moving beyond any notion of effecting 'a precise transcript of ordinary life'. However, the note has also to be taken in conjunction with a statement (4 March 1886) which in my context here, and in any debate about why Hardy gave up writing novels after *Jude* ten years later, must have a crucial place:

'Novel-writing as an art cannot go backward. Having reached the analytic stage it must transcend it by going still further in the same direction. Why not by rendering as visible essences, spectres, etc, the abstract thoughts of the analytic school?'

This notion was approximately carried out, not in a novel, but through the much more appropriate medium of poetry, in the supernatural framework of *The Dynasts* as also in smaller poems. And a further note of the same date enlarges the same idea:

'The human race to be shown as one great network or tissue which quivers in every part when one point is shaken, like a spider's web if touched. Abstract realisms to be in the form of Spirits, Spectral figures, etc.

'The Realities to be the true realities of life, hitherto called abstractions. The old material realities to be placed behind the former, as shadowy accessories.' (177)

Effectively, what Hardy is recognizing is that realism – at least for him as a novelist – is pressing against its limits, that 'abstract realisms' demand a different form to be realized as 'visible essences', and that he must move to the 'more appropriate medium' of epic poetry. He is disingenuous in suggesting that this was not 'carried out . . . in a novel', for the crucial problematic of Hardy's fiction (in *Ethelberta*, but also in most of the later novels) would seem to lie precisely in his attempts to find a form to 'render visible' abstract and analytic 'essences' of contemporary social relations: in particular, the 'fictions' of class and gender hierarchies. A further gloss on the inadequacy of a naturalistic realism is offered in some telling remarks about late Turner paintings in January of the following year (1887):

'I don't want to see landscapes, *i.e.*, scenic paintings of them, because I don't want to see the original realities – as optical effects, that is. I want to see the deeper reality underlying the scenic, the expression of what are sometimes called abstract imaginings.

'The "simply natural" is interesting no longer. The much decried, mad, late-Turner rendering is now necessary to create my interest. The exact truth as to material fact ceases to be of importance in art – it is a student's style – the style of a period when the mind is serene and unawakened to the tragical mysteries of life.' (185)

And in January 1889, again in relation to Turner, he makes the observation: 'Hence, one may say, Art is the secret of how to produce by a false thing the effect of a true' (216).

The concept of 'abstract imaginings' and the problem of their expression in art lie behind the string of related comments in the prefaces to his novels of this period (although some derive from the retrospective 1912 ones when he was editing the 'Wessex Edition'). In the 1891 Preface to *Tess*, he writes that it is 'an attempt to give artistic form to a true sequence of things', and in 1892 that he is concerned with 'impressions' not 'convictions', that 'a novel is an impression, not an argument'. In the 1895 Preface to *Jude*, he makes the most famous of his gnomic prefatory utterances:

> Like former productions of this pen, *Jude the Obscure* is simply an endeavour to give shape and coherence to a series of seemings, or personal impressions, the question of their consistency or their discordance, of their permanence or their transitoriness, being regarded as not of the first moment.

And in the 1912 Preface to *The Well-Beloved*, he writes:

> As for the story itself, it may be worth while to remark that, differing from all or most others of the series in that the interest aimed at is of an ideal or subjective nature, and frankly imaginative, verisimilitude in the sequence of events has been subordinated to the said aim.

Given Hardy's remarks in the *Jude* Preface above and, as we shall see, in the 1895 Preface to *Ethelberta*, the notion here that he usually pursued verisimilitude is highly dubious. Notoriously ironic and defensive as the prefaces are, there is enough continuity in their trajectory at this period (and in their relation to contemporary memoranda in *The Life*) for us to have some confidence that at the very least, Hardy is not trying and failing to write realist fiction, and rather more that he is strategically experimenting with forms and practices which themselves crack open the discourses of realism. As he says of *Jude*, in the assumed voice of a hostile critic: 'it is not the view of life that we who thrive on conventions can permit to be painted' (Preface).

But it is in a couple of memoranda from 1890 (the year before he produced his essay 'The science of fiction', in which he defines realism as 'an artificiality distilled from the fruits of closest observation') that Hardy gives most explicit articulation to a curiously prophetic statement of the aesthetics of twentieth-century Formalism. Early in the year (March–April), he repeats now familiar notions: 'Art consists in so depicting the common events of life as to bring out the features which illustrate the author's idiosyncratic mode of regard; making old incidents and things seem as new' (225). By August, however, the sense of 'making strange' – of 'defamiliarizing' – and of a concomitant rejection of realism is very much more systematically stated:

'Reflections on Art. Art is a changing of the actual proportions and order of things, so as to bring out more forcibly than might otherwise be done that feature in them which appeals most strongly to the idiosyncrasy of the artist.'

'Art is a disproportioning – (*i.e.* distorting, throwing out of proportion) – of realities, to show more clearly the features that matter in those realities, which, if merely copied or reported inventorially, might possibly be observed, but would more probably be overlooked. Hence "realism" is not Art.' (228–9)

It is here, I think, that the core of Hardy's fictional aesthetic is to be found. And it is one which makes it perversely inappropriate to critically recast his fiction in the formal-realist mode – or, indeed, to perceive a 'minor novel' like *Ethelberta* as a failure of decorum in its 'uncharacteristic' content and manner, rather than to recognize it as a subversively artificial 'disproportioning' of the fictions of humanism – in the guise, here, of class relations and a 'probablist' realism.

In *The Hand of Ethelberta* itself questions about realism, artifice, and the illusions of verisimilitude are brought into sharp and explicit focus (I will return to the novel's enactment of them later). The main instances of this – apart from the passage with which I began – occur in chapters 13 and 16 and concern Ethelberta's career as a fictionist. In the former, her first lover, Christopher Julian, happens on her as she is telling one of her tales (rehearsing it, in fact) to her brothers and sisters. She is presented to us – and Christopher believes it too – in these terms: 'Ethelberta's appearance answered as fully as ever to that of an English lady skilfully perfected in manner, carriage, look, and accent' (113). The implication of the artifice ('skilfully perfected') involved in manufacturing this 'appearance' (she is, in the Jamesian sense, 'the real thing') is inescapable. The tale she is telling – and Christopher arrives and eavesdrops *in medias res* – is a highly sensational, not to say gothic, romance; but, with herself as heroine, it purports to be true. Indeed Christopher believes that it is the truth, breaking into the recital with: 'For Heaven's sake, Ethelberta . . . where did you meet with such a terrible experience as that?' She responds 'in a serene voice' – 'but', the novel adds, 'the calmness was artificially done' – thus pointing up Ethelberta's constant and deeply self-divisive acting of 'herself', of her artificial self-representation. Then follows this passage:

'But my concern at such a history of yourself since I last saw you is even more natural than your surprise at my manner of breaking in.'

'That history would justify any conduct in one who hears it –'
'Yes, indeed.'
'If it were true,' added Ethelberta, smiling. 'But it is as false
as –'
She could name nothing notoriously false without raising an image
of what was disagreeable, and she continued in a better manner.
'The story I was telling is entirely a fiction, which I am getting
up for a particular purpose – very different from what appears at
present.' (114)

What the novel sets up here, then, is a complex play on questions
of reality/truth/illusion/deceit, in which these moral absolutes
become questionably relativized: which is the 'real' Ethelberta; is
her fiction fact or not? The chapter proceeds to explain how she has
been cheated out of an inheritance on the death of old Mrs Petherwin
and now has to find some way of supporting her family. She cannot
write poems any more, because she is 'surrounded by gaunt realities'
(116): those of sustaining both the lie that is her life and the reality
of her unacknowledged (because lower-class) family:

'I felt that to write prose would be an uncongenial occupation,
and altogether a poor prospect for a woman like me. Finally I
have decided to appear in public.'
'Not on the stage?'
'Certainly not on the stage. There is no novelty in a poor lady
turning actress, and novelty is what I want. Ordinary powers
exhibited in a new way effect as much as extraordinary powers
exhibited in an old way.'. . .

'I had written a prose story by request, when it was found that I
had grown utterly inane over verse. It was written in the first
person, and the style was modelled after De Foe's. The night
before sending it off, when I had already packed it up, I was
reading about the professional story-tellers of Eastern countries,
who devoted their lives to the telling of tales. I unfastened the
manuscript and retained it, convinced that I should do better by
telling the story.'. . .

'It occurred to me,' she continued, blushing slightly, 'that tales of
the weird kind were made to be told, not written. The action of a
teller is wanted to give due effect to all stories of incident; and I
hope that a time will come when, as of old, instead of an unsocial
reading of fiction at home alone, people will meet together
cordially, and sit at the feet of a professed romancer. I am going
to tell my tales before a London public. As a child, I had a
considerable power in arresting the attention of other children by

165

recounting adventures which had never happened; and men and women are but children enlarged a little.' (117)

There is, in fact, little difference between being the public story-teller of fictions (the novelist Hardy) and the public performance of the 'professed romancer' Ethelberta – except that the latter underscores the degree of artifice and acting involved in any fiction making. With sharp irony, Ethelberta continues that she is going to appear in public as 'Mrs Petherwin, Professed Story-teller' although the one story she is not telling is the fiction of her life as an upper-class lady: 'As a reserved one [notice the pun 'reserved' here: more usually the word would be 'reserve'] I have the tale of my own life – to be played as a last card' (118). As we have seen, she does play it (her last *hand*?), and it is perceived simultaneously as both the truth and a fiction. Hardy too, of course, presents his true 'life' as one of his fictions (*Ethelberta*), and plays 'the tale of my own life' as his 'last card' in producing *The Life* as his true biography (a work which, I have suggested earlier, should instead be regarded as his last fiction).

What is particularly interesting in the passage above is the reference to Defoe, progenitor of the realist novel, whom Ethelberta returns to again:

'Now did you ever consider what a power De Foe's manner would have if practised by word of mouth? Indeed, it is a style which suits itself infinitely better to telling than to writing, abounding as it does in colloquialisms that are somewhat out of place on paper in these days, but have a wonderful power in making a narrative seem real. And so, in short, I am going to talk De Foe on a subject of my own.' (118)

We may note here the emphasis on Defoe's 'wonderful power in making a narrative seem real', reminiscent as it is of that early critic of Defoe who had remarked 'the little art he is master of, of forging a story, and imposing it on the world for truth'. But also, in this context, we should remember the two references to Defoe in *The Life*: one in the section dealing with Hardy's first, unpublished, 'socialistic' novel, *The Poor Man and the Lady*, which notes that its style had the 'affected simplicity of Defoe's (which had long attracted Hardy . . . to imitation of it)'; and the other in Hardy's old age (he was 79):

A curious question arose in Hardy's mind at this date on whether a romancer was morally justified in going to extreme lengths of assurance – after the manner of Defoe – in respect of a tale he knew to be absolutely false. . . . Had he not long discontinued the

writing of romances he would, he said, have put at the beginning
of each new one: 'Understand that however true this book may be
in essence, in fact it is utterly untrue.'[9]

The irony here, in relation to *The Life* itself, is acute; but it is worth
noting, too, both Hardy's use of the word 'romancer' (in the context
of the passage from *Ethelberta* above) and his obvious affinity with
the 'faking' art of the great illusionist, Defoe. *The Life* and prefaces
of course, as we have seen, are full of Hardy's own 'memoranda'
on the art of making the 'uncommon' seem 'real', on the illusion of
truth in fiction, and on the 'impressions' and 'seemings' which
constitute a novel's 'reality'.

The relationship between Hardy, Ethelberta, Defoe, and the
'wonderful power in making a narrative seem real' is reinforced in
chapter 16. This is the occasion of Ethelberta's first public reading,
and the narrative stance of the novel with regard to it is to tell it
in a dispassionate reportage-like prose which emphasizes at once the
artifice and performance of Ethelberta's reading and the authority
and veracity of the novel's own account. 'What was her story to be?'
– many of the audience assume it will be 'some pungent and gratifying revelation of the innermost events of her own life' (131); we,
as readers, know that that is her 'reserved story', and is indeed the
story the novel itself is telling. In fact, what she relates is a fiction
which purports to be authentically real:

Ethelberta's plan was to tell her pretended history and adventures
while sitting in a chair – as if she were at her own fireside,
surrounded by a circle of friends. By this touch of domesticity a
great appearance of truth and naturalness was given, though really
the attitude was at first more difficult to maintain satisfactorily
than any one wherein stricter formality should be observed. She
gently began her subject, as if scarcely knowing whether a throng
were near her or not, and, in her fear of seeming artificial, spoke
too low. This defect, however, she soon corrected, and ultimately
went on in a charmingly colloquial manner. What Ethelberta
relied upon soon became evident. It was not upon the intrinsic
merits of her story as a piece of construction, but upon her
method of telling it. Whatever defects the tale possessed – and
they were not a few – it had, as delivered by her, the one pre-
eminent merit of seeming like truth. A modern critic has well
observed of De Foe that he had the most amazing talent on record
for telling lies; and Ethelberta, in wishing her fiction to appear
like a real narrative of personal adventure, did wisely to make De
Foe her model. His is a style even better adapted for speaking
than for writing, and the peculiarities of diction which he adopts

to give verisimilitude to his narratives acquired enormous additional force when exhibited as *viva-voce* mannerisms. And although these artifices were not, perhaps, slavishly copied from that master of feigning, they would undoubtedly have reminded her hearers of him, had they not mostly been drawn from an easeful section in society which is especially characterized by the mental condition of knowing nothing about any author a week after they have read him. . . . When she reached the most telling passages, instead of adding exaggerated action and sound, Ethelberta would lapse to a whisper and a sustained stillness, which were more striking than gesticulation. All that could be done by art was there, and if inspiration was wanting nobody missed it.

It was in performing this feat that Ethelberta seemed first to discover in herself the full power of that self-command which further onward in her career more and more impressed her as a singular possession, until at last she was tempted to make of it many fantastic uses, leading to results that affected more households than her own. A talent for demureness under difficulties without the cold-bloodedness which renders such a bearing natural and easy, a face and hand reigning unmoved outside a heart by nature turbulent as a wave, is a constitutional arrangement much to be desired by people in general; yet, had Ethelberta been framed with less of that gift in her, her life might have been more comfortable as an experience, and brighter as an example, though perhaps duller as a story. (131–3)

There are three points to note here. First, there is the emphasis again on Defoe, 'that master of feigning' whose 'method of telling' Ethelberta copies to achieve 'the one pre-eminent merit of seeming like truth'. What is striking is that only fifteen pages previously the novel tells us more or less exactly the same about Defoe, including that his style was 'infinitely better [suited] to telling than to writing' (see above p. 166). There is one important difference, however: before it was Ethelberta speaking to Christopher Julian, now it is Hardy informing the reader. What this betrays, in the painstaking account of her 'method of telling' and the emphasis on the deceptions of realism, is both Hardy's own interest in Defoe's 'amazing talent . . . for telling lies' and the consanguinity of author and heroine: they are both 'professed story-tellers' and 'romancers', in fact and in fiction. Ethelberta's life as illusionist, in terms both of her class origins and of her profession, is no more than a displaced version of Hardy's, and the novel then becomes the fictive account of a real life: the author's own. Second, we may register the comment, in the final paragraph, on the effect of this 'romancing' on Ethelberta's character: in 'performing this feat' (of creating a 'true' fiction by art) she discovered 'the full power of that self-command' which was to help her play and win in society's stakes: so too, of course, had the Hardy of *Far From the Madding Crowd* who was now about to enter the social and intellectual life of London on his own terms. The lie of fiction and the lie of 'the life' are intimately connected: Ethelberta 'makes it' by way of fictions – both written and personal – to a cynical marriage with Lord Mountclere which underwrites her social position and gives her the 'freedom' to write an epic poem; Hardy also makes it – by way of similar fictions – to a cynically ambiguous relationship with society and the freedom to write an epic poem. Third, we may savour the strange final sentence of the passage in which, we learn, Ethelberta's ability to dissemble her real self makes the 'story' of her life less dull, but her life itself less 'comfortable'. The alienated image of the fragmented and disconnected elements of her personality in 'a face and hand reigning unmoved outside a heart by nature turbulent as a wave' has a note of personal bitterness which we may judge to be Hardy's. Fiction making of this order costs a great deal; and that, in effect, is what *The Hand of Ethelberta* is all about. As D. H. Lawrence wrote of the novel in his cryptic and penetrating comments on Hardy, it is 'the hard, resistant, ironical announcement of personal failure, resistant and half-grinning. It gives way to violent, angry passions and real tragedy, real killing of beloved people, self-killing; [it is] the one almost cynical comedy [marking] the zenith of a certain feeling in the Wessex novels . . . the end of the happy endings.'[10] In this, and especially in the notion of 'self-killing', Lawrence identifies both the fiercely self-ironic thrust of the novel and its pivotal place in the development of Hardy's fiction.

There is an equally ironic coda to chapter 16 in which Hardy literally 'reproduces' the critics' reviews of Ethelberta's performance. One of these is made to notice (aptly) that the event owes 'its chief interest to the method whereby the teller identifies herself with the leading character in the story'; another – once released from 'the magic influence' of the narration – 'perceive[s] how *improbable, even impossible*, is the tissue of events to which we have been listening with so great a sense of reality, and we feel almost angry with ourselves at having been the victims of such utter illusion' (my italics). And a third, like Christopher Julian earlier, believes Ethelberta's story to be true:

The combinations of incident which Mrs Petherwin persuades her hearers that she has passed through are not a little marvellous;

169

and if what is rumoured to be true, that the tales are to a great
extent based upon her own experiences, she has proved herself to
be no less daring in adventure than facile in her power of
describing it. (135–6)

The fact that it is Hardy himself writing these 'reviews'; that the
stylistic parody is very exact; that he uses the conventional words
'improbable' and 'impossible' (which, as we know, his own novel
was to be continually labelled); that he parades the terms 'reality'
and 'illusion'; and that he once again foregrounds the central
paradox about truth and deception in fiction and in life – suggests
just how self-reflexively obsessed with artifice this novel is.

Everything I have indicated so far, indeed, suggests a strategic and
self-conscious intervention on Hardy's part concerning class mobility
and the making and writing of fictions. What Hardy's intentions
were, we cannot of course know (although we can guess); but even
if we did, we would still face the problem that we face with that
ultimate proof of the intentionalist fallacy, *The Life*: would we
believe what he says? What we can identify, however, is the degree
of self-consciousness in the written discourse of the novel, and infer,
therefore, that its mode and style are not accidental, but are
themselves central to the strategy of the book, whatever that may be.
Hardy himself, as always, is both suggestive and opaque, although
his self-consciousness is everywhere apparent. The title itself, with
its multi-layered play on the word 'hand', should alert us: 'hand' as
in marriage; 'hand' as in cards; 'hand' as in writing; 'hand' as in
paid worker; 'hand' as in Hardy's mother's maiden name. And the
sub-title also – 'A Comedy in Chapters' (which had to be dropped
from the serial version because it might suggest that Hardy was a
'professional joker'(!)[11] but which, significantly, was restored for
book publication) – draws attention to the staged artificiality of the
novel.[12] The Preface, written much later (1895), together with the
1912 'PS', is conscious of its central problematics – while being, in
Robert Gittings's ingenuous phrase, 'curiously defensive'.[13] Hardy
admits the 'somewhat frivolous' nature of the narrative, but himself
questions whether 'comedy' is quite the right word to describe it,
and in 1912 he suggests that it is 'more accurately, satire', thus pointing to a purposive animus which the word 'comedy' does not carry.
He further claims that 'a high degree of probability was not attempted in the arrangement of the incidents'; and in the 'PS' makes the
baldly 'neutral' remark: 'The artificial treatment perceptible in many
of the pages was adopted for reasons that seemed good at the date
of writing for a story of that class, and has not been changed.' Is
'artificial' used positively or negatively here? 'Adopted for reasons

that seemed good at the date of writing' suggests an intended 'artifice/-iality', but what were the 'reasons' and do they or do they not still 'seem good'? What constitutes the 'artificial treatment' anyway, and why was it suitable for 'a story of that class'? Does that last phrase mean 'of that type' or 'about that social class'? All we can know for certain is that Hardy was conscious of 'improbablist' criticism and of the 'artifice/-iality' of the novel. But what the Preface and 'PS' also draw attention to was the critics' irritation at *The Hand of Ethelberta*'s 'unexpectedness' after *Far From the Madding Crowd*, and Hardy's belief that in its 'reversal of the social foreground', it 'appeared thirty-five years too soon'. Taken together with his remarks on 'its choice of medium, and line of perspective . . . to excite interest in a drama – if such a dignified word may be used in the connection – wherein servants were as important as, or more important than, their masters; wherein the drawing-room was sketched in many cases from the point of view of the servants' hall', this would seem to suggest that, many years later, Hardy was still acutely aware of both the class consciousness and the aesthetic self-consciousness of the novel.

However by 1912, as I have shown in chapter 1, the contemporary critical consensus had already sifted Hardy's work to produce a canon of major works which fitted orthodox conceptions of the novel, in the process excising *The Hand of Ethelberta*, amongst others, as irretrievably 'minor'. Hardy's own 'General Preface' of 1912 had, of course, helped to reinforce this categorization by seeming to elevate the 'Novels of Character and Environment' over the 'Romances and Fantasies' and the 'Novels of Ingenuity' (otherwise 'Experiments') like *The Hand of Ethelberta*. It is noteworthy, too, that Hardy there again mentions their 'not infrequent disregard of the *probable* in the chain of events' and 'the *artificiality* of their fable' (my italics). Whether he intended to disparage them and confirm the critics' predilections, once more we cannot know; but what is clear, is Hardy's consciousness of their modal experimentality and his unease with the constraints of 'probablism'. These two tendencies, of course, have become the permanent grounds on which criticism deals with *The Hand of Ethelberta*: improbable plotting, artificiality of treatment, thin characterization, scant knowledge of upper-class London society, strained satire, awkward and mannered style. Most criticism, in other words, either ignores the novel totally or rejects those features which most insistently and pervasively comprise the fabric of its discourse. In accepting 'artificiality' and 'improbability' as unproblematically pejorative terms with which to dismiss the novel, criticism operates myopically within parameters which are themselves drawn up on partial premises.

Before turning more extensively to those insistent discourses of class and artifice in the novel itself, I want to briefly consider Robert Gittings's and Richard Taylor's treatment of *The Hand of Ethelberta*.[14] Gittings has a chapter entitled 'Ethelberta' in *Young Thomas Hardy*, has edited and introduced the 'New Wessex' edition, and writes sympathetically and perceptively – although finally obtusely – about the novel. He well exemplifies how even perceptions which follow the logic of the novel's discourses can be blocked and obscured by the predetermining critical criteria of fictional 'propriety' and literary 'excellence'. In the biography, Gittings deals with Hardy's growing dissociation from his relatives and the necessary concealment of his origins as he married the middle-class Emma Gifford and became successful with *Far From the Madding Crowd*, and he suggests that Hardy made a 'surprising' and 'very personal' decision that his next novel would deal with 'the situation in which he found his own life, as a writer of humble origins acclaimed by a society which might, if knowing, have found them contemptible'. So, Gittings deduces: 'perhaps from an inborn necessity to write the teasing problem somehow out of his system, was evolved the most uneven and contradictory of all Hardy's novels.'[15] Two assumptions inform this: one, that Hardy had to 'write the problem out of his system' – not that it might remain the ground bass for all his subsequent fiction; and two, that the novel is aesthetically damaged. Much of Gittings's chapter, however, is a detailed and convincing account of how much autobiographical material the novel contains; of how Hardy edited the serial version (and indeed extensively revised the first book edition of 1876 for the 1892 re-publication) to conceal the extent of his own background in it; and of how his marriage to Emma Gifford in 1874 both affected the novel and exacerbated the tensions of his class deception. But Gittings is unable to move beyond these factual *aperçu*s to a positive analysis of the novel: the chapter is shot through with the word 'improbable', and where he (rightly) points to 'the theme of class concealment' as 'an obsession', he can only add that 'it throws the novel out of balance in a way which puzzled all reviewers' (292). Where he speaks perceptively of Ethelberta as 'this synthetic character and her dilemmas [which] were meant to express, in secret guise, Hardy's own', he can still only see the novel as 'this manufactured and cryptic book' (293): 'synthetic' characters, 'manufactured', and 'cryptic' writing – which might be symptomatic of Hardy's own tensions – are all implicitly condemned on aesthetic grounds. Again, Gittings rightly notes the similarity between Hardy and Ethelberta as thwarted poets, commenting on Hardy's failure to get into print at this stage – 'so yet another prime passion of his life was driven underground' (297). But personal traumas, for Gittings (as for so many other psycho-biographers), produce a writer-hero who 'from this time . . . shows evidence of the violence that his uprooting from the past had done to his essential being. . . . It was this strain and fixed gloom that pursued him, like a haunted person, all the rest of his long life' (298). Gittings could well be right, but the idealist notion of Hardy's 'essential being', together with the absence of any conception of 'Ideology' and of a critical apparatus which can deal with the 'improbable', means that he can only see the novel as Hardy's 'last gesture from the class to which he really belonged. He wrote out of his system the Hardy who was one of the people who toiled and suffered. From now onward, he surveyed such people as one who had escaped from their world' (295–6). Gittings is right to say that Hardy's class position changes, but wrong to imply the shift was so simple: Hardy never 'really belonged' to one class, but was precisely one of the 'metamorphic classes' he mentions in *The Hand of Ethelberta* (320); it is that which underlies the 'strain' of his work thereafter. The novel is less a farewell to his 'real' class than a recognition of the contradictory position in which he was now situated.

Gittings's later introduction to the 'New Wessex' edition brings these issues into sharper focus. Much of the biographical material is the same, but the check-rein of critical orthodoxy now holds back the earlier perceptions about class and writing; the framing essay to the only accessible modern edition of the novel, therefore, is one which perpetuates all the old-established commonplaces. Its final sentence synopsizes the critical perspective within which the novel is viewed: having discovered that at certain moments the character of Ethelberta comes alive (Gittings has earlier noted that what Hardy 'drew best' in his fiction was 'the full-scale portrait of a real woman'),[16] he concludes: 'It is in moments such as this that the ''Comedy in Chapters'' transcends its artificial and private frame-work to touch the universality of the greater novels' (28). It is within this almost self-parodying literary-critical frame, then, that Gittings sees *The Hand of Ethelberta* as 'the joker in the pack' of Hardy's novels which 'fascinates by its very strangeness' (15). Puzzling though its provenance immediately after *Far From the Madding Crowd* may be, he can only state: 'It is as if written by a different hand and, it must be added, by a far less competent one' – explana-tions as to why this 'joker' should come next being reduced to a suggestion that Hardy may have been imaginatively exhausted (16–17). (Gittings does, however, suggest that Hardy's 'negative' reason for writing the novel, which largely accounts for its 'comparative failure', was his reaction to comparisons with George Eliot (21–2).)

The main aspects of this 'failure' are, not surprisingly, the familiar truisms of Hardy criticism: Ethelberta's situation is not 'even remotely plausible'; 'a large part of *Ethelberta* is badly written'; 'even more disconcerting, Hardy returns to *what we know to be the faults* of his very first novels' (my italics); Hardy had 'reverted' to the 'class bias' criticized by Alexander Macmillan in *The Poor Man and the Lady*; Hardy was 'trying a realistic portrayal of the society into which he himself in real life had just made a move'; there are 'the most delightful and realistic' moments when Hardy is 'completely . . . at home' writing about the lower orders, 'the total improbability of many incidents in the novel', and the 'incredible plot and obsessive criticism of society and conventional manners'.[17] It is notable how the novel's attitudes to social class and the aesthetics of 'improbablism' are hunted down together by conventional criticism. There is one point finally, however, which indicates the almost perverse misrecognition fostered by realist-humanist criticism, and this is Gittings's interesting suggestion that *Ethelberta* is really in the tradition of the 'old-fashioned novelette': rather than being in advance of its time – as Hardy claimed in both *The Life* and the 1895 Preface – the novel 'could have been written for a romantic-magazine audience at any time in the last hundred years'. Historically dubious though this claim is, Gittings goes on to 'admit' that Hardy 'stand[s] the conventional ending on its head', and we expect him to develop this notion of parody. However, without any explanation of the motive for, or effect of, this inversion, he says:

> yet Hardy, although he may have claimed to be writing a comedy, was certainly not writing a parody. His handling is too heavy and obvious for any such interpretation. He is firmly meshed in both the characterization and the style of novels of a much lesser type. (15–16)

The paradox of Gittings's position, despite the biographical critic's innate intentionalism, is to recognize Hardy's perverse response to the success of *Far From the Madding Crowd* and his turning of the novelette convention 'on its head', and yet to blandly claim that he was 'certainly not writing a parody' for the very reasons – 'heavy and obvious handling' – that might suggest Hardy was doing exactly that, or at least something equally self-conscious.

A further instance of an extended and sympathetic reading of *The Hand of Ethelberta* which is also disabled by the constraints of conventional critical discourse, is Richard H. Taylor's essay in his *The Neglected Hardy*. As I noted in chapter 1 (pp. 52–3), Taylor's attitude to all the 'lesser novels' is circumscribed by his acceptance of the standard ranking of Hardy's fiction, and his treatment of

Ethelberta is no exception. However, he does perceive a number of features in the novel which potentially cut below the normal critical commonplaces and point to its seriousness, noting, for instance, Hardy's cynical recognition that he must write what the public wants (a 'novel of manners'), but also seeing that, at the same time, Hardy is satirizing the form itself. He therefore positively identifies the manifest artificiality of the novel and its self-conscious use of irony, farce, improbability, and so on, finding it reminiscent of Restoration comedy. Equally, he notices the seriousness of Ethelberta's character (and how closely Hardy is involved with her): she is 'the first of the moderns', in whom, unlike many of the 'major' protagonists, 'the potentialities of the individual will are explored'; she is 'worldly, ruthless and ambitious'; her final achievement in terms of social status and economic security is ambivalent because of the cost to her personality – alienated and *déracinée* at the end; and the potentialities in her character in some way perturb Hardy himself, who 'never ventur[ed] further in his investigation of this capacity' (i.e. of a woman being in control of her own life).[18] Furthermore, Taylor realizes that the novel 'originates in that most consistent of Hardy's preoccupations: class division' (68); that it 'is a study of the physical and personal deracination which later leads to the personal and social tragedies in *Tess* and *Jude*' (71); and 'what a seminal novel [it] may be in the Hardy canon; his deepest concerns are packed in, and nowhere else are his social beliefs set out with such clarity' (71).

Why, then, is the essay ultimately so blandly conventional and disappointing? The answer may lie in the fact that Taylor cannot put his perceptions together, in a radical reading which follows their logic, precisely because he is controlled by the critical parameters of 'Thomas Hardy' and the ranking of his work. For example, he continually privileges the 'great novels' – in comparison with which (Taylor has intimate knowledge) 'Hardy did not intend [*Ethelberta*] to be taken as seriously' (57). Nor should we 'expect characters on the scale of those in the Novels of Character and Environment': *Ethelberta* is 'more modest and its tone is different' and 'if it is not as good as *The Return of the Native* . . . that is partly to say that Hardy is better at writing a different kind of novel' (74). Within such a critical discourse, therefore, *Ethelberta* is locked unquestionably into position – 'we can', says Taylor, 'glimpse *a more characteristic* Hardy novel running like a stream below the surface' (64, my italics) – and in this context, the novel's perceived radical characteristics will clearly be turned and blunted. So that despite the force of Ethelberta's character, she 'just misses the stature of some of the better-known heroines, since she is trimmed to fit the mode of the novel' – 'the heroine of a comedy, mocked and undermined' whom Hardy does not finally endorse: her 'suppression of emotion by reason and will-power is no solution . . . and he turned away from it' (64–6). Equally, the 'radicalism' of the novel (which had 'over-reached itself' in *The Poor Man and the Lady*, but was 'reasserted more powerfully' in *Ethelberta*) is nevertheless 'tempered with humour', so that it becomes 'not a socialist manifesto, but . . . a humanitarian and compassionate work . . . making a plea for personal dignity while regretting the ironies of prevailing conditions' (68). In this reading (which, as we shall see, the novel nowhere makes as self-evident as Taylor assumes), Ethelberta only 'gets on' by 'dissociating herself from the honest endeavour represented by her family'; and the novel, in its 'outcry against unfair privilege and social advantage, urban pretensions and hypocrisy', becomes 'a celebration of the spiritual and moral superiority of country life' (71). Not only is this an astonishing and unrecognizable claim as regards the 'determinate text' of the novel we have before us, it is also a classic instance of the late twentieth-century reaffirmation of Hardy as rural humanist. However, the incorporation of even such 'social messages' within the mannered and artificial modality of the novel is 'one of the reasons for [its] comparative failure' (71); Ethelberta is too large for it and 'we may prefer to wish her in a more serious work'; the mode of the novel is 'basically inimical to Hardy's tragic imagination'; and this clash produces tensions which 'at least partly dissipate the dramatic stature of the work' (74). The novelist of *Ethelberta*, therefore, is turned back once again to face his real self: not just rural humanist, but also tragic realist. For all his rehabilitation of Hardy's 'lesser fiction', then, Taylor can only do it by showing how a novel like *Ethelberta* 'runs like a stream' below the 'more characteristic' (real) Hardy of character and environment, and not by allowing its socially and formally radical artifice to rise to the surface.

But whatever the recuperative processes of criticism, and whatever Hardy's intentions may have been, the text of the novel, from the outset, unmistakably draws attention to its own artificiality and to its playfulness about literary forms and expectations. A fiction which so self-consciously includes disquisitions on fictions should have its own narrative discourses regarded with great care. And indeed the novel plays on, exploits, parodies, and exposes the conventions of both romantic and realist fiction throughout: from the extraordinary first page on which Ethelberta's prehistory is baldly summarized and her 'romantic' marriage and widowhood dealt with in a single reductive sentence ('He, a minor like herself, died from a chill caught during the wedding tour, and a few weeks later was followed into the grave by Sir Ralph Petherwin, his unforgiving father, who had bequeathed his wealth to his wife absolutely' (33)), to the equally contrary ending in which Ethelberta does not marry her young lover Christopher Julian (he receives a windfall inheritance which is, ironically, not enough – 'a tantalizing sum' (404) – and marries Ethelberta's sister Picotee, whose face 'had grown to resemble her sister's' (408)) but in which, instead, she becomes the wife of the wicked old aristocrat, Mountclere (whom she reforms), takes over the running of his estate, provides for her family, and now 'lives mostly in the library' pursuing her career as an epic poet (409). The novel constructs its ironic and parodic animus in a number of ways: by direct mockery of the conventions; by its mannered and self-conscious style; and by its own wilfully self-destructive fictional strategies and contrivance – chance, coincidence, sensationalism, caricature, authorial intrusion, and so on. Hints of the first of these – of overt exposure of romantic conventions – are apparent early on when Ethelberta, after her renewed acquaintance with Christopher Julian, is described as going 'where all ladies are supposed to go when they want to torment their minds in comfort – to her own room' (44), and again in the following passage:

> The hour grew later, and that dreamy period came round when ladies' fancies, that have lain shut up close as their fans during the day, begin to assert themselves anew. At this time a good guess at Ethelberta's thoughts might have been made from her manner of passing the minutes away. Instead of reading, entering notes in her diary, or doing any ordinary thing, she walked to and fro, curled her pretty nether lip within her pretty upper one a great many times, made a cradle of her locked fingers, and paused with fixed eyes where the walls of the room set limits upon her walk to look at nothing but a picture within her mind. (45)

The curiously external stance of the writing suggests a mockery of the genre of female romance, whilst also producing a sharply alienated sense of Ethelberta's character: there is something mechanical about her here, which, as we shall see, can be perceived throughout the novel. Again, her effect on Christopher is rendered thus: '[she] might soon become . . . an indestructible fascination – to drag him about, turn his soul inside out, harrow him, twist him, and otherwise torment him, according to *the stereotyped form of such processes*' (67, my italics). Much later, during Ethelberta's trip to Rouen (where most of her suitors ridiculously follow her), she muses about Mountclere: 'Thus backed up by Sol and Dan, her aunt, and Cornelia, Ethelberta felt quite the reverse of a lonely female persecuted by a wicked lord in a foreign country' (269–70) – although, in a way, this is an accurate description of her situation at this point. What the novel is doing, of course, is drawing ironic attention to the very fictional convention it is at the same time exploiting, just as it does in the case of Mountclere's marriage to Ethelberta (which both families are trying to stop) by way of the words of a society lady:

> 'What a funny thing!' said the lady, with a wretchedly factitious smile. 'The times have taken a strange turn when the angry parent of the comedy, who goes post-haste to prevent the undutiful daughter's rash marriage, is a gentleman from below stairs, and the unworthy lover a peer of the realm!' (345)

I shall return later to the relation between fictional and class reversals, a confluence which may be said to represent the principal discourse of the novel.

Hardy's style, when it is 'pedantic', 'awkward', and self-conscious, is commonly regarded as one of his major 'flaws'; and Gittings, in the essay considered above, includes it amongst 'what are known to be' Hardy's faults in *Ethelberta*, identifying it as the result of his early penchant for Harrison Ainsworth.[19] Certainly the novel's style is pervasively self-conscious, but its very consistency makes it more a strategic mannerism – one which intensifies the defamiliarizing ('disproportioning') effect of the whole work – than a failure of control. For example, a 'town young man' is described (in terms which call to mind Dickens's reifications of character) as having 'a Tussaud complexion and well-pencilled brows half way up his forehead, so that his upper eyelids appeared to possess the uncommon quality of tallness' (56–7); a letter in which Ethelberta begins to tell Christopher the truth about her class background but then burns, is emblematized as being 'poked and stirred . . . till a red inflammation crept over the sheet' (97); and London under moonlight is rendered in extravagantly over-wrought prose: 'ordinary houses were sublimated to the rank of public buildings, public buildings to palaces, and the faces of women walking the streets to those of calendared saints and guardian-angels, by the pure bleaching light from the sky' (156). Again, Alfred Neigh, the cosmopolitan man of letters, finding himself in love with Ethelberta, paces his room in distress and is undercut by the narrative voice: '"O, the deuce, the deuce!" he continued, walking about the room as if passionately stamping but not quite doing it because another man had rooms below' (164); and his name, which the novel constantly uses for jokes, gives rise to extreme self-conscious

facetiousness when Ladywell expostulates: ' "No, Neigh – never!" '
(163). Equally, Ethelberta's attitude to Neigh is presented in the
following chapter-opening as: 'The question of Neigh or no Neigh
had reached a pitch of insistence which no longer permitted of dally-
ing, even by a popular beauty' (219); and her quandary over
whether to marry him and be honest with him or not is presented
– partly as her own musings, partly as the narrative's – in
elaborately mannered terms:

> One palliative feature must be remembered when we survey the
> matrimonial ponderings of the poetess and romancer. What she
> contemplated was not meanly to ensnare a husband just to provide
> incomes for her and her family, but to find some man she might
> respect, who would maintain her in such a stage of comfort as
> should, by setting her mind free from temporal anxiety, enable
> her to further organize her talent, and provide incomes for them
> herself. Plenty of saleable originality was left in her as yet, but it
> was getting crushed under the rubbish of her necessities.
> She was not sure that Neigh would stand the test of her
> revelations. It would be possible to lead him to marry her without
> revealing anything . . . yet Ethelberta's honesty shrank from the
> safe course of holding her tongue. It might be pleasant to many a
> modern gentleman to find himself allied with a lady, none of
> whose ancestors had ever pandered to a court, lost an army, taken
> a bribe, oppressed a community, or broken a bank; but the added
> disclosure that, in avoiding these stains, her kindred had worked
> and continued to work with their hands for bread, might lead such
> an one to consider that the novelty was dearly purchased. (220)

What is noteworthy here, aside from the abrasive analysis of
marriage and class, is the detachment of tone and the ornate
language of the passage which serve to emphasize the deeply
alienated position of 'the poetess and romancer' who has 'plenty of
saleable originality . . . left' and who is presented as though she
were no more than a series of 'considerations' which can be adduced
in coldly calculating prose. I will return to the novel's mechanistic
presentation of Ethelberta's 'character' in a moment.
But by far the most obtrusive manifestations of the novel's
artificiality are the various narrative strategies employed to get the
story told at all. What criticism would call 'improbablism' is rife
here; but because *Ethelberta* is primarily concerned with class deception and the relativity of fiction and truth, the overtly fictive mode
of articulation is central to the whole statement the novel makes:
fiction here represents fictions. The modes of narration are diverse,
but they invariably 'alienate' the reader by placing her or him where

179

they can actually see the perspective the novel is offering them and by the uncompromising artificiality of the device. One such recurrent perspective is that of characters' views of other characters within the book, often from unseen points of vantage which effectively transmute those observed into actors in a performance or show. An early example of this is in chapter 3 where Ladywell and another 'gentlemanly person' observe Picotee from 'a small square hole' in The Weir House, waiting in the rain for Christopher Julian to pass her in his characteristically unperceiving way (55–6). There is no reason why they should see her thus, nor does the episode have any direct bearing on the plot; but the effect, in keeping with so much of the rest of the novel, is to intensify the staged and artificial social relations of people in this society. Similarly, Christopher and his sister Faith, supplying the music for a dance at which Ethelberta is a principal guest (and who has been instrumental in getting them the job), observe the dancers from behind a 'screen of ivy and holly': 'the whole spectacle deriving an unexpected novelty from the accident of reaching their eyes through interstices in the tracery of green leaves' (62). Here, the (perceived) perspective serves both to emphasize 'Ethelberta Petherwin's performance' (64) and to further distance the upper-class Christopher, who has come down in the world, from the lower-class Ethelberta who is deceptively a lady: in other words, to reinforce the sense that the alienating fiction of class actually proscribes a relationship between the only two people in the novel who might have loved each other with spontaneity and passion. But by far the most extended and structurally ironic of such scenes is the one in which Picotee, aided by a servant of the house, observes Ethelberta at a dinner party (where her father, unbeknown to the guests, is serving as a butler) by way of a mirror which reflects the scene through a 'partly-opened door':

> To Picotee's dazed young vision her beautiful sister appeared as the chief figure of a glorious pleasure-parliament of both sexes, surrounded by whole regiments of candles grouped here and there about the room. She and her companions were seated before a large flower-bed, or small hanging garden, fixed at about the level of the elbow, the attention of all being concentrated rather upon the uninteresting margin of the bed, and upon each other, than on the beautiful natural objects growing in the middle, as it seemed to Picotee. In the ripple of conversation Ethelberta's clear voice could occasionally be heard, and her young sister could see that her eyes were bright, and her face beaming, as if divers social wants and looming penuriousness had never been within her experience. (233)

A little later, Picotee has related to her Neigh's account of how Ethelberta had checked out his estate, and hears the ' ' "Ha-ha-ha-ha-ha-ha" ' ' of the 'boozy men' laughing at it (236). This scene as a whole enacts those issues of class, deception, and alienation which the novel continually exposes: not only are Picotee and her father, the butler, dissociated from their own relative by the fiction of class status, but Ethelberta herself has become no more than a false image displaced in a mirror and in an after-dinner *story*. This, however, is very much her reality: her social being is a fiction exposed in the manifest fictiveness of the discourses which constitute her as 'real': those of the novel itself.

Equally self-conscious is the novel's use of letters. The presence of further 'writings' within a novel so concerned with the writing of fictions is immediately conspicuous and compounds its self-reflexiveness. For the most part, the letters are used to convey the 'truth' about Ethelberta's real position: Mr Chickerill's letter to her in chapter 7, for example, finally reveals her background to the reader, while simultaneously raising questions about the veracity of literature and about the problems of upward class mobility (83–4); and Mrs Chickerill's letter in chapter 34 explains how Menlove the servant has penetrated Ethelberta's secret and is likely to reveal the deception, at the same time reinforcing the cynically opportunistic approach to marriage of which Ethelberta herself is inescapably the creature: ' ' "O, this false position! – it is ruining your nature, my too thoughtful mother!" ' ' (273–4). Most significant in my context here, however, are Ethelberta's two letters to Christopher in chapter 9, one of which tells the truth about her background, which she destroys; the other simply compounding the 'fiction'. It is a striking instance of the novel's self-consciousness that it can proffer both versions of the 'truth' about Ethelberta (and about Hardy), 'destroy' one and retain the other – while in fact preserving both for the reader: it is, in effect, the apotheosis of Hardy's own legerdemain in writing this 'fiction' about his own ('real') class position. Finally, as an example of the extraordinary flouting of the 'probable' in this novel, we may notice the exchange of letters (and the authorial intrusions) between Ethelberta and Lord Mountclere in two more or less adjacent inns in Melchester, negotiations about their possible marriage being conducted, at this point, entirely by letter. After the receipt of one such the following passage occurs:

'Ho-ho-ho – Miss Hoity-toity!' said Lord Mountclere, trotting up and down. But, remembering it was her June against his November, this did not last long, and he frantically replied:–
MY DARLING, – I cannot release you – I must do anything to

181

keep my treasure. Will you not see me for a few minutes, and let bygones go to the winds?

Was ever a thrush so safe in a cherry net before! (317)

The novel moves, here – as it does elsewhere – into a kind of absurd farce, making no pretence of realism. But as an exposure of the shams, deceptions, subterfuges, stratagems, and exploitations involved in the social (class and gender) relations of marriage, it is no more 'unreal' than the conventional fictional representation of courtship and marriage in novels contemporary with it. Its fictions simply do not purport to be 'real'; and, in the process, it calls in question the 'reality' of those other social and fictional representations which *do*.

The Hand of Ethelberta is, indeed, largely constituted by such uncompromisingly fictive contrivance (Ethelberta, with nice irony, herself claims: 'I am a rare hand at contrivances' (226), and she is elsewhere described as knowing 'the ins and outs of contriving' (407)). Coincidence, chance, contingency, improbability, and absurdity smack the reader in the face – to the point, in fact, where it becomes perverse to apply realist criteria at all. There is the ironic coincidence of the guests at Mr Doncastle's commenting on the butler's face after they have unknowingly discussed his daughter's poems in front of him (80–1). There is the implausible scene when Ethelberta, disguised and in the company of her two workman brothers, visits the Royal Academy exhibition to see Ladywell's picture of her and overhears two men discussing how she is to be Neigh's wife – before he has even begun to court her (194). There is the grossly improbable moment when Ethelberta observes the trees which hinder her view of the sea being felled on Mountclere's orders to satisfy her whim: 'One of the trees forming the curtain across it began to wave strangely: it went further to one side, and fell' (255–7). There is the absurd contingency of Mountclere's yacht meeting Ethelberta's boat on the way to France (an event too far-fetched to be an 'error' of fictional decorum); and the ridiculous farce in the hotel in Rouen when three of Ethelberta's suitors are all attending on her in different rooms, and two of them, leaning out of their windows, recognize each other while overhearing the third's conversation with her:

Upon a balcony beneath [Neigh] were the speakers, as he had suspected – Ethelberta and the viscount. Looking right and left, he saw projecting from the next window the head of his friend Ladywell, gazing right and left likewise, apparently just drawn out by the same voice which had attracted himself.

'What – you, Neigh! – how strange', came from Ladywell's lips. (284–5)

'Strange' indeed. But no more so than the inexplicable chapter in which Ethelberta, thinking throughout the night about whether she should marry Mountclere or not, looks up 'a well-known treatise on Utilitarianism', and later a chapter – significantly on ' "the *disciplina arcani*, or, the doctrine of reserve" ' – in 'an old treatise on Casuistry', from which the arguments are rehearsed with literal quotations (295–7). There is, too, the wildly contingent plotting of the journey that Lord Mountclere's brother and Sol Chickerill undertake together to try and prevent the marriage, which includes a sea trip to Knollsea (and the coincidence of a storm sending them back the way they had come (348–54)), at the end of which Mr Chickerill and Christopher Julian, who have been travelling together without knowing it, meet up with Sol and Mr Mountclere – all of them arriving too late (365–9). Finally, there is the crazy gothic 'business' of Ethelberta's note, passed through a window into the wrong hands, and the foiling therefore of her attempt to escape from Mountclere:

> The voice was so different from her brother's that she was
> terrified; her limbs quivered. In another instant the speaker had
> struck a wax vesta, and holding it erect in his fingers he looked
> her in the face.
> 'Hee-hee-hee!' The laughter was her husband the viscount. (394–9
> *passim*)

Mountclere then tells her 'a story' – ' "I have learnt the art from you" ' – after which they agree to negotiate, with Ethelberta congratulating Mountclere on his plot: ' "It was stratagem against stratagem. Mine was ingenious; yours was masterly! Accept my acknowledgment. We will enter upon an armed neutrality" ' (400–2). By these later scenes, the novel is not bothering with the illusion of realism at all: the contrivance is naked, the fiction manifestly fictive. But just as the callous deceptions and illusions of class and gender hierarchies are exposed, as we shall see, by this caricatured melodramatic fiction, so too are the mystifications of a 'probablist' realism which are no less contrived – and often more so – in their pursuit of verisimilitude. 'Improbable' *The Hand of Ethelberta* may be, but that does not mean it is less 'truthful'.

I want now, therefore, to show how the fictional contrivance of the novel exposes the alienating fictions of class and gender relations. Unlike most of Hardy's fiction, so criticism would seem to imply – although my focus here is to question that assumption – *The Hand of Ethelberta* is obsessively and exclusively concerned with social class and, within that, the gender relations involved in courtship and marriage. The *donnée* of the plot – a young woman who deceives society about her class origins and operates successfully within its codes – establishes this from the outset. But the texture of the whole novel is composed, almost line by line, of an extreme sensitiveness to the nuances of class position – a sensitiveness that derives from a perspective which looks both up and down with equal familiarity and with equal unease. At one point the novel registers, parenthetically, a passing reflex of Ethelberta's: 'a word of Christopher's about somebody else's mean parentage, which was spoken in utter forget-fulness of her own position, . . . had wounded her to the quick never-theless' (174). This, in a sense, identifies the ruling consciousness of the novel as a whole. Characters are invariably placed, for example, in exact class stations. Picotee appropriately (and we should remember Hardy's sisters and cousins) is a pupil-teacher, and Ethelberta – intended by her parents for a governess (124) – thinks, in a moment of despair, of teaching as a career (292), which would indeed be, but for her writing, her 'correct' class occupation. Christopher, who has come down in the world, earns a meagre living by his music, but his sensibilities, attitudes, and actions are always those of a leisured gentleman: when he first meets Picotee he immediately perceives her status and 'lowered his method of address to her level at once' (52); and his attitude to Ethelberta, despite her superiority to him in many ways, is often patronizing: for instance, he is enamoured by 'the romantic ubiquity of station that attached to her' – a response accounted for by the novel because 'his faith in society had departed with his own social ruin' (122). Ethelberta's young husband's father, who dismisses the 'homeless governess' when he sees the way the wind is blowing, is 'an ambitious gentleman *just* knighted' (307, my italics – Hardy's irony is very precise). Ethelberta's own consciousness, in particular, continually registers relationships in class terms. She perceives that Neigh and Ladywell 'were both too near her level to be trusted to bear the shock of receiving her from her father's hands'; but goes on to recognize that 'though her genesis might tinge with vulgarity a commoner's household, susceptible of such deprecia-tion', a peer's family might be able to stand it (295) – although earlier she has worried that Mountclere's 'interest in her was not likely, under the ordinary influences of caste feeling, to continue longer than while he was kept in ignorance of her consanguinity with a stock proscribed' (268–9). What is notable in the novel, then, is the iterative and minutely sensitive registering of the characters' class differences. But equally, scenes, places, and gatherings of people are always presented with their class co-ordinates in the foreground. Knollsea, at the begin-ning of chapter 31, is immediately identified in these terms: 'Everybody in the parish who was not a boatman was a quarrier, unless he were the gentleman who owned half the property and had been a quarryman, or the other gentleman who owned the other half, and had been to sea' (243). A dinner party at the Doncasters' – 'who lived in a moderately fashionable square' – is framed by a satirical analysis of smiles and laughter as notations of social class:

> All the friends and relatives present were nice people, who exhibited becoming signs of pleasure and gaiety at being there; but as regards the vigour with which these emotions were expressed, it may be stated that a slight laugh from far down the throat and a slight narrowing of the eye were equivalent as indices of the degree of mirth felt to a Ha-ha-ha! and a shaking of the shoulders among the minor traders of the kingdom; and to a Ho-ho-ho! contorted features, purple face, and stamping foot among the gentlemen in corduroy and fustian who adorn the remoter provinces. (75)

And the house-party at Enckworth Court when Ethelberta stays there is very precisely classified, detailing the new and meretricious *arrivistes'* penetration of the old landed aristocracy and Ethelberta's own *petit-bourgeois* snobbery about them:

> the present assemblage seemed to want much of that old-fashioned stability and quaint monumental dignity she had expected to find under this historical roof. Nobody of her entertainer's own rank appeared. Not a single clergyman was there. A tendency to talk Walpolean scandal about foreign courts was particularly manifest. And although tropical travellers, Indian officers and their wives, courteous exiles, and descendants of Irish kings, were infinitely more pleasant than Lord Mountclere's landed neighbours would probably have been, to such a cosmopolite as Ethelberta a calm Tory or old Whig company would have given a greater treat. (306)

Much of the comedy – which is of a bitterly serious kind – in the journey Sol Chickerill (a carpenter) and Mountclere's brother make to 'rescue' their respective relatives from a marriage which transgresses class codes, derives from mutual recognition of their class position and antagonism and from the irony, therefore, of their being on the same errand from antithetical class perspectives:

> 'If it should come to pass, she would play her part as his lady as well as any other woman, and better. I wish there was no more reason for fear on my side than there is on yours! Things have come to a sore head when she is not considered lady enough for such as he. But perhaps your meaning is, that if your brother were to have a son, you would lose your heir-presumptive title to the cor'net of Mountclere?'. . . .

'The suggestion is as delicate as the – atmosphere of this vile room. But let your ignorance be your excuse, my man. It is hardly worth while for us to quarrel when we both have the same object in view.' (338)

And again, later, Sol says:

'Upon my life I should be inclined to laugh, if I were not so much inclined to do the other thing, at Berta's trick of trying to make close family allies of such a cantankerous pair as you and I! So much of one mind as we be, so alike in our ways of living, so close connected in our callings and principles, so matched in manners and customs!' . . .

Mountclere faintly laughed with the same hideous merriment at the same idea, and then both remained in a withering silence, meant to express the utter contempt of each for the other, both in family and in person. (368)

What we see here, I think, is how the novel's farcical discourse itself articulates the absurdly irrational nature of a class society.

In general, however, the novel's satirical animus – which so upset Hardy's contemporaries and plenty of later critics – is directed against the upper classes. It may well be because of this that he is criticized for his 'ignorance' and 'improbable' rendering of society, and is patronized for being 'at home' only with lower-class rural characters. But Hardy, of course, is no more of one class than the other, and no more 'naturally' realistic about one than the other; indeed, the defamiliarization of class relations perceptible in *The Hand of Ethelberta* (and, in fact, most of his fiction) is determined by his peculiarly contradictory class insertion as *arriviste* professional writer in metropolitan society. What the novel emphasizes in particular about the upper classes is that their superiority is as much a fiction as Ethelberta's own. Christopher Julian, for example, is always shown to be weaker than Ethelberta and without the energy to succeed as an artist, although he is constantly aware of his superior social class; Ladywell, the painter, is condemned in similar terms; guests at various parties are frequently revealed to have been elevated by way of trade or fortuitous circumstance; and their literary and artistic education, significantly, is invariably inferior to Ethelberta's: when she visits Milton's grave in Cripplegate Church, for instance, with the Belmaines and Neigh, it is she who knew it was not in Westminster Abbey and she who reads from his poetry – being 'the only one present who could properly manage blank verse' (212). Alfred Neigh in particular, the society *beau* and man of letters, is revealed, in Ethelberta's 'disillusive discovery', to rest his social standing on the horse-knackering business (see quotation on pp. 203–4); this is the reality behind his façade of breeding, superiority, and misogyny, and it leads to Ethelberta's perception that they are 'too nearly cattle of one colour' for him to be able to forgive her her class background (200).[20] Finally Lord Mountclere, although of genuinely noble descent, is presented melodramatically as the decadence of a noble line, who is said to have an unspeakable past and has let his estate go to ruin. He inhabits a house for which 'art' has been purchased to produce 'illusion' and which is mainly a modern sham – 'a stone mask worn by a brick face' (304)[21] – and keeps a mistress (calling herself 'Lady Mountclere') in a cottage in his grounds. Ironically, however, it is him Ethelberta marries, because he has the cynical realism and the status not to mind her origins or her class deception. As my opening quotation shows; having listened to Ethelberta's 'fictional' account of her real life story, Mountclere tells her not to expose herself to the other guests who 'are no better than you', and pronounces with cynical honesty:

'But my father and friends?' said she.
'Are nothing to be concerned about. Modern developments have shaken up the classes like peas in a hopper. An annuity, and a comfortable cottage –'
'My brothers are workmen.'
'Manufacture is the single vocation in which a man's prospects may be said to be illimitable. Hee-hee! – they may buy me up before they die! And now what stands in the way? It would take fifty alliances with fifty families so little disreputable as yours, darling, to drag mine down.' (308–9)

In a sense, Mountclere appears as the grotesque exposé of the basic premise of a class system: that it must disguise its artificiality and perpetuate the illusion of being natural.

It is in Ethelberta herself, however, that we feel the full force of the novel's obsessive consciousness of class, and it is in her 'character' that the mannered artifice of the fiction and the contradictions of class position most strongly intersect. To discuss Ethelberta as 'a character' at all is difficult, and this problem itself is an important aspect of her significance: because she is so divided – as Ethelberta Chickerill, as Mrs Petherwin, as Professed Story-Teller, as the 'beloved' of four different men – and because the reader experiences her in all these roles, no one of which can be identified definitively as the 'real' Ethelberta, 'her character', if the term still means anything, must comprise all of these roles. She is fashioned by circumstance, and is constituted by the social roles consequent on it:

that is her reality. But it is a reality, equally, which is overtly fashioned by the text: at a number of levels, 'Ethelberta' exists only as a fiction (as a 'lady', as a 'romancer', as a character in the novel), and as such she resists and challenges the character analysis – based on the notion of an individual 'real' personality or unitary subject – of humanist realism and its affiliated critical praxis. If 'Ethelberta' is seen to be composed solely by fictional discourse – as 'representation' – then she draws attention to the fact that so too are all other heroines, however much their 'round', 'knowable', extra-textual 'reality' is admired by literary criticism. Shortly after Ethelberta has become a success by way of her poems, she is the subject of a conversation at the Belmaines' between two society ladies:

'She is one of those people who are known, as one may say, by subscription: everybody knows a little, till she is astonishingly well known altogether; but nobody knows her entirely.' . . .

'She has apparently a very good prospect.'
'Yes; and it is through her being of that curious undefined character which interprets itself to each admirer as whatever he would like to have it. Old men like her because she is so girlish; youths because she is womanly; wicked men because she is good in their eyes; good men because she is wicked in theirs.'
'She must be a very anomalous sort of woman, at that rate.'
'Yes. Like the British Constitution, she owes her success in practice to her inconsistencies in principle.'
'These poems must have set her up. She appears to be quite the correct spectacle. Happy Mrs Petherwin!' (94)

What is emphasized here is Ethelberta's unknowability, the 'inconsistencies' of her character(ization), her being whatever men choose to make her, and her status as 'spectacle'. These are, indeed, all the terms in which she is represented by the novel: as a series of perceived images, of 'seemings', of 'impressions', her reality being that of a social and literary fiction (significantly, a few lines later, during an ironic conversation with Mrs Belmaine about the upward social mobility of servants, Ethelberta refers to original pedigree as 'the first edition' (95)). Her deception as to her class background is constantly presented as playing a part: Christopher, playing music at the dance, watches 'Ethelberta Petherwin's performance' (64), although it is no more than her ordinary social behaviour; and when he next comes across her, rehearsing her fiction to the children in the country (see above pp. 164–5), she is described as at the centre of a 'natural theatre', her 'appearance answer[ing] as fully as ever to that of an

English Lady skilfully perfected in manner, carriage, look, and accent' (112–13). The premeditated and rehearsed artifice conveyed by the phrase 'skilfully perfected' is compounded by its syntactical ambiguity in the sentence: is the phrase in apposition to 'her appearance' or to 'an English lady'? The implications are quite different. The ambiguity of 'being a lady' also crops up with Neigh, who says: '"directly I saw you I felt that nobody ever came so near my idea of what is desirable in a lady"' (203). The irony is complex here, for Neigh – later described by Ethelberta as 'one of those horrid men who love with their eyes' (241), that is, who turn women into visual objects – is himself a sham who misrecognizes Ethelberta as 'the real thing'. But what is significant again is the syntax of the sentence, in which Ethelberta comes as near as anybody ever did to his 'idea of what is desirable in a lady' – nearer, indeed, than the real thing ever could. Ethelberta's 'act' is indeed fetishized by Neigh's perception of her; but effectively, also, her reality is what she seems – the alienating effects of which the novel's prose draws attention to in the description of her face when Neigh tells her he knows she has visited his estate:

> Her face did not change, since a face must be said not to change while it preserves the same pleasant lines in the mobile parts as before; but anybody who has preserved his pleasant lines under the half-minute's peer of the invidious camera, and found what a wizened, starched kind of thing they stiffen to towards the end of the time, will understand the tendency of Ethelberta's lovely features now. (204)

The detached language and ironic stance – combined with the reference to the new 'mechanical' visual art of photography – turn 'Ethelberta's lovely features' into an object dissociated from her being; just as, in the scene at the Belmaines' above when the topic of servants arises, the novel says: 'The face of Ethelberta showed caution at once' and then: 'The face of Ethelberta showed venture-someness' (94), where the full genitive, in place of 'Ethelberta's face', implies the mask-like reification of her features. Earlier, during a conversation with Christopher in which he is deceived about her class, there is a moment when 'Ethelberta smiled a smile of many meanings' (41) as though smiling strategically and instrumentally; and much later, negotiating with Mountclere, she is presented in the following terms: 'But none of this reached her face'; 'Ethelberta flung at Lord Mountclere a look which clipped him like pincers'; 'Ethelberta's show of passion went as quickly as it had come' (314–15). The point is that because of the deception she practices, Ethelberta can never be an integrated being; she is always an alienated 'performance'.

This alienation is given most emphatic focus in Ethelberta's relations with her family. The unnaturalness of the deceit required by the codes of class society is evidenced by the 'improbability' of her living two discrete lives: one as a member of her family and the other as a total stranger to it; lives which are not allowed to meet except as they traverse the 'Ethelberta' the novel itself realizes. Picotee strikes the note when she says to Ethelberta: '"I have told nobody that we are sisters, or that you are known in any way to me or to mother or to any of us"' (71); and her little sister tells Christopher: '"She lives there along wi' mother and we. But she don't want anybody to know it, sir, cause she's celebrate, and 'twouldn't do at all"' (110–11). This destructive split is re-emphasized by her carpenter brothers who draw attention at once to the dehumanizing deception of Ethelberta's own life, to their (and indeed the whole family's) complicity in it and to Ethelberta's contradictory liking for it:

> ' 'Twould demean her to claim kin wi' her in London – two
> journeymen like us, that know nothing besides our trades.'
> 'Not at all,' said Christopher. 'She would be pleased to see any
> straightforward honest man and brother, I should think,
> notwithstanding that she has moved in other society for a time.'
> 'Ah, you don't know Berta!' said Dan, looking as if he did.
> 'How – in what way do you mean?' said Christopher uneasily.
> 'So lofty – so very lofty! Isn't she, Sol? Why she'll never stir out
> from mother's till after dark, and then her day begins; and she'll
> traipse about under the trees, and never go into the high-road, so
> that nobody in the way of gentle-people shall run up against her
> and know her living in such a little small hut after biding in a big
> mansion-place. There, we don't find fault wi' her about it; we like
> her just the same, though she don't speak to us in the street; for a
> feller must be a fool to make a piece of work about a woman's
> pride, when 'tis for her good that he should not. Yes, her life has
> been quare enough. I hope she enjoys it, but for my part I like
> plain sailing. None of your ups and downs for me.' (124)

Later, Sol brings into high relief the 'absurdity' of this family relationship – and the reiteration of the word 'absurd' reverberates well beyond the limited sense it has within the conversation in the text:

> 'So Berta and Mr Julian, if you'll go on and take no more notice
> o' us, in case of visitors, it would be wiser – else, perhaps, if we
> should be found out intimate with ye, and bring down your

gentility, you'll blame us for it. I get as nervous as a cat when I
think I may be the cause of any disgrace to ye.'
'Don't be so silly, Sol,' said Ethelberta, laughing.
'Ah, that's all very well,' said Sol, with an unbelieving smile;
'but if we bain't company for you out of doors, you bain't
company for us within – not that I find fault with ye or mind it,
and shan't take anything for painting your house, nor will Dan
neither, any more for that – no, not a penny; in fact, we are glad
to do it for 'ee. At the same time, you keep to your class, and
we'll keep to ours.' . . .

The two brothers then turned their backs upon their visitors, and
went on working, and Ethelberta and her lover left the room. 'My
brothers, you perceive,' said she, 'represent the respectable British
workman in his entirety, and a touchy individual he is, I assure
you, on points of dignity, after imbibing a few town ideas from
his leaders. They are painfully off-hand with me, absolutely
refusing to be intimate, from a mistaken notion that I am ashamed
of their dress and manners; which, of course, is absurd.'
'Which, of course, is absurd,' said Christopher.
'Of course it is absurd!' she repeated with warmth, and looking
keenly at him. But, finding no harm in his face, she continued as
before: 'Yet, all the time, they will do anything under the sun that
they think will advance my interests. In our hearts we are one.
All they ask me to do is to leave them to themselves, and
therefore I do so.
'Two more sisters of mine, whom you have never seen at all, are
also here. They are older than any of the rest of us, and had,
broadly speaking, no education at all, poor girls. The eldest,
Gwendoline, is my cook, and Cornelia is my housemaid. I suffer
much sadness, and almost misery sometimes, in reflecting that
here are we, ten brothers and sisters, born of one father and
mother, who might have mixed together and shared all in the
same scenes, and been properly happy, if it were not for the
strange accidents that have split us up into sections as you see,
cutting me off from them without the compensation of joining me
to any others. They are all true as steel in keeping the secret of
our kin, certainly; but that brings little joy, though some
satisfaction perhaps.' (139–41)

The passage reveals the consonance between 'the absurd' and
'alienation' in a class system which dissociates like from like by the
fictions of differential status. The novel keeps returning us to the
question: which is the real Ethelberta? The answer this passage gives
is 'both'. Her reality is the split personality apparent here in

Ethelberta's emphasis on the family's common humanity ('in our hearts') and her ability simultaneously to use obviously acquired and condescending class language about her brothers (who 'represent the respectable British workman in his entirety') and her sisters ('poor girls').

It is this deeply divided consciousness of Ethelberta's which dominates the novel. As an earlier quotation suggests, she is made up of 'inconsistencies'; she herself says: '"Experimentally, I care to succeed in society; but at the bottom of my heart, I don't care"' (141). The novel enacts the polarity of 'society' and 'heart' – just as the passage above with her brothers shows that, although she may hang on to both terms, they are in fact irreconcilable. On a number of occasions, Ethelberta wishes she could die:

> Often at such conjunctures as these, when the futility of her great undertaking was more than usually manifest, did Ethelberta long like a tired child for the conclusion of the whole matter; when her work should be over, and the evening come; when she might draw her boat upon the shore, and in some thymy nook await eternal night with a placid mind. (218)

This, however, is a 'Comedy in Chapters' in which physical death is not an option. But the desire to pull out of her deception and return to simplicity is insistent:

> 'I wish I could get a living by some simple humble occupation, and drop the name of Petherwin, and be Berta Chickerill again, and live in a green cottage as we used to do when I was small. I am miserable to a pitiable degree sometimes, and sink into regrets that I ever fell into such a groove as this. I don't like covert deeds, such as coming here to-night.' (225)

And again:

> 'I have decided to give up romancing because I cannot think of any more that pleases me. . . . I will never be a governess again: I would rather be a servant. If I am a school-mistress I shall be entirely free from all contact with the great, which is what I desire, for I hate them, and am getting almost as revolutionary as Sol. Father, I cannot endure this kind of existence any longer. I sleep at night as if I had committed a murder: I start up and see processions of people, audiences, battalions of lovers obtained under false pretences – all denouncing me with the finger of ridicule. Mother's suggestion about my marrying I followed out as far as dogged resolution would carry me, but during my journey here I have broken down; for I don't want to marry a second time

192

among people who would regard me as an upstart or intruder. I am sick of ambition. My only longing now is to fly from society altogether, and go to any hovel on earth where I could be at peace.' (293)

What these passages reveal is Ethelberta's destructive consciousness of the falsity of her life (her 'self-killing', in D. H. Lawrence's phrase, see p. 169) and her longing to return to an earlier self, another 'reality' which pre-exists the one that now constitutes her life – one which is theoretically her 'true' self. But what the trajectory of the novel confirms is the delusion of these dreams: she cannot escape the logic of her life. Indeed she marries Lord Mountclere – the ultimate symbol of her incorporation by the fiction of class, and the agency which, while enabling her to fulfil her 'duty' to her family, alienates her most completely from them; so that, by the end, she controls the estate, runs all her family's lives, but has herself disappeared from the novel – except as a distant figure who passes in a coach and is talked about with awe by her sister and erstwhile lover. Ethelberta is what the fiction has made her: a woman with a 'will of iron', severe on the servants, respected by everyone, and writing that 'epic poem' (409). In the course of this process, she is presented as the creature of circumstance: at once the victor and the victim of social class. Her 'character' is susceptible to 'those devious impulses and tangential flights which spoil the work of every would-be schemer who instead of being wholly machine is half heart' (306); and she registers 'that old sense of disloyalty to her class and kin by feeling as she felt now which caused the pain, and there was no escaping it' (179). At the same time, she knows she must cynically continue to construct the fiction of herself, a class image which makes her acceptable to that other class of which she is also a part (185). She is honest with herself about her plight – 'melancholy and mistaken thoughts of herself as a counterfeit had brought her to this' (205); but she is also the dehumanized victim of her own deception: 'She had at this juncture entered upon that Sphinx-like stage of existence in which, contrary to her earlier manner, she signified to no one of her ways, plans, or sensations, and spoke little on any subject at all. There were occasional smiles now which came only from the face, and speeches from the lips merely' (217; note here the suggestion of an automaton in the use of 'the' instead of 'her'). When she does tell the 'truth' about herself, as we have seen, it is taken as a fiction and is curtailed by the cynical realist she marries for convenience, before all has been revealed. Increasingly she sees herself as 'a thing' (251), as 'public property' (280), as 'ready for my role' (297), as so totally alienated from 'herself' that, in one highly significant passage, she thinks of herself as a different woman to the one she thought she was:

> In looking back upon her past as she retired to rest, Ethelberta could almost doubt herself to be the identical woman with her who had entered on a romantic career a few short years ago. For that doubt she had good reason. She had begun as a poet of the Satanic school in a sweetened form; she was ending as a *pseudo-*utilitarian. Was there ever such a transmutation effected before the action of a hard environment? It was not without a qualm of regret that she discerned how the last infirmity of a noble mind had at length nearly departed from her. She wondered if her early notes had had the genuine ring in them, or whether a poet who could be thrust by realities to a distance beyond recognition as such was a true poet at all. Yet Ethelberta's gradient had been regular: emotional poetry, light verse, romance as an object, romance as a means, thoughts of marriage as an aid to her pursuits, a vow to marry for the good of her family; in other words, from soft and playful Romanticism to distorted Benthamism. Was the moral incline upward or down? (297)

We may notice in passing the effects of a 'hard environment' and 'realities' on the career of a 'true poet', and remember Hardy as a similar protagonist in *The Life*. But more to the point here, the passage fractures any conception of 'character' as unitary subject: 'Ethelberta' – within her story and within the novel – is no more than what class and the novel make her: a set of contradictory discourses artificially held together by the 'illusionism' of both these fictions. And is there any more definitive answer to the passage's concluding question, which raises again the relativity of absolutes, than there is to the one the novel continuously poses: which is the 'real' Ethelberta?

At this point, and in conclusion, I return to Robert Gittings and Hardy's 'negative' reason for writing *The Hand of Ethelberta* (see p. 173): that his irritation at the comparisons with George Eliot after *Far From the Madding Crowd* led him to write a novel totally dissimilar to hers. Gittings comments characteristically:

> The novel's part-failure comes from this negative pattern. In it, Hardy cut himself off very largely from the deep, ancestral, archetypal Dorset family past, on which he always drew so successfully. *Far From the Madding Crowd* had been entirely written in the low, large cottage, his birthplace, only a few miles

from all the scenes of the novel. It is full of the fireside influence and folk-memory of Hardy's mother, the most powerful inspiration of his life. To allot such a small space in *Ethelberta* to these essential influences was to maim the story at the outset. Again, to produce a brittle, semi-theatrical novel of ingenuity, in an attempt to be unlike the deep and philosophic texture of George Eliot's novels, once more weakened Hardy by substituting negative reasons for positive.[22]

We see here, at their most explicit, a number of the tendencies I have earlier identified in the production of 'Hardy' as 'great writer': *The Hand of Ethelberta* is 'maim[ed] . . . at the outset' by not deal-ing with the 'essential influences' of the rural life Hardy knew best; Hardy's own phrase from the 1912 General Preface – 'novel of ingenuity' – is used without attribution, thus granting it unproblematical and definitive status; the novel is characterized as 'brittle' and 'semi-theatrical', and is then compared to the 'deep and philosophic texture' of George Eliot's fiction – Hardy's reaction being seen as 'negative'. In effect, George Eliot's humanist realism is being used as a measure of Hardy's work when it is not about Wessex; *Ethelberta*, therefore, is found wanting and can be deemed a 'minor' deviation from the main thrust of the 'great' works – a necessary tactic for a humanist-realist criticism based on liberal-bourgeois conceptions of 'character' and common-sense 'probablism' if its own 'fictions' are not to be exposed and demystified.

On the other hand I do not wish to suggest that Hardy intentionally wrote a novel which challenged George Eliot's fiction at every point; I have merely tried to look 'positively' at *The Hand of Ethelberta*, to read its discourses beyond the limiting perspectives of humanist-realist criticism, and to note how radically, in the event, it challenges the work of, say, George Eliot. Eliot's fiction affirms, even in the late works, the possibility of moral maturation in individual human subjects which contains the seeds of the reform of the social organism as a whole – a world view conveyed by way of 'rounded' and 'consistent' characters who 'live' in the discourses of a 'convincing' and 'truthful' realism. The account given of their lives and of their moral triumphs in the complex web of a class society purports to be authoritative and authentic, and therefore underwrites the belief that human individuals (of 'character') are effective in resisting and reforming the structurally exploitative and unjust mechanisms of a capitalist class society. By parading the fiction of class, and by articulating this in a fiction which foregrounds its own artifice, *Ethelberta* exposes both how destructive of the individual the class system is (alienation equals impotence), and how illusory is the conception of 'character', of the unitary, efficacious human subject, in humanist-realist fiction. At a stroke, as it were, the novel threatens the coterminous notions of 'the individual' and of 'character' which lie at the heart of bourgeois liberal-humanist ideology and its dominant literary form. 'Artificiality' parallels 'alienation', 'fiction' parallels 'class'; and the character 'Ethelberta' is no more than the amalgam of discourses which structure her in the novel. To ask who is the 'real' Ethelberta, or which is the 'true' story of her life (indeed, what is the real 'Hardy'), is to receive the answer: the fictional discourses which determine and represent them – contradictory, discontinuous, fractured, 'unreal'. And if the 'character/individual' is perceived to be no more than this – either in fictional or social terms – then the whole organicist world view of humanist-realism is called to account. But to bring to bear on the novel a critical paradigm derived from such a world view will indeed be to render it a 'failure', a 'joker', an 'improbable' fiction; will be to exorcize its subversive force as a text bitterly inscribed by hostility to the destructive illusions of a class society and the literary ideology which sustains them. Throughout this chapter I have, instead, deployed a different paradigm to show how, in its aggressive fictionality, *The Hand of Ethelberta* can be made to yield its force, while at the same time demonstrating, by extensive quotation, that the determinate discourses of the text permit this strategy. I have not, however, suggested that Hardy intentionally encapsulated these meanings within it – although it is clear that his own contradictory insertion in the class system, displaced in the form of 'Ethelberta', is the matrix in which the novel is *produced*. Rather my point is, as I have been at pains to establish throughout, that *how* the novel is read, and what meanings and effects it renders, is a matter of how it is *reproduced* – of its, and its reader's, ideological location in history and culture. Conventional bourgeois criticism has shut it out; I have reintroduced and remodelled it, if only because the perceptions it permits – of class, gender, and fictional representation – thrust into relief similar issues and practices in those 'major novels' which have been appropriated for the realist-humanist 'Wessex' canon of 'character and environment'. *The Hand of Ethelberta* is a novel deeply marked by the alienating class experience of its author – himself one of the 'metamorphic classes of society' (320) who 'gets a living' (181) by story-telling, torn between the 'delusion of appearances' (281) that status brings and the 'old class where your feelings are' (84); and it is one which registers this tension in its own uneasy fictionality. It is what Christopher Julian, in this most self-conscious novel, calls a 'satire of circumstance' (112; Hardy was later to entitle a volume of his poems *Satires of Circumstance* (1914)). Why should we assume, then, that Hardy's other fiction is any different?

6

Another 'Wessex'; another 'Thomas Hardy'

Literary criticism, as we have seen in Part I, 'writes' the kind of writer it wants, constructs a figure and a landscape which serve its own cultural presuppositions. My readings of *The Life* and *The Hand of Ethelberta* were intended to break the frame in which that critical picture is mounted, and to set up another perceptual frame in which different landscapes can be created – of history, of Hardy's work, *in* Hardy's work. The processes of deconstructing the one and reconstructing the other are, it goes without saying, on behalf of a different cultural ideology – one which, even in this apparently marginal matter of literature and criticism, attempts to foster the consciousness necessary, at all levels of experience, to bring about radical social change. I do not intend, of course, to overbid my hand by constructing 'Hardy' as a closet revolutionary – he wasn't, and the discourses of his writing are determinate enough to make any such enterprise a foolish one. However, the point of my critiography has been to prove that meanings are constructed, with partiality, *on* the text, in the name of an accurate reading of the 'determinate text'. What I want to propose, then, is not that Hardy is 'really a socialist', but that he can just as well be mobilized on socialism's behalf as he can on the naturalized behalf of liberal humanism. The determinate text, as literary criticism itself constantly proves, is determinate only to the extent of what it will permit (Hardy is not about Hinduism?). But the 'text' of Hardy's work, perceived through the frame of *The Life* and *Ethelberta*, is emphatically determinate in its obsession with the alienations of class and gender roles, and with the related illusions of realist art. And so it is by no means any more a false reproduction of Hardy to present him as a subversive writer, and to claim his assistance in attacking false consciousness, than it is to represent him as the 'poet of Wessex'. This final chapter, therefore, sketches in some of the lines with which this 'Thomas Hardy' may be drawn.

First of all, it is quite apparent that 'the true romance of country life', the 'timeless order' of the rural community, the 'real', 'essential', 'old England', so beloved of much Hardy criticism, is historically a pernicious myth. Dorsetshire labourers – Hardy's 'Shakespearean peasants' – lived in appalling poverty throughout the nineteenth century, often earning less than 7s 6d a week (thus making them the worst-paid labourers in England), working extremely long hours and living in small, dirty, tied cottages. Hardy's novels were written during the two 'great depressions' of English agriculture, when there was massive migration from the land in Dorset and when trade-union activity was extensive and relatively successful. Marx describes the process whereby 'the action of capital on landed property' transforms the agricultural economy into one based on 'wage labour' and hence 'clears' the land of its 'excess mouths' (those who do not work for wages and so no longer 'belong' there). And in *Capital* he writes, as it were, the true history of 'Wessex':

> The continual emigration to the towns, the continual formation of surplus-population in the country through the concentration of farms, conversion of arable land into pasture, machinery, etc., and the continual eviction of the agricultural population by the destruction of their cottages, go hand in hand . . . The packing together of knots of men in scattered little villages and small country towns corresponds to the forcible draining of men from the surface of the land. The continuous superseding of the agricultural labourers, in spite of their diminishing number and the increasing mass of their products, gives birth to their pauperism. Their pauperism is ultimately a motive to their eviction and the chief source of their miserable housing which breaks down their last power of resistance, and makes them mere slaves of the landed proprietors and the farmers. Thus the minimum of wages becomes a law of Nature to them.[1]

George Wotton, Merryn Williams, and Raymond Williams have all convincingly indicated what the 'real relations' of nineteenth-century agricultural society were like, and I do not intend to go over the ground again.[2] However, it is still worth asking: to what, then, does Hardy's 'Wessex' allude? Was he writing about the 'universal' themes of Man, Fate, and Nature set in a mythic and elemental rural environment? Was he elegizing the loss of the 'peasant community' beset by Victorian capitalism and industrialism? Or was he, from his own contradictory *déclassé* and *déraciné* position of meritocratic, metropolitan, professional man of letters, refracting the historically determinate process of the transformation of the rural community of which he both was, and was not, a part? As George Wotton points out, 'there is no identity between Wessex and history . . . it is neither a mechanical reflection nor an idealist creation, but a system of reality which is produced out of a combination of elements – the time, place, relations and means of production – involved in the productive process of writing itself'.[3] I have discussed something of the complex contradictions produced by Hardy's class position in relation to both *The Life* and *The Hand of Ethelberta* and will return to them later in this chapter. Here it is merely worth noting that Hardy was certainly sharply conscious of the historical process at work, as his essay 'The Dorsetshire labourer' of 1883 confirms; and in his 1895 Preface to *Far From the Madding Crowd*, that most 'pastoral' and popular of the Wessex novels, he offers what amounts to a gloss on Marx's account above, of the processes of pauperization and emigration, noting 'the recent supplanting of the class of stationary cottagers . . . by a population of more or less migratory labourers'.[4] Indeed, the 'rural idyllist' is remarkably precise in his detailing of the social relations of the agricultural economy. It is worth remembering, for example, that in three of the novels the 'fate' of main characters hinges on dispossession from their homes because of owners' rights on lifehold properties: in Hardy's first 'melodramatic' novel, *Desperate Remedies*, Farmer Springrove's leases on the cottages which burn down revert to the Aldclyffe family because they are not insured;[5] in *The Woodlanders*, Giles Winterbourne loses his house for similar reasons (combined, significantly, with the displeasure of his 'landlord', the *arriviste* 'outsider', Felice Charmond, who 'contemplates pulling the houses down' – 'pulling down is always the game', comment the labourers);[6] and in *Tess*, the last stages of the heroine's destruction are set in motion by the loss of the family home. It is worth reading Hardy's description of this carefully, if only to note how unsentimental and unelegiac – indeed how ironic – the tone is ('till the other word was introduced from without'; 'humorously designated by statisticians'; 'by some means the village had to be kept pure'); how detailed and specific the notation of the process is; and again, how close it is to the Marx passage quoted above:

> At length it was the eve of Old Lady-Day, and the agricultural world was in a fever of mobility such as only occurs at that particular date of the year. It is a day of fulfilment; agreements for outdoor service during the ensuing year, entered into at Candlemas, are to be now carried out. The labourers – or 'workfolk', as they used to call themselves immemorially till the other word was introduced from without – who wish to remain no

longer in old places are removing to the new farms.

These annual migrations from farm to farm were on the increase here. When Tess's mother was a child the majority of the field-folk about Marlott had remained all their lives on one farm, which had been the home also of their fathers and grandfathers; but latterly the desire for yearly removal had risen to a high pitch. With the younger families it was a pleasant excitement which might possibly be an advantage. The Egypt of one family was the Land of Promise to the family who saw it from a distance, till by residence there it became in turn their Egypt also; and so they changed and changed.

However, all the mutations so increasingly discernible in village life did not originate entirely in the agricultural unrest. A depopulation was also going on. The village had formerly contained, side by side with the agricultural labourers, an interesting and better-informed class, ranking distinctly above the former – the class to which Tess's father and mother had belonged – and including the carpenter, the smith, the shoe-maker, the huckster, together with nondescript workers other than farm-labourers; a set of people who owed a certain stability of aim and conduct to the fact of their being life-holders like Tess's father, or copyholders, or, occasionally, small freeholders. But as the long holdings fell in they were seldom again let to similar tenants, and were mostly pulled down, if not absolutely required by the farmer for his hands. Cottagers who were not directly employed on the land were looked upon with disfavour, and the banishment of some starved the trade of others, who were thus obliged to follow. These families, who had formed the backbone of the village life in the past, who were the depositaries of the village traditions, had to seek refuge in the large centres; the process, humorously designated by statisticians as 'the tendency of the rural population towards the large towns,' being really the tendency of water to flow uphill when forced by machinery. The cottage accommodation at Marlott having been in this manner considerably curtailed by demolitions, every house which remained standing was required by the agriculturist for his work-people. Ever since the occurrence of the event which had cast such a shadow over Tess's life, the Durbeyfield family (whose descent was not credited) had been tacitly looked on as one which would have to go when their lease ended, if only in the interests of morality. It was, indeed, quite true that the household had not been shining examples either of temperance, soberness, or chastity. The father, and even the mother, had got drunk at times, the younger children seldom had gone to church, and the eldest daughter had made queer unions. By some means the village had to be kept pure. So on this, the first Lady-Day on which the Durbeyfields were expellable, the house, being roomy, was required for a carter with a large family; and Widow Joan, her daughters Tess and 'Liza-Lu, the boy Abraham and the younger children, had to go elsewhere.[7]

Furthermore, 'Wessex', it is easy to forget, contains a great deal of hard labour: 'comical' the rustics of *The Return of the Native* may be, but furze-cutting is clearly not funny; nor is the experience of turnip-grubbing for the women ('female field-labour was seldom offered now, and its cheapness made it profitable for tasks which women could perform as readily as men') at Flintcombe Ash in *Tess*, where 'the rain . . . raced along horizontally upon the yelling wind, sticking into them like glass splinters till they were wet through'; nor again mechanical labour on the steam threshing-machine, whose engineer 'was in the agricultural world, but not of it';[8] nor that of Marty South in *The Woodlanders* making spars at 'eighteenpence a thousand' (she can make 2s 3d for a day and half a night's work);[9] nor that of the 11-year-old Jude who (like Joseph Arch, the Agricultural Labourers Union leader) scares birds for 6d a day. Equally, the bucolic landscape of Wessex also contains Mixen Lane, the slum district of *The Mayor of Casterbridge*, where amongst 'much that was sad, much that was low, some things that were baneful . . . much that was bad, needy respectability also found a home':

> Under some of the roofs abode pure and virtuous souls whose presence there was due to the iron hand of necessity, and to that alone. Families from decayed villages – families of that once bulky, but now nearly extinct, section of village society called 'liviers', or lifeholders – copyholders and others, whose roof-trees had fallen for some reason or other, compelling them to quit the rural spot that had been their home for generations – came here, unless they chose to lie under a hedge by the wayside.[10]

This is, of course, the 'packing together of knots of men in . . . small country towns' of the quotation from *Capital* once more. 'Wessex' also means the hamlet of Marygreen, where the rootless Jude is brought up and where

> many of the thatched and dormered dwelling-houses [have] been pulled down of late years, and many trees felled on the green. Above all, the original church, hump-backed, wood-turreted, and quaintly hipped, had been taken down, and either cracked up into heaps of road-metal in the lane, or utilized as pig-sty walls,

garden seats, guard-stones to fences, and rockeries in the flower-beds of the neighbourhood. In place of it a tall new building of modern Gothic design, unfamiliar to English eyes, has been erected on a new piece of ground by a certain obliterator of historic records who had run down from London and back in a day. The site whereon so long had stood the ancient temple to the Christian divinities was not even recorded on the green and level grass-plot that had immemorially been the churchyard, the obliterated graves being commemorated by the eighteenpenny cast-iron crosses warranted to last five years.[11]

There are also the various urban settings in *Jude* – most especially the poor end of Christminster and the tiny lodging-house room in the shadow of Sarcophagus College where Little Father Time kills himself and the other children. There is 'The Slopes', the Stoke d'Urberville house in *Tess*, red-brick and brand new where 'everything looked like money', built in 'one of the few remaining woodlands in England of undoubted primaeval date' by *nouveau-riche* Northern money, and presented as a pernicious influence on its neighbouring village, Trantridge, which, amongst other vices, drinks heavily 'the curious components sold to them as beer by the monopolizers of the once independent inns'.[12] And there is Farn-field Park in *The Hand of Ethelberta*, family estate of the London man-about-town, Neigh, but again the property of an *arriviste* entrepreneur:

Ethelberta could not resist being charmed with the repose of the spot, and hastened on with curiosity to reach the other side of the pool, where, by every law of manorial topography, the mansion would be situate . . .

But where should have been the front door of the mansion was simply a rough rail fence, about four feet high. They drew near and looked over.

In the enclosure, and on the site of the imaginary house, was an extraordinary group. It consisted of numerous horses in the last stage of decrepitude, the animals being such mere skeletons that at first Ethelberta hardly recognized them to be horses at all. . . . These poor creatures were endeavouring to make a meal from herbage so trodden and thin that scarcely a wholesome blade remained; the little that there was consisted of the sourer sorts common on such sandy soils, mingled with tufts of heather and sprouting ferns . . .

Adjoining this enclosure was another and smaller one, formed of high boarding, within which appeared to be some sheds and out-houses. Ethelberta looked through the crevices, and saw that

in the midst of the yard stood trunks of trees as if they were
growing, with branches also extending, but these were sawn off at
the points where they began to be flexible, no twigs or boughs
remaining. Each torso was not unlike a huge hat-stand, and
suspended to the pegs and prongs were lumps of some substance
which at first she did not recognize; they proved to be a
chronological sequel to the previous scene. Horses' skulls, ribs,
quarters, legs, and other joints were hung thereon, the whole
forming a huge open-air larder emitting not too sweet a smell . . .

'We are close to a kennel of hounds,' said Ethelberta, as
Picotee held tightly to her arm . . . 'These poor horses are
waiting to be killed for their food.' . . .

The experience altogether, from its intense melancholy, was
very depressing, almost appalling to the two lone young women,
and they quickly retraced their footsteps. The pleasant lake, the
purl of the weir, the rudimentary lawns, shrubberies, and avenue,
had changed their character quite . . .

'The man owning that is one of the name of Neigh,' said the
native; wiping his face. ' 'Tis a family that have made a very large
fortune by the knacker business and tanning, though they be only
sleeping partners in it now, and live like lords. Mr. Neigh was
going to pull down the old huts here, and improve the place and
build a mansion – in short, he went so far as to have the grounds
planted, and the roads marked out, and the fish-pond made, and
the place christened Farnfield Park; but he did no more . . . He's a
terrible hater of women, I hear, particularly the lower class.'[13]

What is particularly striking here is the juxtapositioning of the crude
reality with 'pastoral' expectations of the country house (note the
opening sentence, for example, and later the 'picturesque' language:
'the pleasant lake, the purl of the weir').

I adduce these elements of an other than 'pastoral' Wessex not to
claim that Hardy is, indeed, a 'social realist', but to indicate, first,
that if one shifts the frame it is fairly easy to produce from the
'determinate text' a writer who is historically specific, not a rural
idyllist, and very precise in his sociological detail. Second, and
related to the last point, the common factor in all these instances is
a sharp awareness of the practice and effects of entrepreneurial
capitalism as the informing structure of economic and social relations. Again, I do not wish to suggest that the 'socialistic' young
Hardy of *The Poor Man and the Lady* lurks behind all the novels,
but it is equally partial not to perceive that in all of his 'social
history' the eye is firmly on exploitation and dispossession as the
reflex of the economic (and related, legal) system. Perhaps the

fiercest and most symbolic formulations of this are in *The Woodlanders* when Marty South sells her hair, in order to ease the crushing labour of spar-cutting, to adorn the property-owning and indolent *arriviste*, Felice Charmond; and Grammer Oliver sells her head for ten pounds to the scientific dilettante, Dr Fitzpiers, who wishes to dissect it after her death;[14] in this world, it appears, anything is a commodity. I merely draw attention, here, to the specific cast of Hardy's perception of social relations in all these cases, a cast of mind perhaps not unrelated to his experiencing of the commodification and exploitation of writing in the London literary market.

But it is certainly a cast of mind aligned with another insistent element in Hardy's fiction, and one again brought strongly into relief by the frame-changing effect of taking *The Hand of Ethelberta* seriously: the treatment of social class. As I pointed out earlier (see p. 130), Merryn and Raymond Williams have shown Hardy's class of origin to be that most threatened and unstable 'intermediate' class of dispossessed rural artisans and small business people, while failing to consider the more complex and contradictory position Hardy finds himself in by way of his career as a professional literary man. I am not so much concerned here, therefore, with the representation of people from the rural 'intermediate' class in his fiction, but more with how his novels are imbued with an obsessive class consciousness – and especially with the minutiae of class distinctions and with the problems of relationship between those who are *déclassé*. This will then lead me to look, in a little more detail and in relation to the gender politics of Hardy's novels, at the women characters whose upward social mobility or ambiguous class position is central to them. The 'poor man and the lady' theme is indeed at the heart of all Hardy's fiction, although its inflexions are diverse and in no way constrained by the specific gender orientation of the title of that first novel.

One of the most striking aspects of the novels, when one begins to look at them in this way, is that without exception they hinge on class relations, on individuals' uncertainties as to what class or class fraction they belong to, or on the problems of a radical shift in class position. Whatever else Hardy may have had in mind, their basic structural and textural crux was not so much 'Wessex' and the agricultural community, but the problematical relations of a class society in rapid change. This is immediately and obviously apparent in the early novel, *A Pair of Blue Eyes*. From the opening paragraph, which emphasizes the importance of understanding 'the circumstances of her history',[15] of the heroine Elfride, the narrative foregrounds the nuances of class distinction. There is the early comic story of Lord Luxellian's forebears being 'hedgers and ditchers by rights' (44–5) – a clear sounding-note of the arbitrariness of class position – followed by the Revd Swancourt's snobbish belief that Stephen Smith is one of the 'Fitzmaurice Smiths', 'a well-known ancient county family': 'Mr. Smith, I congratulate you on your blood; blue blood, sir; and, upon my life, a very desirable colour, as the world goes' (52). (The theme of a spurious 'heredity' and its destructive tendencies will re-emerge with *Tess* and with Fitzpiers in *The Woodlanders*, and the old Hardy will much later reveal his obsession with his own family's decline in *The Life* (see p. 143).) Stephen Smith himself is always sharply conscious of his problematical class status: he can't play chess, mispronounces his Latin, and cannot ride (83–4, 87–8); and when he 'confesses' his true background to Elfride, he is absolutely precise: he went to 'a dame school originally, then to a national school', his father is 'a cottager and a working master-mason', his mother's people 'had been well-to-do yeomen for centuries, but she was only a dairy-woman, having been left an orphan' (104–5). Having learnt that Stephen's family work for Lord Luxellian, Elfride is equally exact, remembering that she had not been able to think of marrying a 'large farmer' because he 'was not good enough' (109). Lord Luxellian himself is described as resembling 'a good-natured commercial traveller of the superior class' (170 – note the punctilious specificity of the description), and the snobbish 'new' Mrs Swancourt instructs Elfride not to use the word 'gentleman' any more: '"We have handed over 'gentleman' to the lower middle class, where the word is still to be heard at tradesmen's balls and provincial tea-parties, I believe. It is done with here"' (170). And so it goes on, both in terms of the characters' perceptions of their class relations, and of the narrative voice's own continual and scrupulous commentary on them. But it is also worth noting that one of the central characters in the triangle, Knight, a London literary man who has several characteristics of the young Hardy, nevertheless assumes a condescending manner to his protégé Stephen: 'to the essayist, Smith was still the country lad whom he had patronized and tended' (285). It is as though in Smith, the aspiring architect, and in Knight, the cosmopolitan 'man of letters' – both of whom love Elfride (herself a tyro writer of 'romances') – Hardy has produced a split version of himself on either side of the class divide over which he was currently straddled. Significantly, perhaps, the object of 'their' love in the end marries Lord Luxellian and dies from a wasting illness and miscarriage. Elfride does not have the force of Ethelberta, the successful 'romancer' and 'illusionist', and is sacrificed on the deadly altar of class propriety. Smith and Knight can do no more than observe the failure of their hopes, and only Hardy, that other 'professed romancer', can rescue anything from the destructive fictions of class distinction: a fiction which is itself hag-ridden with the punctilios of a class complex.

It is a consciousness, I am insisting, which is the matrix for all of Hardy's ironic 'tragedies of modern life'. If his characters are indeed 'victims', they are victims of a class society which arbitrarily discriminates human beings by the artifice of social status: a system which claims to be centrally concerned with the individual human subject, but which operates, behind its ideological screen of humanism, precisely to destroy individual aspiration by way of social mechanisms that dispossess people through the fiction of superiority/ inferiority. I have already drawn attention to the phrase at the beginning of *A Pair of Blue Eyes* about 'the circumstances of [Elfride's] history'. 'Circumstance/circumstances' are crucial Hardyan terms ('Satires of Circumstance', for example); but those words, in English, do not merely suggest the determinate conditions in which a person is situated – they also have, significantly, an inflexion of class position (as in 'of some circumstance', 'in straitened/reduced circumstances'). It is with this undertone, I think, that the words function in Hardy's fiction; and it is therefore no surprise to find that, throughout the novels, 'the circumstances of [a character's] history' are exactly and scrupulously drawn in terms of their class insertion, both as a way of defining their 'character' and as the spring for the character's trajectory in the action of the book.

Examples from each of Hardy's novels will confirm this. In *Desperate Remedies*, he is at great pains in the early chapters to 'place' Cytherea and Owen Graye precisely as ' "like those of other people similarly circumstanced" ',[16] in other words, of good professional background (reinforced by mother's money) but impoverished by their imprudent architect father's death, and much of the novel's plot hinges on their relations with the lady-squire, Miss Aldclyffe. Fancy Day, in *Under the Greenwood Tree*, is very exactly located as the daughter of a superior rural worker (of the 'intermediate' class): 'head gamekeeper, timber steward, and general over-looker for this district' on the Earl of Wessex's estates. However, she has been 'in training' and is now the new village schoolmistress[17] – she is, in other words, part of that process of upward social mobility for many lower-class women in the second half of the nineteenth century which followed the development of teacher training for primary education.[18] And this elevation is the cause of her (comically) problematical relations with her suitors (tranter's son and clergyman). Much the same is true, too, of Bathsheba Everdene in

Far From the Madding Crowd, significantly 'an excellent scholar [who] was going to be a governess once', whose father was 'a gentleman-tailor really' ('of a higher circle of life', 'worth scores of pounds', and 'a very celebrated bankrupt') but who inherits her uncle's farm.[19] Again, the novel's action centres on the 'elevated' heroine's relations with a social spectrum of males: shepherd, soldier, gentleman-farmer.

Paula Power, in *A Laodicean*, who is the daughter of 'the great railway contractor', an MP, and 'a great Nonconformist', inherits an 'ancient' estate which her father had bought and is now the owner of the castle and property of the displaced old aristocrats, the de Stancys.[20] She is thus part of the same entrepreneurial class that produces the *arrivistes* Alec d'Urberville, Alfred Neigh, and Felice Charmond, and she too has tense socio-sexual relations with her suitors (an architect and a de Stancy scion). *The Return of the Native* is even more scrupulously specific in the social location of its main characters – as in the case of Mrs Yeobright, the aspiring mother of Clym: 'though her husband had been a small farmer she herself was a curate's daughter, who had once dreamt of doing better things'; Clym, of course, is well educated ('he went to school early'), has become 'manager to a diamond merchant' in Paris, and has returned, disillusioned with business, to 'keep a school' on Egdon; Wildeve has been an engineer 'in an office in Budmouth', but now keeps The Quiet Woman inn on the heath – 'a clever, learned fellow in his way . . . brought up to better things'; and Eustacia, whose 'native place' was the fashionable seaside resort of Budmouth, is 'the daughter of the bandmaster of a regiment which had been quartered there – a Corfiote by birth' and of an old sea-captain's daughter (the captain himself being 'a man of good family' with 'a cousin in the peerage').[21]

Anne Garland, in *The Trumpet-Major*, is the reduced genteel daughter of 'a landscape painter's widow' – 'two ladies of good report, though unfortunately of limited means', and the Lovedays are 'an ancient family of corn-grinders' who had 'formed matrimonial alliances with farmers not so very small, and once with a gentleman-farmer' (note again the specificity of Hardy's definition), but who were derived from 'the rank known as ceorls or villeins, full of importance to the country at large, and ramifying throughout the unwritten history of England'.[22] Both the sons, however, who are in love with Anne, are very much of the 'intermediate' class. In *Two on a Tower*, Viviette, Lady Constantine, is the wife of Sir Blount Constantine of ancient family, the only true 'lady' in all of Hardy's fiction; and in the strange class pastoral of this overtly 'poor man and the lady' novel, she falls in love with Swithin St Cleeve, the son of an 'erratic' curate and a farmer's daughter, well educated and with a small independent income. Perhaps it is significant, too, that Viviette, who has offended all the proprieties of the class and gender system (she rejects the advances of a bishop for Swithin), should fade and die at the end (like Elfride) – the last sentence of the novel being: 'The Bishop was avenged.'[23] Lucetta Templeman, in *The Mayor of Casterbridge*, is also 'of good family, well bred and well educated' – 'the daughter of some harum-scarum military officer who had got into difficulties'; she has dropped into genteel poverty but then inherits a sizeable fortune from a relative in Bristol which enables her to take High-Place Hall in Casterbridge; Henchard, of course, is originally a hay-trusser, whose work, the novel is careful to insist, however, was that 'of the skilled countryman' as distinct from that of 'the general labourer'; and Farfrae, a Scottish 'new man' on his way to the New World, has 'some inventions useful to the [corn] trade'[24] (in other words, like Wildeve, trained as an engineer).

In *The Woodlanders*, class tensions are central to the movement of the novel, and its precision in locating the characters is uncompromising. Mr Melbury is 'the chief man of business hereabout . . . the timber, bark and copse-ware merchant'; he is 'of the sort called self-made, and had worked hard'; he sends his daughter away to boarding-school 'at the figure of near a hundred a year', to assuage the shame of his own lack of education; and he is acutely conscious of her elevated position as a result: 'your sphere ought not to be middling.' Grace herself becomes, at one level, no more than an investment – 'You'll yield a better return' – and in the process she is displaced from the communities to which she could theoretically belong. Mrs Charmond is the young widow of a 'rich man engaged in the iron trade in the north' whose fortune had bought Hintock House and the surrounding woodlands (cf. Paula Power and Alec d'Urberville). Her mother had known that ' "my face was my only fortune" '; she had been 'a play-actress for a short while' on Mr Charmond's money; but she is now the landlord of most of the inhabitants of the area. And Fitzpiers, 'so modern a man in science and aesthetics', is the last scion of an old family: ' "Mr. Fitzpiers's family were lords of the manor for I don't know how many hundred years. . . . Why, on the mother's side he's connected with the long line of the Lords Baxby of Sherton." '[25]

Tess, of course, is also the last flowering of a noble old family who are now hagglers and whose name has been bought by the Stoke d'Urbervilles with money made 'in the North' by old Mr Simon Stoke, 'an honest merchant (some said money lender)'. Alec, therefore, is a second-generation *arriviste* 'gentleman'. Tess herself is both of, and not of, her community: she 'had passed the Sixth Standard in the National School under a London-trained mistress [and] spoke two languages', and she 'had held a leading place' in the village school, but as soon as she left she lent 'a hand at haymaking or harvesting on neighbouring farms; or, by preference, at milking or butter-making processes'. Angel Clare, the third son of an old evangelical clergyman, becomes a 'free-thinker' who decides not to go to Cambridge and take orders, but trains to become a farmer 'in the Colonies, America, or at home' in order to protect his 'intellectual liberty'.[26] In *Jude the Obscure* the class location is equally exact: Jude, an orphan living with his aunt, is 'crazy for books', but has to scare birds for a farmer, assist his aunt in the bakery and then learn the trade of stonemason, all the while dreaming of going to the university at Christminster; Sue is the daughter of 'an ecclesiastical worker in metal', who passes the Queen's Scholarship examination to enter the teacher-training school at Melchester in order to become (like Fancy Day) a schoolmistress, but who is also a religious free thinker; and Arabella is the daughter of a pig-breeder who emigrates to Australia and then moves into the licensing trade.[27] Finally, there is Jocelyn Pierston in *The Well-Beloved* who is the son of 'an inartistic man of trade and commerce', but himself a 'sculptor of budding fame'. The three generations of Avices with whom he falls in love are, however, from much less prosperous stock of 'quarrying' freehold cottagers – although the third Avice is herself refined, educated, and thence also upwardly socially mobile: she elopes with the son of a 'Jersey gentleman' who 'teaches French'.[28]

What is apparent from this list – aside from the punctilious detailing of class co-ordinates – is that the vast majority of Hardy's main characters are in an unstable class position and that the plots of the novels crucially depend on the uneven relations between such people. Either they are in 'reduced circumstances' through unforeseen impoverishment or the financial/legal activities of others; or they are 'elevated' by inheritance or the graft of their parents; or they are out of place in their present social milieu; or they are educated to a point at which they are ill at ease in the circumstances where they 'belong'. Invariably they come into contact with others who have one or more of the same displacements, and, conversely, with those who are more stably situated in their class position. What Hardy's acutely attuned class consciousness registers are the tensions and social disasters attendant on the interaction of these 'metamorphic classes of society'. For example, it is perhaps not too obvious to suggest that *The Return of the Native* is not so much a playing-out of human tragedy against the cosmic presence of elemental nature, but a complex sociological narrative in which too many 'displaced' persons come into contact with each other in an alien environment. The *petit-bourgeois*, proto-cosmopolitan Eustacia is so athwart the culture of a lumpen (not idyllic) rural community that any hope of release by way of others who also do not 'belong' attracts her. In this respect, Wildeve, himself alienated and *déraciné*, is more significant than Clym; for he fuels Eustacia's frustration by his very presence, whereas Clym merely presents her with a fortuitous and more romantic opportunity. However, Clym's education – fired by his mother's social aspirations – effectively disables him for any of his possible *loci* (cf. Grace Melbury): he can neither function happily in the metropolitan society where he is successful (and which Eustacia aspires to), nor can he fulfil his idealist dream of once more becoming 'a native' while 'teaching' his fellow natives. Furthermore, he cannot have a satisfactory marriage with Eustacia because, although they are 'drawn' to each other (as are Eustacia and Wildeve) by their common 'metamorphic' nature, they are at entirely different stations in their class dislocation. Clym could perhaps only resolve the impossible contradictions of his class position by becoming – like Hardy – a novelist, whose fiction is, none the less, traversed by them.

Again, we can see in *The Woodlanders* that the intersection of problematical class relations lies at its centre. George Melbury is doing well as a self-made businessman; his way of proving this – to himself as much as to others – is to educate Grace to a level where she can no longer comfortably be a 'native', cannot regard Giles Winterbourne socially as marriage partner, is not a part of the 'society' which her fellow pupils at the boarding-school inhabit, and cannot relate to the 'sophisticated' parasitic world of Felice Charmond or Fitzpiers. Her trance-like state throughout the novel, and her passivity in the face of all the social exploitation she is subject to (cf. Tess), are the product of the impasse of class relations she experiences in her displacement. Giles, too, is blocked and immobilized by the disintegration of his social and economic *locus*; his skills are fast becoming redundant, his business does not have the entrepreneurial clout of Melbury's, and he is susceptible to the depredations of a different kind of economic organization – the capital-backed proprietorship of an 'inorganic' landlord. Mrs Charmond, while no more a part of the Hintock community than Wildeve or Eustacia were of Egdon, is more disruptive because she has financial and legal power too. That she uses it irresponsibly, however, is not so much a criticism of her personally, as it is a reflex of her own social dislocation: poor-genteel society girl become wealthy heiress and owner of a rural community. Like Eustacia, any release from her displacement is welcome, and Fitzpiers, whom she 'recognizes' as of her world, represents this. The fact that their affair is presented in such stagey and artificial terms (a point I will return to later) signals its fortuitousness: that they, too, albeit again at different points on the 'metamorphic' scale, are destructively drawn to each other only by dint of their common deracination. Fitzpiers's attraction for George Melbury, on the other hand, is his (worthless) family lineage; for Grace, significantly, it is the sense she (wrongly) has that he is her kind because he too is not a 'native', and he is educated and sophisticated (notice how dangerously slippery is a unitary notion of 'sophistication' for the 'metamorphic classes'). Sophisticated he certainly is – abstract, 'intellectual', dilettantish – but he is also short of money: there is a pointed, but easily overlooked, moment when he mentions that it is with the help of Mr Melbury's money that he is to set up a medical practice in Budmouth.[29] Fitzpiers is just as dispossessed as Giles, but in a very different inflexion. My point simply is that *The Woodlanders* sets up a complex and finely-tuned scenario in which the tensions and potential destructions of social mobility in a class society can be observed. What is of interest is less the personal 'tragedy' of the individuals involved, and rather the revelation of the inimical social relations consequent on the conjuncture of people differentially located in the factitious hierarchies of a class system.

Finally, in this context, we may read *Tess of the d'Urbervilles*, Hardy's most admired tragedy, in the same terms. It is, after all, Tess's difference, not her representativeness (as 'country maiden'), which attracts her to both Alec and Angel – the two other displaced people in the novel. She combines great physical beauty with a consciousness which is embryonically the same as theirs: one which simply does not know what its 'place' is. Her trance-like passivity throughout much of the action of the novel is, like Grace Melbury's, a product of this, and it draws her towards those with whom she seems to have an affinity. Certainly she is 'victimized' at once by the past (her 'heredity') and by the present (Alec's irresponsible economic power and Angel's intellectual dishonesty), but to simply blame the past and the present as external instruments in Tess's destruction is to fail to see that the business of the Durbeyfields' relationship to the noble old d'Urbervilles is symptomatic of the pernicious arbitrariness of class position (compare the Luxellians in *A Pair of Blue Eyes*), and that Alec and Angel's behaviour to her is itself more an aspect of the 'ache of modernism' than merely reprehensibly 'modern' social abuse. For at the centre of this 'ache' is the historically-determined consciousness of not knowing what one is – in terms of social place, function, and identity – and Tess is as disabled by this as she is by the exploitation of external social predators such as Alec and Angel are usually regarded as being. But they too, socially adrift and displaced from a class community (inherited new wealth, immature 'free-thinking'), are equally alienated consciousnesses (hence Alec's 'improbable' conversion to preaching and Angel's schizoid changes of mind about Tess). This is not to deny that they are personally blameworthy, nor that they have power (economic, sexual, intellectual) which Tess does not, nor that they are determined by these male power discourses, nor that 'symbolically' they represent precisely those social forces as destroying Tess; it is merely to bring into view class displacement as a crucial determinant in forming individuals so that they act in the way they do. For Hardy's deeply alienated class consciousness 'perceives' individual social interpellation as more complex, more determinate, than do notions of instrumental or mechanistic social action. Tess, Alec, and Angel are so formed by 'circumstance', especially of class location, that – in proximity to each other in an 'alien' environment – they *must* interact in the way they do. Men like Angel and Alec *will* turn women like Tess into fetishistic objects (or 'images') of their own fantasies, and women like Tess – between two worlds – will both become and not become those object-images. How can she then, in the ontological or essentialist sense, be 'a pure woman', and also, what exactly is the novel's 'stance' on her fate?

My final general point here, then, is to try and resolve the recurrent critical 'problem' implied by that last question: whose side is Hardy on? Does he like or dislike Eustacia Vye and Clym Yeobright? Is he really hostile to Fitzpiers and Mrs Charmond, to Alec and Angel? Why are Giles and Grace and Tess made to do nothing to help themselves? Was Tess raped or complicit in her seduction? In what sense is she 'a pure woman'? Are the tragic protagonists mere victims, or in part responsible for their own fate? Is Hardy really against the 'modern world', his novels an elegy to the destruction of the organic community? Does he believe in the 'President of the Immortals'? All these questions are reflexes of a humanist-realist critical perspective unhappy with the disconcertingly ambivalent stance of the novels, but they all seem to me beside the point. I do not for a moment wish to suggest that Hardy was 'neutral' – a disinterested, and therefore 'realistic', observer of social process; I want to say, rather, that there is no blame of individuals. Characters are ideologically and socially determined, 'circumstanced' by the subject-positions they occupy; struggle and aspire they may, but they do not control their own destiny, can neither free nor fulfil themselves. What controls them, weak or powerful, in this reading, is a class system which reproduces the dynamics of social and economic power in an 'absurd', arbitrary, and divisive way. This bitterly deterministic view of the individual is, I think, the 'gloom' and 'pessimism', the anti-humanism – mystified as metaphysics – which has so harried criticism; and it is this too, as we shall see, that results in an anti-realism itself recalcitrant to orthodox literary ideology. Nevertheless, it would be quite wrong to imply that Hardy transcends this social despair in his fiction, that somewhere lurking in his secret consciousness was a socialist dream, a recognition that collective action would destroy the hegemony of bourgeois class society. On the contrary, Hardy is himself a product of that growing crisis within liberal humanism which shortly afterwards was to produce in modernism some of the twentieth century's most admired monuments to cultural pessimism. Indeed, it is this which has made him, I believe, at once so suscept-ible to recuperation as a proto-modernist ('Hardy to Lawrence'), and so popular now in a society whose *mentalité* is imbued with cultural despair. But I wish now – as another way of 'explaining' Hardy's simultaneously radical perception of class relations and his inability to break through the social despair it engendered – to look at the sexual politics of his fiction.

As we have seen in Part I (see pp. 41–3), Hardy from the start has been regarded as a novelist who excels in creating powerful 'women characters' and, more recently, as a kind of proto-male-feminist. My intention here is to relate this gender consciousness – especially of the nature and social place of women – to his obsessive concern with class and to the contradictions which seem to traverse all his fiction. It has often been observed that the mainspring of Hardy's tragedy is a sexual relationship between people of different social class – 'the poor man and the lady' theme once more. Now it should already be clear, first, that the cross-class relationships are not always that simple: Eustacia Vye, for example, is no more a 'lady' than Clym and Wildeve are 'gentlemen', nor is Sue in relation to Jude, and *Tess* is more about 'the poor woman and the gentlemen' than vice versa. But second, and more importantly, it is apparent from my list above of characters from the 'metamorphic' classes that many of those displaced are, in fact, women, and that most of the 'ladies' are ones who have been artificially elevated by education, marriage, or inheritance. In other words, it is not so much that these female characters actually are 'ladies', but that they are upwardly socially mobile – either in terms of self-perception and aspiration, or of finding themselves wealthy, or of unlooked-for, *de facto* relocation through education. What Hardy seems to focus on, within his 'metamorphic' classes, is a dynamically 'rising' group which is principally female. Sometimes this is associated with intellectual 'emancipation' (Ethelberta, Paula Power, Sue Bridehead, even Tess), sometimes with simple social location (Fancy Day, Eustacia, Grace Melbury), more often it is to do with the 'freedom' and 'power' of status and wealth (Bathsheba, Miss Aldclyffe, Mrs Charmond, Paula again, Lucetta). But whichever way it is presented or perceived, the sense is of women as a dynamically emergent social group. A reflex of this is the often noted 'weakness' of the male protagonists – Stephen Smith and Knight, Christopher Graye, Christopher Julian, Clym, Giles, and Angel, for example. They, too, are part of the unstable class fraction that Hardy pin-points, but they do not seem to have the potential energy of the rising female group. At the heart, in other words, of Hardy's displaced class are women with greater potential for upward social mobility than men – or, to put it another way, for emancipation from the constraints of a disabling class society predicated on patriarchy.

There are various ways of reading this in relation to the fiction. We could see Hardy, crudely, as critics have done, as in the long line of (male) tragedians for whom women are *'fatale'*, bringing men low in their susceptibility to female charms. We could, conversely, see a group of 'noble' female characters whose tragedy it is to love not wisely but too well. We could, more sociologically, see the crux of Hardy's 'tragedy' in the impossibility of successful sexual relationships which cross class boundaries; or, in terms of my analysis above, in the relations of a group profoundly displaced and unstable in their class location, but where the most dynamically unstable sub-group is female. We could present Hardy's fiction, as feminist critics have done, as displaying the double morality of a patriarchal society and its suppression of women and their aspirations: 'The woman pays', as the title of 'Phase the fifth' in *Tess* puts it; or we could refine that to suggest, with Patricia Stubbs, that Hardy, while in tune with contemporary Victorian feminist thinking, is nevertheless constrained by his own imprisonment within male literary stereotypes of women. What I think is quite certain is that the 'determinate text' of Hardy's fiction permits a Hardy to be reproduced who is emphatically concerned with the gender/class issue, who 'reveals' the injustices of a patriarchal class society, and who sees at the core of the problematical class/sexual relations of his displaced group the rising dynamic of women as the most potentially destabilizing force. And in no necessarily negative sense, either: for the artificial constructions of a gender-biased class society are seen to oppress women more destructively than men – *vide* Elfride, Grace, Eustacia, Tess, Viviette – even Lucetta and Felice Charmond. The frustrated upward and emancipating drive of Hardy's 'heroines' can, then, be deployed in criticism and in teaching to lay bare the mechanisms by which the fiction of gender/class 'difference' operates at the ideological heart of liberal-bourgeois society. And this is a 'Hardy' I would like to see more of.

However, in so far as it does not engage with one insistent feature of the novels, it leaves one problem intact: in the end, the women do indeed 'pay'. The novels are not, of course, nor could they be, unproblematically 'feminist', and I mention again Patricia Stubbs's sense of Hardy's 'contradictoriness': his consciousness of gender injustice and yet his residual patriarchalism (see p. 43). There may be every possibility, as I have indicated, for a modern critic to strategically reproduce a 'feminist Hardy', but it would be historically suspect, if nothing else, to hypothesize a male author in the second half of the nineteenth century as having a conscious and coherent feminist philosophy in view. As Stubbs says, Hardy 'shared in a culture which, though changing under pressure from an increasingly articulate women's movement, was still essentially patriarchal, so that its available images and forms were likely to be able to accommodate only an attenuated version of what women themselves were feeling and thinking'.[30] Hardy, after all, was shaped by his cultural location, even if he was in conflict with it. But Stubbs's suggestion that Hardy's women are limited by his inability to liberate himself from the forms and literary 'types' of conventional usage, still fails to consider both the narrative trajectory of his fiction and Hardy's *class* consciousness in relation to the gender issue. For one thing is obvious about most of the novels: the women, and especially the 'rising' ones, are destroyed or constrained at the end. There are some exceptions: Cytherea Graye gets man and money; Fancy Day marries happily – although the ending is ironic; so too does Bathsheba the second time around; Paula Power remains wealthy and is engaged to the 'middling' George Somerset, although the final words of the novel are 'But I wish you were a de Stancy'; Thomasin marries the reddleman – but only in one version of the two endings; and Ethelberta, as we have seen, triumphs over all, but at some cost (I shall return to Ethelberta). Otherwise, the 'heroines' are dead or trapped in unwanted marriages (as Grace and Sue). Now it is perfectly possible to contend that it is 'society' which is responsible for this thwarting and destroying, and that Hardy, as a clear-sighted critic of the system, merely reflects reality in their fates. But this is to indulge the reflectionist fallacy of realism; to forget that it is the narrative discourse of Hardy's fiction – not 'life' – which brings about these 'fates', that it is the dominant trajectory of plot and structure which negates female aspiration, which prohibits these rising women from fulfilling themselves. Certainly, it may seem that the logic of the world in which Tess lives means that she must be destroyed; that Eustacia cannot survive because there is no place for her; that Grace cannot escape her marriage to Fitzpiers. But there is no necessary logic to these resolutions – except in so far as the text itself 'writes' the logic – just as there isn't in the more contrived cases: Felice Charmond, for example, does not have to be shot by a former lover, Lucetta does not have to be so upset by the skimmety-ride that she miscarries and dies, nor does Sue have to lose her nerve so totally that she has to return to Phillotson and Mother Church. Symptomatic they may be; but it is still Hardy's fiction which establishes such 'logic'.

This strange contradiction in the novels – between a positive liberating consciousness and a negative neutralizing structure – might be explained by positing that psychologically Hardy was a misogynist. More convincing to my mind, is the notion that Hardy did indeed fear women, but in terms of their threatening upward social mobility, and therefore as a dimension of his acute class consciousness. We have seen from reading *The Life* how insecure and contradictory were Hardy's own class position and his perception of it; and we have also seen how much of his fiction is focused on the instability of the 'metamorphic classes' and on the potential for social disaster therein. As Hardy becomes successful as a '*man* of letters' and lives out the fiction of his own new class position, so anything that threatens it is to be feared; and the dynamic of women as a rising social group is the most immediately threatening. A hint of Hardy's neurosis is caught in a memorandum of July 1888, when he writes of a woman he met at Walter Pater's: 'Met Miss ——, an Amazon, more, an Atlanta, most, a Faustine. Smokes: handsome girl: cruel small mouth: she's of the class of interesting women one would be afraid to marry.'[31] Clearly Miss —— is a 'new woman', by whom Hardy is at once attracted and repelled. This socio-sexual apprehension, then, becomes at once the subject of his fiction and the object of its repression, for Hardy's own profession, even more sharply, was one of the areas most susceptible to the entry of aspiring and emancipated women (and George Eliot may, again, be a significant name in this context). It is worth noting that in the early novel, *A Pair of Blue Eyes*, there are a number of disparaging or ambiguous references to women and novel writing. The foolish, snobbish Mrs Swancourt, in conversation with Elfride who has written a 'romance', is made to tell her: '"Publish it, by all means. All ladies do that sort of thing now; not for profit, you know, but as a guarantee of mental respectability to their future husbands."' Later Knight, the literary man (only partly satirized), says to Elfride who has declared that she will never write another romance: '"Well, you may be right. That a young woman has taken to writing is not by any means the best thing to hear about her.'' ''What is the best?'' . . . ''I suppose to hear that she has married . . . Then to hear no more about her.''' And later again, Knight (Hardy?) comments, in a significantly contradictory and self-reflexive utterance: '''Every literary Jack becomes a gentleman if he can only pen a few indifferent satires upon womankind: women themselves, too, have taken to the trick; and so, upon the whole, I begin to be rather ashamed of my companions.'''[32]

Whatever Hardy had in mind here, and however sympathetic or not the portrait of Knight is, the conjunction of writing, women, and class is quite overt. And that, in inverse form, brings me back to Ethelberta. It seems to me highly revealing that Hardy should displace himself into a woman – herself a fictionist (both in life and literature) and the most successful of all his heroines, who is writing 'an epic poem' at the end having achieved the necessary social status and prosperity to give up 'romancing' – in order at once to 'expose' his own class origins and to subvert the alienating fictions of a class society. What it suggests, surely, is that the matrix in which Hardy's contradictory fictional discourses are shaped is composed of his insecurities and fears about class and gender, and that this permits the consciousness of the novels to 'perceive' the very conditioning it is itself subject to. It only remains for me now, in constructing a subversive 'Thomas Hardy', to secure this alienated consciousness to the anti-realist nature of the fiction.

Throughout this study, I have suggested that criticism has manufactured a 'realist' Thomas Hardy by foregrounding those aspects of his fiction which most nearly approximate to humanist realism, and by ignoring, suppressing, or rejecting those which run counter to or challenge it. Specifically, a number of novels are disenfranchised as 'minor', and the problematical elements in the 'major fiction' are excised as 'faults' or 'flaws' – failures of realist decorum. By reappropriating *The Hand of Ethelberta*, I tried to show that such elements of Hardy's fiction are as substantive a part of the discourse as any other, that they are indeed a mode of representation necessary for the demystification of class and gender relations and their auxiliary, fictional realism. It seems to me quite absurd to purport to be discussing a writer's 'work', if one deletes from it substantial amounts of its constituent discourse. What we must do, if we choose to discuss Hardy or indeed any other writer, is to try and comprehend, make sense of, the whole discourse; for its potential meanings are to be activated only by way of the 'determinate text' in its entirety. So, finally, I want to glance selectively at the implications for the 'great' but 'flawed' humanist realist of 'character and environment' of returning to full status those discourses in the text which most disturb a realist reading: the mannered and intrusive style; the improbable use of chance and coincidence; the 'sensational', 'melodramatic', and 'gothic' modes; the self-conscious and self-reflexive obsession with the artifice of art, the fictiveness of fiction, the ambiguity of illusion and reality, the 'veracity' of appearances; those discourses, indeed, which relate to Hardy's own comments about his fiction as being a 'series of seemings', to his rejection of realism as 'Art', and to his notion of 'disproportioning'.

From the beginning, with the 'melodramatic' first-published novel *Desperate Remedies*, there is a curious ambiguity of mode – usually put down to Hardy's immature 'touch' and his desire to break into a popular market. But from the disconcerting section headings ('September the twentieth. Three to four P.M.'; 'From 1843 to 1861'; 'The fifth of January. Before dawn'; 'Noon') to the incredibly convoluted plotting of the later part of the novel, there is an insistent possibility that this novel is simultaneously mocking the conventions of the genre it is imitating. And once this has been perceived, then the status of a paragraph like the following one shifts significantly from seeming to be, in its context, the 'awkward', 'sententious' moralizing of a self-educated journeyman novelist indecorously showing off, to becoming a potentially subversive comment on the romantic social fictions of 'love' and 'marriage'. How far, for example, in the first sentence, is Hardy ironically echoing the famous opening statement of *Pride and Prejudice*?

> It is a melancholy truth for the middle classes, that in proportion as they develop, by the study of poetry and art, their capacity for conjugal love of the highest and purest kind, they limit the possibility of their being able to exercise it – the very act putting out of their power the attainment of means sufficient for marriage. The man who works up a good income has had no time to learn love to its solemn extreme; the man who has learnt that has had no time to get rich.[33]

And if this is the case, then the over-wrought and mannered language of the 'Queen of night' chapter in *The Return of the Native* may equally become less a matter of Hardy displaying his learning in 'fine writing', and more unambiguously an ironic configuration of Eustacia's 'type' and of the kind of writing to which she would be most susceptible:

> Her presence brought memories of such things as Bourbon roses,

rubies, and tropical midnights; her moods recalled lotus-eaters and the march in 'Athalie', her motions, the ebb and flow of the sea; her voice, the viola. In a dim light, and with a slight rearrangement of her hair, her general figure might have stood for that of either of the higher female deities. The new moon behind her head, an old helmet upon it, a diadem of accidental dewdrops round her brow, would have been adjuncts sufficient to strike the note of Artemis, Athena, or Hera respectively, with as close an approximation to the antique as that which passes muster on many respected canvases. . . .

Her high gods were William the Conqueror, Strafford, and Napoleon Buonaparte, as they had appeared in the Lady's History used at the establishment in which she was educated. Had she been a mother she would have christened her boys such names as Saul or Sisera in preference to Jacob or David, neither of whom she admired. At school she had used to side with the Philistines in several battles, and had wondered if Pontius Pilate were as handsome as he was frank and fair.[34]

Armed, then, with this recognition that Hardy's language and style may be complex and self-conscious, rather than 'pedantic', waywardly successful, or merely evocatively 'descriptive', we may turn now to a famous passage in *Tess*:

Being so often – possibly not always by chance – the first two persons to get up at the dairy-house, they seemed to themselves the first persons up of all the world. In these early days of her residence here Tess did not skim, but went out of doors at once after rising, where he was generally awaiting her. The spectral, half-compounded, aqueous light which pervaded the open mead, impressed them with a feeling of isolation, as if they were Adam and Eve. At this dim inceptive stage of the day Tess seemed to Clare to exhibit a dignified largeness both of disposition and physique, an almost regnant power, possibly because he knew that at that preternatural time hardly any woman so well endowed in person as she was likely to be walking in the open air within the boundaries of his horizon; very few in all England. Fair women are usually asleep at mid-summer dawns. She was close at hand, and the rest were nowhere. . . .

It was then, as has been said, that she impressed him most deeply. She was no longer the milkmaid, but a visionary essence of woman – a whole sex condensed into one typical form. He called her Artemis, Demeter, and other fanciful names half teasingly, which she did not like because she did not understand them.[35]

What becomes immediately apparent is that this is not a 'set-piece' of romantic description on Hardy's part, but a presentation of the way in which Angel perceives Tess, and of the nature of their relationship. The second paragraph makes this quite clear, of course ('the visionary essence of woman', 'Artemis', 'Demeter'), but the language and frame of reference of the first proclaim it too. Did *they* really *both* think of themselves as Adam and Eve? And whose words are the academic, latinate 'spectral', 'aqueous', 'pervaded', 'inceptive', 'disposition', 'physique', 'regnant', 'preternatural'? What we have, in fact, is an instance of the novel's technique of presenting the 'character' of Tess as an amalgam – often destructively contradictory – of 'images' of her as she is 'perceived' by individuals or by society. Here then, typically, she is imaged in the abstract, male-intellectual, and idealist terms of Angel's discourse (ironically undercut by her presence as sex-object – 'any woman so well endowed in person'). In a sense – and as a reflex of her social displacement and insecure identity – Tess has no 'character' at all: she is only what others construct her as (*vide* Ethelberta), and so is herself merely a 'series of seemings'. Such a perception, of course, gives a wholly new dimension to the notion of her being 'a pure woman'. For if the phrase is read in the ontological, rather than ethical, sense then it becomes sharply ironic, since there can indeed be no such thing as 'essential character' in a situation where women are no more than the focus of male socio-sexual images of their desired forms. This is at once a radical subversion of the liberal-bourgeois conception of the individual and of the humanist-realist conception of 'character'; and as we saw with Ethelberta, it is precisely related to class/gender alienation.

The technique is used extensively in Hardy's fiction (but most obviously in the 'minor novels'), and accounts for the frequent criticism of the characters as 'flat' or 'stagey'. Take, for example, the presentation of Alec d'Urberville as stage-melodrama villain:

> He had an almost swarthy complexion, with full lips, badly moulded, though red and smooth, above which was a well-groomed black moustache with curled points, though his age could not be more than three- or four-and-twenty. Despite the touches of barbarism in his contours, there was a singular force in the gentleman's face, and in his bold rolling eye.
> 'Well, my Beauty, what can I do for you?' said he, coming forward. . . .

> The driver was a young man of three- or four-and-twenty, with a cigar between his teeth; wearing a dandy cap, drab jacket,

breeches of the same hue, white neckcloth, stick-up collar, and
brown driving-gloves – in short, he was the handsome, horsey
young buck who had visited Joan a week or two before to get her
answer about Tess. . . .

D'Urberville looked round upon her, nipped his cigar with the
tips of his large white centre-teeth, and allowed his lips to smile
slowly of themselves.
'Why, Tess,' he answered, after another whiff or two, 'it isn't a
brave bouncing girl like you who asks that? Why, I always go
down at full gallop. There's nothing like it for raising your
spirits.'[36]

This may not necessarily be a 'failure of imagination' on Hardy's
part to realize Alec's character fully, but rather a formal strategy to
'locate' Alec immediately, and to enact the artificiality of his
'character', also, as a constructed class subject. Indeed, as I noted
earlier, Alec's character shifts radically and disconcertingly (see, for
example, the passage when he has become a preacher[37]) because he
too has no identity other than that which the social trappings of
entrepreneurial new wealth image him as. Again, we do not need to
see this as Hardy carelessly caricaturing the predatory wealthy male,
but as a symptomatic representation of the alienation consequent on
class and gender construction. Felice Charmond, in *The
Woodlanders*, can be seen in a similar way. Take the passage when
Fitzpiers first visits her:

He was shown into a room at the top of the staircase, cosily and
femininely draped, where by the light of the shaded lamp he saw
a woman of elegant figure reclining upon a couch in such a
position as not to disturb a pile of magnificent hair on the crown
of her head. A deep purple dressing-gown formed an admirable
foil to the peculiarly rich brown of her hair-plaits; her left arm,
which was naked nearly up to the shoulder, was thrown upwards,
and between the fingers of her right hand she held a cigarette,
while she idly breathed from her delicately curled lips a thin
stream of smoke towards the ceiling. . . .

Mrs. Charmond did not move more than to raise her eyes to him,
and he came and stood by her. She glanced up at his face across
her brows and forehead, and then he observed a blush creep
slowly over her decidedly handsome cheeks. Her eyes, which had
lingered upon him with an inquiring, conscious expression, were
hastily withdrawn, and she mechanically applied the cigarette
again to her lips.[38]

This is the 'fast' society woman of sensational fiction, the *femme fatale* of conventional typology. Is it an error of literary tact on Hardy's part to include such a figure in the bucolic environs of *The Woodlanders*? Or is it an attempt to convey the peculiarly artificial nature of Felice's 'character' instantly and directly, to express emblematically her 'inorganic' class location and social relations (rural landowner) as the mannered, stagey product of 'circumstance'? It is not fortuitous that we learn she has been thrust on the marriage market by her mother because 'her only fortune was her face' (with all its implication of theatre), that she has indeed been a 'play-actress',[39] nor that she should lie there adorned with hair bought off Marty South's head. Mrs Charmond is, in fact (like Ethelberta), no more than the performance which social determinations have cast her as: a factitious type of the *arriviste* 'nobility', a gold-digging actress, funded by inherited 'new money' and wearing the spoils of class exploitation. And finally, in this analysis of Hardy's anti-realist characterization, it is possible, as George Wotton has suggested, to perceive the 'rustic chorus' so beloved of Hardy criticism not as Hardy's celebration of 'Hodge', but as a kind of Bahktinian 'carnivalization' in which the 'workfolk', dispossessed and uncivilized, mock the ideological deceptions and mystifications of the dominant classes 'by their laughter which degrades and materializes the idea, the abstract, the spiritual'.[40] We may remember, as an example, Robert Creedle and the slug on Grace Melbury's plate at Giles's supper-party: '"Well, 'twas his native home, come to that; and where else could we expect him to be? I don't care who the man is, slugs and caterpillars always will lurk in close to the stump of cabbages in that tantalizing way."'[41] So much for Mr Melbury's social aspirations.

We may also regard positively the long catalogue of 'chance' or 'melodramatic' events on which the plots of Hardy's novels are built. Critics have thought of these as the crudely obtrusive representations of the workings of fate or, with E. M. Forster, as the 'hammering and sawing' of a flawed craftsman.[42] But again, in the frame set up by the manifest anti-realism of *The Hand of Ethelberta*, they take on a different character. For example, the extraordinary set of coincidences which result in Mrs Yeobright's death in *The Return of the Native* no longer appear as the creaking mechanism of 'plot as fate', but as a structural metaphor for the inescapably contingent relations the 'metamorphic' characters of that novel find themselves in. Again, the 'improbable' presentation of Little Father Time in *Jude the Obscure* and his death with the other children – '"Done because we are too menny"' – becomes in itself a formal demystification of the illusory fictions of realism and humanism. He is, as the text itself self-consciously puts it, 'their nodal point, their focus, *their expression in a single term*' (my italics).[43] What that 'single term' enacts is an alienation which sees through the 'improbable' injustices of Christminster's humanism, a humanism disguised by ideology as the disinterested pursuit of culture and truth and which a humanist realism (like George Eliot's) shores up by its affirmation of the sanctity of the human individual. Equally, the fortuitous discovery by one of Angel's brothers and Mercy Chant, his erstwhile 'intended', of Tess's boots when she goes to visit the Clare family at the vicarage; the sensational business of the sleep-walking Angel placing Tess in the 'empty stone coffin of an abbot' after her confession; the painted signs saying 'THY, DAMNATION, SLUMBERETH, NOT' and 'THOU, SHALT, NOT, COMMIT . . .' that Tess comes upon on her journey home from Alec; and the strange coda when Angel and 'Liza-Lu, Tess's sister whom the novel has hitherto ignored, watch Tess's hanging and then walk off hand in hand[44] – all imply a consciousness which is not merely straining at the limits of a 'probablist' realist discourse (after *Jude* and the uncompromisingly fictive *The Well-Beloved*, Hardy did indeed give up novels and move to an explicitly non-realist mode in the epic-drama of *The Dynasts*), but one which is strategically anti-realist. This is further compounded, in the later novels especially, by the self-conscious parading of the fictiveness of fiction as itself a mode of 'disproportioning'. There are the *Tristram-Shandy*-like typographical devices THITHER J.F. ☞; and the intrusively inserted literary and other 'quotations': 'He could have declared with a contemporary poet'; 'there was ghastly satire in the poet's lines'; '"By experience", says Roger Ascham.'[45] There is the undisguised commentary of the narrative voice: on the railway in *Tess*, for example: 'Modern life stretched out its stern feeler to this point three or four times a day, touched the native existences, and quickly withdrew its feeler again, as if what it touched had been uncongenial';[46] or on Sarcophagus College in *Jude*: 'the outer walls . . . silent, black and windowless – threw their four centuries of gloom, bigotry, and decay into the little room she occupied, shutting out the moonlight by night and the sun by day.'[47] There is the grotesquely 'indecorous' comedy, in *Jude* again, of the 'farcical yet melancholy' 'general scuffle' in Phillotson's schoolroom:

wherein a blackboard was split, three panes of the school-windows were broken, an inkbottle was spilled over a town-councillor's shirt-front, a churchwarden was dealt such a topper with the map of Palestine that his head went right through Samaria, and many black eyes and bleeding noses were given, one of which, to everybody's horror, was the venerable incumbent's, owing to the zeal of an emancipated chimney-sweep, who took the side of Phillotson's party.[48]

There are the obtrusively artificial and mannered 'presentations' of character or scene; for instance, the following (Brechtian) moment in *Tess*:

> From the foregoing events of the winter-time let us press on to an October day, more than eight months subsequent to the parting of Clare and Tess. We discover the latter in changed conditions; instead of a bride with boxes and trunks which others bore, we see her a lonely woman with a basket and a bundle in her own porterage, as at an earlier time when she was no bride; instead of the ample means that were projected by her husband for her comfort through this probationary period, she can produce only a flattened purse.[49]

And there are the overtly non-realist scenes in which symbolic significance disallows any semblance of verisimilitude: for example, the contingent business with the mantrap at the end of *The Woodlanders*; the moment when Alec surprises Tess by arising from the sarcophagus in the d'Urberville tomb after she has mistaken him for a stone effigy; or the scene when Jude first arrives in Christminster and meets the 'spectres' of its famous poets and philosophers:

> There were poets abroad, of early date and of late, from the friend and eulogist of Shakespeare down to him who has recently passed into silence, and that musical one of the tribe who is still among us. . . . Jude found himself speaking out loud, holding conversations with them as it were, like an actor in a melodrama who apostrophizes the audience on the other side of the footlights.[50]

Who, we might ask, in such manifestly self-conscious and fictive discourses as these, is 'apostrophizing the audience'? Whose 'melodrama', in its straining to give form to the real relations of a class society disguised by the ideological veil of humanism, rips apart the fictions and illusions of a realism which passes off its depiction of that ideology as 'telling things as they really are'?

This 'Thomas Hardy', critiographically released from his conventional guises, waits to be read. Once perceived, the 'determinate text' of his fiction can be seen to be pervasively inscribed by the contradictory consciousness which 'wrote' it. We might, indeed, ask what happened to and within Thomas Hardy in that fierce struggle to succeed in the literary and social jungle of nineteenth-century London, and what it cost to become the Grand Old Man of English Letters by the early twentieth century. But this is not, I hasten to add, to slip back into fallacies of 'intentionalism' and 'intrinsic meaning' – traps which I have continuously manoeuvred to avoid. Rather, this book's lengthy and dogged presentation of evidence should bear witness to the amount of late twentieth-century critical labour involved in rescuing a radical Thomas Hardy, or indeed any canonized writer, from their critical niche. But just as 'good little Thomas Hardy' was forged out of the raw material, so too can this rather more spirited figure.

Notes

Introduction

1 Letter to the author from Professor John Lucas, Loughborough University, 2 September 1983. I would like to register here my gratitude for the years of friendship and support which John Lucas has given me.

2 Terry Eagleton, *Walter Benjamin or Towards a Revolutionary Criticism*, London: Verso, 1981, 126–7.

3 I am indebted for this insight to Asha Kanwar, an ex-Ph.D. student at Sussex University, now in the Department of English at the University of Punjab, India. The reference is from her Ph.D. thesis: 'The fictional theories of Arnold Kettle and Raymond Williams with special reference to selected nineteenth-century novels.'

1 The critical constitution of 'Thomas Hardy'

What is a critiography?

1 E. H. Carr, *What is History?* (1961), Harmondsworth: Penguin, 1965, 11. All further references to this book appear as bracketed numbers in the text.

2 Tony Bennett, 'Text and history', in Peter Widdowson, ed., *Re-reading English*, London: Methuen, 1982, 224–5. All further references to this essay appear as bracketed numbers in the text.

To 1914

3 R. G. Cox, ed., *Thomas Hardy: The Critical Heritage*, London: Routledge & Kegan Paul, 1970, Introduction, xv.

4 Charles Whibley, 'Thomas Hardy', *Blackwood's Magazine*, June 1913, in Cox, op. cit., 416.

5 Harold Williams, 'The Wessex novels of Thomas Hardy', *North American Review*, January 1914, in Cox, op. cit., 429.

6 Unsigned review of *Far From the Madding Crowd*, *Saturday Review*, 9 January 1875, in Cox, op. cit., 42.

7 Unsigned review of *The Return of the Native*, *Saturday Review*, 4 January 1879, in Cox, op. cit., 51.

8 Richard le Gallienne, review of *Tess of the d'Urbervilles*, *Star*, 23 December 1891, in Cox, op. cit., 178–9.

9 The former phrase is R. H. Hutton's in a review of *The Mayor of Casterbridge*, 5 June 1886, in Cox, op. cit., 138. 'Gloom' appears *passim* in popular reviewing of Hardy's work in the period.

10 W. L. Phelps, 'Thomas Hardy', *Essays on Modern Novelists*, 1910 (originally in *Atlantic Monthly*, Boston), in Cox, op. cit., 398.

11 Edward Wright, 'The novels of Thomas Hardy', *Quarterly Review*, April 1904, in Cox, op. cit., 360–1.

12 H. Williams, op. cit., in Cox, op. cit., 433, 423–4.

13 Review in the *Pall Mall Gazette*, 25 October 1873, quoted in Cox, op. cit., Introduction, xvi.

14 The above references, all from Cox, op. cit., (page numbers appear in brackets), are as follows: the *Spectator* and *The Times*, 25 January 1875, Introduction (xvii); *Athenaeum*, 5 December 1874 (20); *Westminster Review*, January 1875 (32–3); R. H. Hutton, *Spectator*, 19 December 1874 (22, 24); Henry James, *Nation*, 24 December 1874 (27–31, *passim*).

15 Unsigned survey article, *British Quarterly Review*, 1881, in Cox, op. cit., 78–9, 94.

16 Wright, op. cit., in Cox, op. cit., 363.

17 Florence Emily Hardy, *The Life of Thomas Hardy 1840–1928* (1962), London: Macmillan, 1975, 98 (see references for fuller publication details of this work).

18 ibid., 103.

19 'Thomas Hardy's novels', *Westminster Review*, April 1883, in Cox, op. cit., 116–17; and 'Concerning *Jude the Obscure*', *Savoy Magazine*, October 1896, in Cox, 306–7.

20 8 February 1896, in Cox, op. cit., 280, 283.

21 Unsigned survey article, *New Quarterly Magazine*, October 1879, in Cox, op. cit., 60–70 *passim*.

22 'Novels of character and environment', *Spectator*, 7 September 1912, in Cox, op. cit., 408–10.

To the present

23 David Cecil, *Hardy the Novelist*, London: Constable, 1943, 153. All further references to this book appear as bracketed numbers in the text.

24 For fuller discussion of this see George Wotton, *Thomas Hardy: Towards a Materialist Criticism*, Dublin: Gill & Macmillan, 1985, 202–7. Wotton's book in fact complements my own work at a number of points.

25 There is further analysis of this construction of Hardy, and of Douglas Brown's text in relation to it, in Wotton, op. cit., ch. 12, especially pp. 165–9.

26 Raymond Williams, *Politics and Letters* (1979), London: Verso, 1981, 245–6.

27 Terry Eagleton, *Walter Benjamin or Towards a Revolutionary Criticism*, London: Verso, 1981, 127. Leavis, of course, writes rather more

extensively and positively about Hardy as *poet*: cf. the pages on him in *New Bearings in English Poetry*, London: Chatto & Windus, 1932.

28 F. R. Leavis, *The Great Tradition* (1948), Harmondsworth: Penguin, 1962, 32–3, 139–40, 248.

29 See Cox, op. cit., Introduction, xxxii.

30 F. R. Leavis, *The Common Pursuit* (1962), Harmondsworth: Penguin, 1978, 237.

31 R. Williams, op. cit., 245. Williams is here speaking about the period when he himself was writing *The English Novel from Dickens to Lawrence* (1970), in which, of course, Hardy figures significantly.

32 Eagleton, op. cit., 127–8.

33 Michael Millgate, *Thomas Hardy: His Career as a Novelist*, London: Bodley Head, 1971, 25. All further references to this book appear as bracketed numbers in the text.

34 I am thinking particularly here, for example, of F. B. Pinion's *A Hardy Companion* (1968) and his editing, amongst many other things, of the *Thomas Hardy Society Review*; of R. L. Purdy's *Thomas Hardy: A Bibliographical Study* (1954) and his editing, with Michael Millgate, of *The Collected Letters* (1978–   ); of Lennart Björk's editing of *The Literary Notebooks of Thomas Hardy* (1985); of Richard H. Taylor's editing of *The Personal Notebooks* (1978); of P. N. Furbank's general editing of the 'New Wessex' edition of Hardy's work and Samuel Hynes's editing of *The Complete Poetical Works* (1982, 1984); of M. E. Chase's *Thomas Hardy: From Serial to Novel* (1927); John Paterson's *The Making of* The Return of the Native (1960); Patricia Ingham's 'The evolution of *Jude the Obscure*', *Review of English Studies* (1976); and John Laird's *The Shaping of* Tess of the d'Urbervilles (1975).

35 John Laird, *The Shaping of* Tess of the d'Urbervilles, Oxford: Oxford University Press, 1975, 4.

36 Carl Weber, *Hardy of Wessex* (1940), rev. edn, London: Routledge & Kegan Paul, 1965, 295, 97.

37 Roy Morrell, *Thomas Hardy: The Will and the Way* (1965), Oxford: Oxford University Press, 1978, xii. All further references to this book appear as bracketed numbers in the text.

38 Richard Carpenter, *Thomas Hardy* (1965), London: Macmillan, 1976, 39. All further references to this book appear as bracketed numbers in the text.

39 One other influential book of the same period should also be noted here: J. I. M. Stewart's *Thomas Hardy, A Critical Biography*, Harlow: Longman, 1971. This is rather more *belles-lettrist* although often incisive, but it operates very much within the same critical parameters as other monographs reviewed in this section and is again extensively recommended as critical reading in student 'study guides'.

40 Jean Brooks, *Thomas Hardy: The Poetic Structure*, London: Elek Books, 1971, 8. All further references to this book appear as bracketed numbers in the text.

41 Ian Gregor, *The Great Web*, London: Faber, 1974, 79. All further

references to this book appear as bracketed numbers in the text. In a later essay Gregor (with Michael Irwin) does address himself to the 'minor novels'. See 'Either side of Wessex' in Lance St John Butler, ed., *Thomas Hardy After Fifty Years*, London: Macmillan, 1977. This essay is more extensively considered on p. 44.

42 Penelope Vigar, *The Novels of Thomas Hardy: Illusion and Reality*, London: Athlone Press, 1974, ch. 1 *passim*. All further references to this book appear as bracketed numbers in the text.

43 See Gregor, op. cit., Preface, 19. Gregor refers there to an article of that title which he wrote 'some years ago' for *Essays in Criticism* (xvi, 3 July 1966), but which remains the burden of his present book.

44 J. Hillis Miller, *Thomas Hardy: Distance and Desire*, Oxford: Oxford University Press, 1970, Preface *passim*, and 208.

45 Dale Kramer, *Thomas Hardy: The Forms of Tragedy*, London: Macmillan, 1975, 28.

46 Peter Casagrande, *Unity in Hardy's Novels*, London: Macmillan, 1982, 11, 223.

47 J. B. Bullen, *The Expressive Eye*, Oxford: Oxford University Press, 1986, 89.

48 Albert J. Guerard, *Thomas Hardy* (1949), rev. edn, London: New Directions, 1964, ix. All further references to this book appear as bracketed numbers in the text.

49 Arnold Kettle, *An Introduction to the English Novel* (1953), London: Hutchinson, 1967, 45, 48, 55.

50 Open University course 'The nineteenth-century novel and its legacy', units 17–18, '*Tess of the d'Urbervilles*', prepared by Arnold Kettle, Milton Keynes: Open University Press, 1982.

51 Richard H. Taylor, 'Thomas Hardy: a reader's guide', in Norman Page, ed., *Thomas Hardy: The Writer and his Background*, London: Bell & Hyman, 1980, 247, 220, 246.

52 Merryn Williams, *Thomas Hardy and Rural England*, London: Macmillan, 1972, 199–200.

53 Raymond Williams, *The English Novel from Dickens to Lawrence*, London: Chatto & Windus, 1970, 95.

54 Terry Eagleton, *Criticism and Ideology* (1976), London: Verso, 1978, 94–5, 131–2.

55 Eagleton, *Walter Benjamin*, op. cit., 127–30.

56 Wotton, op. cit., 183.

57 John Lucas, *The Literature of Change*, Brighton: Harvester, 1977, 188.

58 John Goode, 'Women and the literary text', in Juliet Mitchell and Ann Oakley, eds, *The Rights and Wrongs of Women*, Harmondsworth: Penguin, 1976, 217–18. All further references to this essay appear as bracketed numbers in the text.

59 John Goode, 'Sue Bridehead and the new woman', in Mary Jacobus, ed., *Women's Writing and Writing about Women*, Beckenham: Croom Helm, 1979, 100, 107–8.

60 Patricia Stubbs, *Women and Fiction* (1979), London: Methuen, 1981, 59.

A note on the case of the 'minor novels'

61 R. H. Taylor, op. cit., in Page, op. cit., 222.
62 I. Gregor and M. Irwin, 'Either side of Wessex', op. cit., in Butler, op. cit., 104.
63 R. H. Taylor, op. cit., in Page, op. cit., 221.
64 Unsigned article, 'The Hardy industry', *Observer*, 22 October 1967.
65 See James Gibson, *Tess of the d'Urbervilles*, Macmillan Master Guides, London: Macmillan, 1986.
66 Thomas Hardy, *A Laodicean*, ed., Barbara Hardy, with Introduction, 'New Wessex' edn, London: Macmillan, 1975, 13.
67 Thomas Hardy, *Desperate Remedies*, ed., C. J. P. Beatty, with Introduction, 'New Wessex' edn, London: Macmillan, 1975, 12, 31, 32.
68 Thomas Hardy, *A Pair of Blue Eyes*, ed., Ronald Blythe, with Introduction, 'New Wessex' edn, London: Macmillan, 1975, 14, 17.
69 Thomas Hardy, *A Pair of Blue Eyes*, ed., Alan Manford, with Introduction, 'World's Classics' edn, Oxford: Oxford University Press, 1985, xvii–xviii.
70 Thomas Hardy, *The Hand of Ethelberta*, ed., Robert Gittings, with Introduction, 'New Wessex' edn, London: Macmillan, 1975, 15, 18, 21, 27.
71 R. L. Purdy and Michael Millgate, eds, *The Collected Letters of Thomas Hardy, IV: 1909–13*, Oxford: Oxford University Press, 1984, 209. I am grateful to Norman Page for pointing this reference out to me. The 1912 'General Preface' is reproduced at the end of all the texts in both the 'New Wessex' and Penguin editions of Hardy's novels.
72 All references are to Cox, op. cit., 67, 97, 102, 148.
73 J. M. Barrie, 'Thomas Hardy: the historian of Wessex', *Contemporary Review*, lvi, 1889, in Cox, op. cit., 159.
74 Edmund Gosse, 'Thomas Hardy', *The Speaker*, 13, September 1890, in Cox, op. cit., 168.
75 Wright, op. cit., in Cox, op. cit., 356; and Phelps, op. cit., in Cox, 394–406 *passim.*
76 Whibley, op. cit., in Cox, op. cit., 411, 418.
77 H. Williams, op. cit., in Cox, op. cit., 429.
78 B. Ifor Evans, *A Short History of English Literature* (1940), Harmondsworth: Penguin, 1958, 171; Harry Blamires, *A Short History of English Literature*, London: Methuen, 1974, 378–9.
79 Albert C. Baugh, ed., *A Literary History of England* (1967), London: Routledge & Kegan Paul, 1970, 1466–8.
80 Cox, op. cit., xiii.
81 Butler, op. cit.; Page, op. cit.; Dale Kramer, ed., *Critical Approaches to the Fiction of Thomas Hardy*, London: Macmillan, 1979.
82 Richard H. Taylor, *The Neglected Hardy*, London: Macmillan, 1982. This, and the following quotations, are from the Introduction, 1–5 *passim.*
83 ibid.: this, and the following quotations, are from the Conclusion, 174–83 *passim.*

Hardy, 'Wessex', and the making of a national culture

84 Timothy O'Sullivan, *Thomas Hardy: An Illustrated Biography*, London: Macmillan, 1975.

85 Preface to 1895 edition of *Far From the Madding Crowd*; also 'General Preface' to the Wessex edition of 1912.

86 Roy Hattersley, 'Endpiece: how I came to Casterbridge by way of Reykjavik', *Guardian*, 23 January 1982.

87 I am indebted to Lyn Pykett of University College, Aberystwyth for this information.

88 Unsigned review, *Athenaeum*, 15 June 1872; and unsigned 'Survey', *British Quarterly Review*, 1881, both in Cox, op. cit., 9, 83.

89 Gosse, op. cit., in Cox, op. cit., 169.

90 Phelps, op. cit., in Cox, op. cit., 400.

91 Wright, op. cit., in Cox, op. cit., 347, 349, 351, 359.

92 H. Williams, op. cit., in Cox, op. cit., 429–34 *passim*.

93 Whibley, op. cit., in Cox, op. cit., 415.

94 I am indebted to Charles Swann of Keele University for this quotation. It appeared some years ago in a paper first given by him at Thames Polytechnic; I am not aware that it has ever been published.

95 Victoria Mann, 'Far from the boring classroom: a different way to study': an untitled and undated ripsheet from a magazine (in the author's possession).

96 For a fuller discussion of this, see Peter Brooker and Peter Widdowson, 'A literature for England, *c.* 1900–14', in R. Colls and P. Dodd, eds, *The Idea of Englishness, 1880–1920*, Beckenham: Croom Helm, 1985.

97 Sir Henry Newbolt, 1921 Board of Education Report, *The Teaching of English in England*, 312.

98 ibid., 252–3, 255, 202. For more extended discussion of this, see Derek Longhurst, 'Not for all time, but for an age: an approach to Shakespeare studies', in Peter Widdowson, ed., *Re-reading English*, op. cit., and his 'Shakespeare in education: reproducing a national culture', *Red Letters*, 11, Spring 1981.

99 Martin J. Weiner, *English Culture and the Decline of the Industrial Spirit, 1850–1980* (1981), Harmondsworth: Penguin, 1985, 51–3.

100 'Survey', 1881, op. cit.; Whibley, op. cit. Both in Cox, op. cit., 85, 411.

101 ibid., 421, 416.

102 H. Williams, op. cit., in Cox, op. cit., 428.

103 Henry Newbolt, 'A new departure in English poetry', *Quarterly Review*, January 1909, in Cox, op. cit., 386–7, 393.

104 Edmund Blunden, *Thomas Hardy*, London: Macmillan, 1942, 212, 251.

105 Cecil, op. cit., 45, 147–9, 153.

106 Douglas Brown, *Thomas Hardy* (1954), Harlow: Longman, 1961, 30–1, 90, 63, 111.

107 Irving Howe, *Thomas Hardy* (1966), London: Weidenfeld & Nicolson, 1968, 19, 32, 17–18, 21–3.

108 See, for example, the West Country & Southern Tourist Board pamphlet, 'Discover the Hardy country' and the Thomas Hardy Society pamphlets by M. R. Skilling, 'Walk round Dorchester (Casterbridge) with Thomas Hardy', 1975, and 'Walk round Weymouth (Budmouth) with Thomas Hardy', 1983. The filmstrip is Stella Mary Newton, *Writers and Their Times* series, 1, 'Thomas Hardy', Cheltenham: Visual Publications. The quotation is from the advertising pamphlet, 'English and drama: audio-visual resources from Visual Publications', 1987.

109 Hermann Lea, *Thomas Hardy's Wessex* (1913); Clive Holland, *Thomas Hardy's Wessex Scene* (1971). See also J. Stevens Cox, ed., *Thomas Hardy: Materials for a Study of his Life, Times and Works* (1968) and *More Materials* (1971); Ruth Firor, *Folkways in Thomas Hardy* (1931); Denys Kay-Robinson, *Hardy's Wessex Reappraised* (1972).

110 Andrew Enstice, *Thomas Hardy: Landscapes of the Mind*, London: Macmillan, 1979, ix.

111 M. Williams, op. cit., 193, 199.

112 David Lodge, *Working with Structuralism*, London: Routledge & Kegan Paul, 1981, 91, 101.

113 For a fuller discussion of this, see Peter Widdowson, 'The anti-history men: Malcolm Bradbury and David Lodge', *Critical Quarterly*, 26, 4, Winter 1984, 5–32.

114 Donald Davie, *Thomas Hardy and British Poetry*, London: Routledge & Kegan Paul, 1973, ix. All subsequent references to this book appear in brackets in the text.

115 Davie is here (pp. 102–3) quoting F. E. Hardy, *The Life of Thomas Hardy*, op. cit., 204, which reproduces a memorandum of Hardy's for 24 January 1888.

A disruptive 'Thomas Hardy'

116 Eagleton, *Walter Benjamin*, op. cit., 128–30.

117 For a fuller discussion of this in relation, specifically, to *Adam Bede*, see Peter Widdowson, Paul Stigant, and Peter Brooker, 'History and literary "value": *Adam Bede* and *Salem Chapel*', *Literature and History*, 5, 1, Spring 1979.

118 Catherine Belsey, 'Re-reading the great tradition', in Widdowson, *Re-reading English*, op. cit., 122, 127, and *passim*.

119 ibid., 122–3.

120 The phrase belongs to Henry James in a letter to R. L. Stevenson, 19 March 1892.

2 'Thomas Hardy' in education

1 Holly Goulden and John Hartley, '"Nor should such topics as homosexuality, masturbation, frigidity, premature ejaculation or the menopause be regarded as unmentionable"', *Literature Teaching Politics* (*LTP*) 1, 1982, 6.

2 Much of the research for this chapter was done in the Department of

Education and Science Library and Library Store, and in the archives of the University of Cambridge Local Examinations Syndicate. My thanks to the patient people who helped me there. I give no detailed references for the examination papers and questions in this chapter, except – in brackets in the text – their provenance and date. If anyone wishes further to establish their authenticity, they are welcome.

3 Letter from John Lucas to author, 2 September 1983.

4 I am afraid that my sample here is even more sketchy and random than it was for secondary education. I am grateful to friends and colleagues up and down the country and elsewhere in the world who have sent me examples of the kinds of question their institutions set on Hardy.

3 'Tragedies of modern life'? 'Thomas Hardy' on radio, TV, and film

1 See James Gibson, *Tess of the d'Urbervilles*, Macmillan Master Guides, London: Macmillan, 1986.

2 *Mayfair*, 2, 7, 1967, 72–3.

3 Terry Coleman, 'The lady beyond the hero's grasp', *Guardian*, 19 March 1982.

4 The most overtly proto-filmic of Hardy's works is *The Dynasts*, with its large-scale panning shots of European conflict in the Napoleonic wars, its ironic cutting-down to individual scenes of human action, and its cosmic 'supernatural' overviews. But similar techniques appear in the fiction, especially long shots of human individuals in the landscape which rapidly focus down onto them (e.g. in *The Return of the Native* and in *Tess*). David Lodge has noted this in his essay 'Thomas Hardy as a cinematic novelist', in Lance St John Butler, ed., *Thomas Hardy After Fifty Years*, London: Macmillan, 1977, 78–89. Lodge does not appear to have read John Wain's Introduction to *The Dynasts*, London: Macmillan, Papermac, 1965, ix ff., which claims that Hardy's imagination and the devices it uses in the epic drama are 'cinematic' and that the text of *The Dynasts* is, in fact, 'a shooting-script'.

5 The information here mainly derives from the British Film Institute (BFI) Film Index. The silent 1913 version of *Tess* was made by Famous Players Film Co./Monopol Film Co., directed by J. Searle Dawley and acted, amongst others, by Minnie Maddern Fiske and Raymond Bundel. The 1924 version (Metro-Goldwyn, 7000 ft, cert. A) was directed by Marshall Neilan and acted by Blanche Sweet, Conrad Nagel, Stuart Holmes, George Fawcett, Courtenay Foote, and Kate Price. *Far From the Madding Crowd* (1911) was made by the Edison Co. and ran for 12 minutes. Trimble's version (1915, 4600 ft) had in its cast Florence Turner, Campbell Gullan, Malcolm Cherry, Marion Grey, and Henry Edwards. Lachman's *Under the Greenwood Tree* (1929, 8386 ft) starred Marguerite Allan, John Batten, Nigel Barrie, Billy Shine, and Robert Abel. The BFI have the script for this film. Morgan's *Mayor of Casterbridge* (1921) had as its cast Fred Groves, Pauline Peters, Mavis Clare, and Warwick Ward. There are notes on the script and sets of the

abandoned post-war *Mayor*, by Thorald Dickinson in *Sight and Sound*, January 1951, 363.

6 The BBC Programme Index for both TV and Radio is a comprehensive record of all broadcasts, however small, transmitted by the BBC and catalogued under 'Contributor's' name (e.g. 'Hardy, Thomas'). I studied it for the period 1945 to 1980, and am grateful for access to it. From the start it contains basic information (date and time of transmission, title of work, programme); later it adds the names of producers, adaptors, readers, actors, etc., the particular slot (e.g. 'Closedown', 'The Monday Play'), and details of repeats. Given that actual audio and visual access to past programmes is wellnigh impossible for the lay researcher, the Index is of considerable value. Most of the following material in this part of the chapter derives from it.

7 These were: 'The Withered Arm' (dram. Rhys Adrian); 'Fellow Townsmen' (dram. Douglas Livingstone); 'A Tragedy of Two Ambitions' (dram. Dennis Potter); 'An Imaginative Woman' (dram. William Trevor); 'The Melancholy Hussar' (dram. Ken Taylor); 'Barbara of the House of Glebe' (dram. David Mercer).

8 An article by Trevor Johnson, '"Pre-critical innocence" and the anthologist's Hardy', *Victorian Poetry*, 17, 1979, 9–29, presents interesting statistical information about the incidence of Hardy's poetry in anthologies and about which poems appear most frequently. 'The Darkling Thrush', 'The Oxen', and 'The Convergence of the Twain' are the top three, with all the others (bar 'The Ruined Maid') amongst the next most popular. I am grateful to Edward Neill for pointing out this article.

9 John Coleman, 'The Wessex set', *New Statesman*, 20 October 1967. I am indebted to the British Film Institute (BFI) Library for access to its catalogue and collection of reviews and press cuttings. This reference, and most of the following ones to material on TV and film versions of Hardy's work, derive from that source.

10 James M. Welsh, 'Hardy and the pastoral, Schlesinger and the shepherds: *Far From the Madding Crowd*', *Literature/Film Quarterly*, 9, 2, 1981, 79–84. George Wotton, *Thomas Hardy: Towards a Materialist Criticism*, Dublin: Gill & Macmillan, 1985, 200, makes a similar point.

11 Unfortunately I could only view five of the seven parts – episodes three and six being missing (the latter including, sadly, the 'skimmington ride' scenes). I am absolutely indebted, however, to Carrie who works (worked?) in the Drama Department of the BBC and who loaned me the old video tapes which she had discovered at the back of a cupboard, together with some of the production stills from the series which illustrate this chapter. Without those tapes, it would have been extremely difficult to write this section of chapter 3, so my thanks to Carrie for them and for her unfailing friendliness and verve.

12 Unsigned review, *Television Today*, 26 January 1978.

13 *Radio Times*, 21–7 January 1978, 66–9.

14 Philip Phillips, 'The man who sold his wife', *Sun*, 21 January 1978.
15 *Television Today*, op. cit.
16 *Sun*, op. cit.; Sally Brompton, *Daily Mail*, 21 January 1978; Robert Gittings, review of *The Mayor of Casterbridge*, *Radio Times* 4–10 March 1978, 78.
17 See Sean Day-Lewis, 'What Potter made of Hardy', *Daily Telegraph*, 6 March 1978; Bernard Davies in 'One man's television', *Broadcast*, 6 February 1978; Robert Gittings, *Radio Times*, op. cit.; Potter's introduction is quoted by both Sean Day-Lewis, above, and Paul Madden, 'The tide of fate', *The Listener*, 9 March 1978.
18 *The Listener*, 26 January 1978 (under 'Television' in 'The Arts' review section).
19 *The Hollywood Reporter*, 27 September 1967, 3.
20 *The Film Daily*, 21 September 1967.
21 '*Far From the Madding Crowd*: general coverage story': 'With the compliments of Mike Russell, Press and Public Relations Manager', Warner Pathe Distributors Ltd.
22 *Moving Picture Herald*, 4 October 1967; *Kinematograph Weekly*, 21 October 1967; *Variety*, 27 September 1967; *The Hollywood Reporter*, 27 September 1967; *The Daily Cinema*, 20 October 1967.
23 *Far From the Madding Crowd*, St Martin's Library edition, London: Macmillan (1957), 1963.
24 James Price, review, *Sight and Sound*, Winter 1967/8, 39–40.
25 *Sun*, 17 October 1967; *Evening Standard*, 19 October 1967; Cecil Wilson, *Daily Mail*, 17 October 1967.
26 See *ABC Film Review*: 'Alan Bates talks about Gabriel Oak', October 1967; 'Peter Finch talks about Boldwood', September 1967; 'Terence Stamp talks about Sergeant Troy', August 1967; 'Julie Christie talks about Bathsheba Everdene', July 1967.
27 John Coleman, *New Statesman*, op. cit.
28 Thomas Hardy, *Far From the Madding Crowd*, Harmondsworth: Penguin, 1978, 440–1.
29 '*Far From the Madding Crowd*: general coverage story', op. cit.
30 In 'Schlesinger: "Crowd" an "epic" challenge', *The Film Daily*, 22 September 1967.
31 David Austen, review, *Films and Filming*, December 1967, 24. In fact, Austen is quoting an interview in *The Times* while the film was in production.
32 *ABC Film Review*, op. cit.
33 *Monthly Film Bulletin*, December 1967, 186 (by 'J. A. D.'); *Evening Standard*, op. cit.; *Sun*, op. cit.
34 *The Hollywood Reporter*, op. cit.
35 *The Daily Cinema*, op. cit.
36 *Sight and Sound*, op. cit.
37 Interview in *Continental Film Review*, 26, 5 (March 1979), 14–15.
38 Columbia Press Release (in BFI Archive), 5.
39 Harlan Kennedy, '*Tess*: Polanski in Hardy country', *American Film*, 5, 1 (October 1979), 65.

40 Andrew Rissik, 'Laurels for Hardy – but less for "Tess"', *Films Illustrated*, 10, 117 (June 1981), 352.

41 Mike Sarne, 'Tess', *Films*, 1, 6 (May 1981), 35.

42 *Motion Picture Product Digest*, 18 February 1981, 72; *Variety*, 7 November 1979, 18; Marjorie Bilbow, *Screen International*, 25 April 1981, 59.

43 *Variety*, ibid.

44 Ann Totterdell, '*Tess*: a second view', *Films*, 1, 7 (June 1981), 39; John Coleman, 'Country matters', *New Statesman*, 10 April 1981; William V. Costanzo, 'Polanski in Wessex . . . filming *Tess of the d'Urbervilles*', *Literature/Film Quarterly*, 9, 2 (1981), 78; Richard Roud, 'Taking the sex out of Wessex', *Guardian*, 17 November 1979; Costanzo, op. cit., 73.

45 Melanie Wallace, 'Tess', *Cineaste*, 11, 1 (Winter 1980/1), 36; Tom Milne, *Monthly Film Bulletin*, May 1981, 98; Rissik, op. cit., 353.

46 Wallace, op. cit., 37; Rissik, op. cit., 353; Milne, op. cit., 97; Jane Marcus, 'A Tess for child molesters', *Jump Cut*, 26 (December 1981), 3.

47 Costanzo, op. cit., 77–9 *passim*; Coleman, 'Country matters', op. cit.; Roud, op. cit.

48 Neil Sinyard, *Filming Literature: The Art of Screen Adaptation*, Beckenham: Croom Helm, 1986, 49.

49 Costanzo, op. cit., 72.

50 Colin Vaines, 'Hardy task for Roman in love', *Screen International*, 24 February 1979, 14–15.

51 *Continental Film Review*, op. cit.

52 Kennedy, op. cit., 62.

53 ibid., 66–7, 62.

54 Rissik, op. cit., 355.

55 Kennedy, op. cit., 67.

56 Blurb on video case, Thorn/EMI video, 1982.

57 Cf. Rissik, op. cit., and Costanzo, op. cit.

58 Milne, op. cit.; Wallace, op. cit.; Costanzo, op. cit.

59 Profile of Nastassia Kinski in Kennedy, op. cit., 64.

60 Quoted in Columbia Press Release, 5.

61 Kennedy, op. cit., 67.

62 Thomas Hardy, *Tess of the d'Urbervilles*, Harmondsworth: Penguin, 1978, 125.

63 Kennedy, op. cit., 66.

4 Hardy and social class: reading *The Life*

1 Terry Eagleton, *Criticism and Ideology* (1976), London: Verso, 1978, 130–1.

2 And from surmise: see, e.g., Robert Gittings, *Young Thomas Hardy* (1975), Harmondsworth: Penguin, 1978, 148–57.

3 Merryn and Raymond Williams, 'Hardy and social class', in Norman Page, ed., *Thomas Hardy: The Writer and His Background*, London: Bell & Hyman, 1980.

4 ibid.; George Wotton in *Thomas Hardy: Towards a Materialist Criticism*, Dublin: Gill & Macmillan, 1985, has also written extensively about Hardy's class position; see especially Part I: 'The conditions of production of Hardy's writing', 15–73 *passim*.

5 The following pages draw, *passim*, on Hardy's modern biographers, but in particular on Robert Gittings, *Young Thomas Hardy* (1975), Harmondsworth: Penguin, 1978 (hereafter *YTH*).

6 ibid., 24.

7 ibid., 34.

8 ibid., 34.

9 M. and R. Williams, op. cit., in Page, op. cit.

10 Memorandum, 28 April 1888, quoted in Florence Emily Hardy, *The Life of Thomas Hardy* (1962), London: Macmillan, 1975, 208. This is the well-known passage on the 'germ' of *Jude the Obscure*; to his comment 'and I am the one to show it to them', Hardy adds: 'though I was not altogether hindered going, at least to Cambridge, and could have gone up easily at five-and-twenty.' Robert Gittings in *The Older Hardy*, London: Heinemann, 1978, 55, doubts this.

11 Gittings, *YTH*, op. cit., 89.

12 See Gittings, *YTH*, op. cit., 66.

13 John Gross, *The Rise and Fall of the Man of Letters* (1969), Harmondsworth: Penguin, 1973, 76, 82.

14 ibid., 182–3.

15 F. E. Hardy, op. cit., 182 (hereafter *The Life*; all further references are to this edition, and appear as bracketed numbers in the text). The passage ends: 'He went about the business mechanically' (183); 'by this time' is 1886 – just after Hardy had completed *The Mayor of Casterbridge* and was starting *The Woodlanders*.

16 Parts of Morley's comments to Macmillan are quoted in *The Life*, op. cit., 58–9. A fuller version is in Gittings, *YTH*, op. cit., 154.

17 Quoted in Gittings, *YTH*, op. cit., 205. It is not clear how much of Morley's criticism Macmillan passed on to Hardy.

18 ibid., 206–7, 212.

19 Unsigned review, 22 April 1871, in R. G. Cox, ed., *Thomas Hardy: The Critical Heritage*, London: Routledge & Kegan Paul, 1970, 3–5.

20 Gittings, *YTH*, op. cit., 216.

21 ibid., 22, 223, 226.

22 Unsigned review, 15 June 1872, in Cox, op. cit., 9.

23 See Gittings, *YTH*, op. cit., 227.

24 R. L. Purdy and Michael Millgate, eds, *The Collected Letters of Thomas Hardy*, Oxford: Oxford University Press, 1978– .

25 Gittings, *YTH*, op. cit., 277–8.

26 *The Life*, op. cit., 108.

27 ibid., 222.

28 *Jude* was first published, in serial form, in *Harper's New Monthly* (1895) under the title *Hearts Insurgent*.

29 The novel was first published in serial form in *Belgravia* (January–December 1878), the editor insisting that it should not end totally

unhappily – hence Hardy's change of direction in not letting Diggory Venn inexplicably disappear at the end, but instead marry Thomasin. In the 'Wessex' edition of 1912, Hardy inserted a note between the penultimate and final chapters of the book. This reads:

> The writer may state here that the original conception of the story did not design a marriage between Thomasin and Venn. He was to have retained his isolated and weird character to the last, and to have disappeared mysteriously from the heath, nobody knowing whither – Thomasin remaining a widow. But certain circumstances of serial publication led to a change of intent.

> Readers can therefore choose between the endings, and those with an austere artistic code can assume the more consistent conclusion to be the true one.

30 The now well-known story of this deception is recounted in the first chapter of Gittings, *YTH*, op. cit., 15–22.

31 A further example of Hardy's (disingenuous) sense of his own modesty is: '[he] often said – and his actions showed it – that he took no interest in himself as a personage' (378).

32 The only other work I have seen which offers serious analysis of *The Life* as a text in its own right, and which also sees Hardy's social dislocation through upward mobility and his hypersensitive class consciousness as mainsprings of his fictional production, is Patricia Alden's chapter on Hardy (mainly about *Jude*) in *Social Mobility in the English Bildungsroman*, Ann Arbor: UMI Research Press, 1986. This essay was only pointed out to me (by a colleague, David Grylls) as my own work was in the last stages of completion, and so I can confess no debt. However, it is reassuring to acknowledge that Dr Alden, *inter alia*, sees Hardy's *déclassé* unease and his sense of class 'betrayal and deception' as informing most of his work, and *The Life*'s 'self-image' as 'an understandable way of dealing with ideological contradictions about social mobility' (44). She points to many similar features as I do in the *The Life*'s discourse which reveal the tension of at once disguising one's class of origin and despising the class society which requires one to do so. But Dr Alden's most interesting argument is that Hardy's presentation of himself as passively unambitious – one who rises without effort or intent – is a significant reflex of this. (See my pp. 146–7 for comment on this prominent feature of *The Life*.)

33 Gittings, *YTH*, op. cit., 19.

34 *The Life* repeats this slippage when it comments on her death in 1904, noting her 'good taste in literature . . . in circumstances in which opportunities for selection were not numerous' (321). Perhaps the circumlocution of this sentence is significant.

35 This 'namesake' had already been mentioned on p. 5 of *The Life* (see above p. 142), and again when he was invited to become a governor of the school in 1909 – he being 'influenced to accept' because his namesake was its founder (343).

36 The square brackets are those of the 'biographer' of *The Life*, i.e.

Hardy, in later life, who is pretending not to know what the 'germ' of *Jude* had been. For a comment on the last part of the quotation see note 10 above.

37 See *The Life*, op. cit., 33–4. Also Gittings's chapter 'Religion' in *YTH*, op. cit., *passim*.

38 Gittings, *YTH*, op. cit., 66–8.

39 For example, the elderly 'biographer' notes that its 'naive realism . . . was so well assumed' that it took in Morley and Macmillan: 'to Hardy's surprise, when he thought the matter over in later years, that his inexperienced imagination should have created figments that could win credence from such experienced heads' (61); and later he ranks *Desperate Remedies* 'quite below the level of *The Poor Man and the Lady*' (64).

40 Matthew Arnold, *Culture and Anarchy* (1869), Cambridge: Cambridge University Press (1932), 1969. Arnold sees the 'men of culture', the 'true lovers of culture', as representing no particular interest except that of the 'best self' of the state. They are the 'true apostles of equality' and culture seeks to 'do away with classes'.

41 See, e.g., pp. 115, 127, 135–6, 138, 140, 180, 195, 210–11, 212, 214, 220, 224, 226–7, 229, 237–8, 251, 259.

42 See note 17.

5 Hardy and social class: *The Hand of Ethelberta*

1 Thomas Hardy, *The Hand of Ethelberta* (1876), London: Macmillan 'New Wessex' edn, 1975, 307–8. All further references to this novel appear as bracketed numbers in the text.

2 Florence Emily Hardy, *The Life of Thomas Hardy* (1962), London: Macmillan, 1975, 102–3.

3 Robert Gittings, Introduction to the 'New Wessex' edition of *The Hand of Ethelberta*, op. cit., 15.

4 *The Life*, op. cit., 108.

5 In the *Cornhill* serialization of the novel (from July 1875), the poems were entitled 'Metres by Me'; in the volume version, they became 'Metres by E'. See Robert Gittings, *Young Thomas Hardy* (hereafter *YTH*), Harmondsworth: Penguin, 1978, 290, and his 'New Wessex' Introduction, op. cit., 26.

6 *The Life*, op. cit., 106.

7 The main sources for these are: Harold Orel, ed., *Thomas Hardy's Personal Writings* (1966), London: Macmillan, 1967, and Lennart Björk, ed., *The Literary Notebooks of Thomas Hardy*, London: Macmillan, 1985.

8 19 December 1863; in *The Life*, op. cit., 40.

9 *The Life*, op. cit., 61, 391–2.

10 D. H. Lawrence, *Study of Thomas Hardy* (1914), in Edward D. McDonald, ed., *Phoenix* (1936), London: Heinemann, 1970, 413.

11 Leslie Stephen to Hardy *re* the *Cornhill* serialization (1875), quoted in *The Life*, op. cit., 104.

Notes

12 Michael Millgate, _Thomas Hardy: His Career as a Novelist_, London:
   Bodley Head, 1971, 111, has interesting suggestions to make about
   Hardy's 'deliberate' reference, in this novel, to Restoration and
   eighteenth-century 'patterns of stage comedy'.
13 Gittings, Introduction, op. cit., 17.
14 Three other sympathetic and perceptive accounts of _The Hand of
   Ethelberta_ are: Michael Millgate, _Thomas Hardy: His Career as a
   Novelist_, op. cit., which recognizes it as 'almost . . . a parable of social
   revolution' (107) and as a successful 'experiment' by no means
   disconnected from the rest of Hardy's work (115–16); Peter
   Casagrande, _Unity in Hardy's Novels: 'Repetitive Symmetries'_, London:
   Macmillan, 1982, which sees it – in common with many of Hardy's
   novels – as concerning 'the troubled consciousness of an uprooted
   native' (119) and as inflecting the author's own such consciousness; and
   John Bayley, _An Essay on Hardy_, Cambridge: Cambridge University
   Press, 1978, which emphasizes how much 'Hardy is here . . .
   completely his own heroine' (150), 'wryly envisaging the possible
   effects on himself of his own social and literary success' (151). None of
   these critics finally breaks with convention, however, by according the
   novel in formal terms the status of being a sophisticated anti-realist
   fiction whose discourses 'match' its deracinated social consciousness.
15 Gittings, _YTH_, op. cit., 289. All further references to this work appear
   as bracketed numbers in the text.
16 Gittings, Introduction, op. cit., 15. All further references to this essay
   appear as bracketed numbers in the text.
17 These comments are distributed _passim_ throughout Gittings's
   Introduction.
18 Richard H. Taylor, _The Neglected Hardy: Thomas Hardy's Lesser
   Novels_, London: Macmillan, 1978, 57, 65, 66. All further references to
   this essay appear as bracketed numbers in the text.
19 Gittings, Introduction, op. cit., 19.
20 Gittings, _YTH_, op. cit., 291–2, indicates how much more obtrusive was
   the closeness to Hardy's own background in the serial and first editions
   of the novel compared to the extensively revised 1895 edition, and
   points out that Neigh's father in the earlier version had married his
   cook. Hardy's mother had herself been a cook.
21 I am sure keen Hardy watchers will know this, although I have not
   myself seen it said anywhere: Enckworth Court is almost certainly
   based on the house Kingston Lacy in Dorset. Bequeathed to the
   National Trust on the death of its reclusive owner, Ralph Bankes, in
   1982, the house was extensively restored and opened to the public in
   August 1985. For many years it had been more or less unknown as a
   significant country house. The house was designed for the Bankes
   family, after the Restoration, by Sir Roger Pratt – a red brick building
   with Portland cornerstones. When William John Bankes succeeded to
   the estate in 1834, he immediately employed Sir Charles Barry to
   remodel Kingston Lacy. Pratt's red-brick house was covered with a
   'skin' of Chilmark stone and, amongst many other alterations and

241

additions, a 30-foot-wide white Carrara marble staircase was installed. Hardy's description of the 'thin freestone slabs' covering the whole brick exterior of Enckworth Court, and of 'the principal staircase, constructed of a freestone so milk-white and delicately moulded as to be easily conceived in the lamplight as of biscuit-ware', suggest that he knew Kingston Lacy quite well. See the opening of chapter 38 for the full description of the 'false' house, pp. 303–5. Hardy apparently visited the house as a guest during the Edwardian period.

22 Gittings, Introduction, op. cit., 21–2.

6 Another 'Wessex'; another 'Thomas Hardy'

1 Karl Marx in *Grundrisse*, and *Capital 1*. I am indebted to George Wotton, *Thomas Hardy: Towards a Materialist Criticism*, Dublin: Gill & Macmillan, 1985, 17, 19–20, for these quotations.

2 See Wotton, op. cit., Part I; Merryn Williams, *Thomas Hardy and Rural England*, London: Macmillan, 1972, Part I, ch. 1 and Part II, ch. 1; and Merryn and Raymond Williams, 'Hardy and social class', in Norman Page, ed., *Thomas Hardy: The Writer and His Background*, London: Bell & Hyman, 1980.

3 Wotton, op. cit., 39–40.

4 'The Dorsetshire labourer' was first published in *Longman's Magazine* in July 1883; it is reprinted in Harold Orel, ed., *Thomas Hardy's Personal Writings* (1966), London: Macmillan, 1967. The 1895 Preface to *Far From the Madding Crowd* appears in most modern editions of the novel.

5 Thomas Hardy, *Desperate Remedies* (1871), London: Macmillan 'New Wessex' edn, 1975, 212–14.

6 Thomas Hardy, *The Woodlanders* (1887), London: Macmillan 'New Wessex' edn, 1974, 130–1, 137–8.

7 Thomas Hardy, *Tess of the d'Urbervilles* (1891), Harmondsworth: Penguin, 1978, 435–6.

8 *Tess*, op. cit., 359, 361, 405.

9 *Woodlanders*, op. cit., 42.

10 Thomas Hardy, *The Mayor of Casterbridge* (1886), Harmondsworth: Penguin, 1978, 328–30.

11 Thomas Hardy, *Jude the Obscure* (1895), Harmondsworth: Penguin, 1978, 50.

12 *Tess*, op. cit., 77, 105.

13 Thomas Hardy, *The Hand of Ethelberta* (1876), London: Macmillan 'New Wessex' edn, 1975, 198–200.

14 *Woodlanders*, op. cit., 150–1.

15 Thomas Hardy, *A Pair of Blue Eyes* (1873), London: Macmillan 'New Wessex' edn, 1975, 39. All further references to this novel appear as bracketed numbers in the text.

16 *Desperate Remedies*, op. cit., 49.

17 Thomas Hardy, *Under the Greenwood Tree* (1872), London: Macmillan 'New Wessex' edn, 1974, 110, 46.

18 See Frances Widdowson, *Going Up Into the Next Class: Women and Elementary Teacher Training, 1840–1914* (1980), London: Hutchinson, 1983.

19 Thomas Hardy, *Far From the Madding Crowd* (1874), Harmondsworth: Penguin, 1978, 76, 111, 97.

20 Thomas Hardy, *A Laodicean* (1881), London: Macmillan 'New Wessex' edn, 1975, 61–2.

21 Thomas Hardy, *The Return of the Native* (1878), Harmondsworth: Penguin, 1978, 83, 162, 229, 92, 73, 120–1.

22 Thomas Hardy, *The Trumpet-Major* (1880), London: Macmillan 'New Wessex' edn, 1974, 39, 47.

23 Thomas Hardy, *Two on a Tower* (1882), London: Macmillan 'New Wessex' edn, 1975, 179, 292.

24 *Mayor*, op. cit., 149, 69, 115.

25 *Woodlanders*, op. cit., 47, 60, 61, 118, 119, 257, 218, 190–1.

26 *Tess*, op. cit., 78, 58, 76, 172.

27 *Jude*, op. cit., 52, 77.

28 Thomas Hardy, *The Well-Beloved* (1897), London: Macmillan 'New Wessex' edn, 1975, 30, 194–5.

29 *Woodlanders*, op. cit., 214.

30 Patricia Stubbs, *Women and Fiction: Feminism and the Novel 1880–1920* (1979), London: Methuen, 1981, 58.

31 Florence Emily Hardy, *The Life of Thomas Hardy* (1962), London: Macmillan, 1975, 212.

32 *Pair of Blue Eyes*, op. cit., 155–6, 185–6, 328.

33 *Desperate Remedies*, op. cit., 79.

34 *Return of the Native*, op. cit., 119, 122.

35 *Tess*, op. cit., 186–7.

36 ibid., 79, 92, 94.

37 ibid., 383–4.

38 *Woodlanders*, op. cit., 216–17.

39 ibid., 257.

40 Wotton, op. cit., ch. 5, especially p. 70.

41 *Woodlanders*, op. cit., 110.

42 E. M. Forster, *Aspects of the Novel* (1927), Harmondsworth: Penguin, 1970, 100–3.

43 *Jude*, op. cit., 410–11.

44 *Tess*, op. cit., 374–7, 320, 128–9, 488–90.

45 *Jude*, op. cit., 120; *Woodlanders*, op. cit., 208; *Tess*, op. cit., 441, 149.

46 *Tess*, op. cit., 251.

47 *Jude*, op. cit., 406.

48 ibid., 313.

49 *Tess*, op. cit., 346.

50 *Woodlanders*, op. cit., ch. 47; *Tess*, op. cit., 448–9; *Jude*, op. cit., 126–7.

References

[In no sense is this a comprehensive bibliography of works by and about Thomas Hardy: the works listed here are those referred to directly in this book.]

Alden, Patricia, *Social Mobility in the English Bildungsroman*, Ann Arbor: UMI Research Press, 1986.

Arnold, Matthew, *Culture and Anarchy* (1869), ed. J. Dover Wilson, Cambridge: Cambridge University Press (1932), 1969.

Austen, David, '*Far From the Madding Crowd*', *Films and Filming*, December 1967.

Baugh, Albert C., ed., *A Literary History of England* (1967), London: Routledge & Kegan Paul, 1970.

Bayley, John, *An Essay on Hardy*, Cambridge: Cambridge University Press, 1978.

Belsey, Catherine, *Critical Practice*, London: Methuen, 1980.

—— 'Re-reading the great tradition', in Peter Widdowson, ed., *Re-reading English*, London: Methuen, 1982.

Bennett, Tony, *Formalism and Marxism*, London: Methuen, 1979.

—— 'Text and history', in Peter Widdowson, ed., *Re-reading English*, London: Methuen, 1982.

Björk, Lennart, ed., *The Literary Notebooks of Thomas Hardy*, London: Macmillan, 1985.

Blamires, Harry, *A Short History of English Literature*, London: Methuen, 1974.

Blunden, Edmund, *Thomas Hardy*, London: Macmillan, 1942.

Boumelha, Penny, *Thomas Hardy and Women: Sexual Ideology and Narrative Form* (1982), Brighton: Harvester, 1984.

Brompton, Sally, 'Kismet, Hardy . . .', *Daily Mail*, 21 January 1978.

Brooker, Peter and Widdowson, Peter, 'A literature for England, *c*. 1900–1914', in R. Colls and P. Dodd, eds, *The Idea of Englishness, 1880–1920*, Beckenham: Croom Helm, 1985.

Brooks, Jean, *Thomas Hardy: The Poetic Structure*, London: Elek Books, 1971.

Brown, Douglas, *Thomas Hardy* (1954), Harlow: Longman, 1961.

Bullen, J. B., *The Expressive Eye: Fiction and Perception in the Work of Thomas Hardy*, Oxford: Oxford University Press, 1986.

Butler, Lance St John, ed., *Thomas Hardy After Fifty Years*, London: Macmillan, 1977.

Byatt, Antonia, 'Hardy rules OK', *Times Educational Supplement*, 21 January 1981.

Carpenter, Richard, *Thomas Hardy* (1965), London: Macmillan, 1976.

Carr, E. H., *What is History?* (1961), Harmondsworth: Penguin, 1965.

Casagrande, Peter, *Unity in Hardy's Novels: 'Repetitive Symmetries'*, London: Macmillan, 1982.

Cecil, David, *Hardy the Novelist*, London: Constable, 1943.

Chase, M. E., *Thomas Hardy: From Serial to Novel*, Minneapolis: Minnesota Press, 1927.

Coleman, John, 'The Wessex set', *New Statesman*, 20 October 1967.

—— 'Country matters', *New Statesman*, 10 April 1981.

Coleman, Terry, 'The lady beyond the hero's grasp', *Guardian*, 19 March 1982.

Collins, Philip, 'Hardy and education', in Norman Page, ed., *Thomas Hardy: The Writer and His Background*, London: Bell & Hyman, 1980.

Colls, R. and Dodd, P., eds, *The Idea of Englishness, 1880–1920*, Beckenham: Croom Helm, 1985.

Costanzo, William V., 'Polanski in Wessex . . . filming *Tess of the d'Urbervilles*', *Literature/Film Quarterly*, 9, 2 (1981).

Cox, R.G., ed., *Thomas Hardy: The Critical Heritage*, London: Routledge & Kegan Paul, 1970.

Creighton, T. R. M., ed., *Poems of Thomas Hardy*, London: Macmillan, 1974.

Daisne, Johan, *A Filmographic Dictionary of World Literature*, Ghent: Story-Scientia, 1971.

Davie, Donald, *Thomas Hardy and British Poetry*, London: Routledge & Kegan Paul, 1973.

Davies, Bernard, 'One man's television', *Broadcast*, 6 February 1978.

Day-Lewis, Sean, 'What Potter made of Hardy', *Daily Telegraph*, 6 March 1978.

Draper, R. P., ed., *Hardy: The Tragic Novels*, London: Macmillan (Casebook), 1975.

Eagleton, Mary and Pierce, David, *Attitudes to Class in the English Novel*, London: Thames & Hudson, 1979.

Eagleton, Terry, *Criticism and Ideology* (1976), London: Verso, 1978.

—— *Walter Benjamin or Towards a Revolutionary Criticism*, London: Verso, 1981.

Enstice, Andrew, *Thomas Hardy: Landscapes of the Mind*, London: Macmillan, 1979.

Firor, Ruth, *Folkways in Thomas Hardy* (1931), New York: Russell & Russell, 1968.

Forster, E. M., *Aspects of the Novel* (1927), Harmondsworth: Penguin, 1970.

Gibson, James, *Tess of the d'Urbervilles*, London: Macmillan (Master Guides), 1986.

References

Gittings, Robert, *Young Thomas Hardy* (1975), Harmondsworth: Penguin, 1978.
—— *The Older Hardy*, London: Heinemann, 1978.
—— 'The Mayor of Casterbridge', *Radio Times*, 4–10 March 1978.
Goode, John, 'Women and the literary text', in Mitchell and Oakley, eds, *The Rights and Wrongs of Women*, Harmondsworth: Penguin, 1976.
—— 'Sue Bridehead and the new woman', in Mary Jacobus, ed., *Women's Writing and Writing About Women*, Beckenham: Croom Helm, 1979.
Goulden, Holly and Hartley, John, '"Nor should such topics as homosexuality, masturbation, frigidity, premature ejaculation or the menopause be regarded as unmentionable"', *Literature Teaching Politics* (*LTP*), 1, 1982.
Gregor, Ian, 'What kind of fiction did Hardy write?', *Essays in Criticism*, XVI, 3 (July 1966).
—— *The Great Web: The Form of Hardy's Major Fiction*, London: Faber, 1974.
Gregor, Ian and Irwin, Michael, 'Either side of Wessex', in Lance St John Butler, ed., *Thomas Hardy After Fifty Years*, London: Macmillan, 1977.
Gross, John, *The Rise and Fall of the Man of Letters* (1969), Harmondsworth: Penguin, 1973.
Guerard, Albert J., *Thomas Hardy* (1949), revised edition, London: New Directions, 1964.
Halliwell, Leslie, *Filmgoer's Companion*, 8th edition, London: Granada, 1984.
Hardy, Florence Emily, *The Life of Thomas Hardy 1840–1928* (1962), London: Macmillan, 1975. This was originally published in two volumes: *The Early Life of Thomas Hardy* (1928) and *The Later Years of Thomas Hardy* (1930).
Hardy, Thomas [NB The works listed here – in order of original book publication – are only the works and editions used in the preparation of this book. For the most part they are from the Macmillan 'New Wessex' edition of 1974–5 (general editor: P. N. Furbank) and the Penguin English Library edition of 1978; notes in the chapters indicate which edition is referred to in any given case. There are, in addition, the Macmillan 'Students Edition' of 1975, and several volumes in the modern Oxford 'World's Classics' series.]
—— *Desperate Remedies* (1871), London: Macmillan 'New Wessex', 1975, with Introduction by C. J. P. Beatty.
—— *Under the Greenwood Tree* (1872), London: Macmillan 'New Wessex', 1974, with Introduction by Geoffrey Grigson.
—— *A Pair of Blue Eyes* (1873), London: Macmillan 'New Wessex', 1975, with Introduction by Ronald Blythe.
—— *A Pair of Blue Eyes*, Oxford: Oxford 'World's Classics', 1985, with Introduction by Alan Manford.
—— *Far From the Madding Crowd*, London: Macmillan 'St. Martin's Library' (1957), 1963.
—— *Far From the Madding Crowd* (1874), London: Macmillan 'New Wessex', 1974, with Introduction by John Bayley.

—— *Far From the Madding Crowd*, Harmondsworth: Penguin, 1978, with Introduction by Ronald Blythe.

—— *The Hand of Ethelberta* (1876), London: Macmillan 'New Wessex', 1975, with Introduction by Robert Gittings.

—— *The Return of the Native* (1878), London: Macmillan 'New Wessex', 1974, with Introduction by Derwent May.

—— *The Return of the Native*, Harmondsworth: Penguin, 1978, with Introduction by George Woodcock.

—— *An Indiscretion in the Life of an Heiress* (1878; a long short story drawn from the unpublished first novel *The Poor Man and the Lady*), ed. Terry Coleman, London: Hutchinson, 1976.

—— *The Trumpet-Major* (1880), London: Macmillan 'New Wessex', 1974, with Introduction by Barbara Hardy.

—— *A Laodicean* (1881), London: Macmillan 'New Wessex', 1975, with Introduction by Barbara Hardy.

—— *Two on a Tower* (1882), London: Macmillan 'New Wessex', 1975, with Introduction by F. B. Pinion.

—— *The Mayor of Casterbridge* (1886), London: Macmillan 'New Wessex', 1974, with Introduction by Ian Gregor.

—— *The Mayor of Casterbridge*, Harmondsworth: Penguin, 1978, with Introduction by Martin Seymour-Smith.

—— *The Woodlanders* (1887), London: Macmillan 'New Wessex', 1974, with Introduction by David Lodge.

—— *Tess of the d'Urbervilles* (1891), London: Macmillan 'New Wessex', 1974, with Introduction by P. N. Furbank.

—— *Tess of the d'Urbervilles*, Harmondsworth: Penguin, 1978, with Introduction by A. Alvarez.

—— *Jude the Obscure* (1895), London: Macmillan 'New Wessex', 1974, with Introduction by Terry Eagleton.

—— *Jude the Obscure*, Harmondsworth: Penguin, 1978, with Introduction by C. H. Sisson.

—— *The Well-Beloved* (1897), London: Macmillan 'New Wessex', 1975, with Introduction by J. Hillis Miller.

—— *The Dynasts* (1903–8), London: Macmillan (Papermac), 1965, with Introduction by John Wain.

—— 'General Preface' (to the 'Wessex' edition of 1912), reprinted in all the 'New Wessex' and Penguin editions.

Hattersley, Roy, 'Endpiece: how I came to Casterbridge by way of Reykjavik', *Guardian*, 23 January 1982.

Hillis Miller, J., *Thomas Hardy: Distance and Desire*, Oxford: Oxford University Press, 1970.

Holland, Clive, *Thomas Hardy's Wessex Scene* (1948), New York: Haskell House, 1971.

Holloway, John, *The Victorian Sage*, London: Macmillan, 1953.

—— *The Charted Mirror*, London: Routledge & Kegan Paul, 1960.

Howe, Irving, *Thomas Hardy* (1966), London: Weidenfeld & Nicolson, 1968.

Hynes, Samuel, ed., *The Complete Poetical Works of Thomas Hardy*,

2 vols, Oxford: Oxford University Press, 1982, 1984.

Ifor Evans, B., *A Short History of English Literature* (1940), Harmondsworth: Penguin, 1958.

Ingham, Patricia, 'The evolution of *Jude the Obscure*', *Review of English Studies*, 1976.

Jacobus, Mary, ed., *Women's Writing and Writing about Women*, Beckenham: Croom Helm, 1979.

Johnson, Trevor, '"Pre-critical innocence" and the anthologist's Hardy', *Victorian Poetry*, 17 (1979).

Kay-Robinson, Denys, *Hardy's Wessex Reappraised*, Newton Abbot: David & Charles, 1972.

Kennedy, Harlan, '*Tess*: Polanski in Hardy country', *American Film*, 5, 1 (October 1979). Contains an interview with Roman Polanski and a 'profile' of Nastassia Kinski.

Kettle, Arnold, *An Introduction to the English Novel* (1953), London: Hutchinson, 1967.

—— '*Tess of the d'Urbervilles*' ('The nineteenth-century novel and its legacy', units 17–18, prepared by A. K.), Milton Keynes: Open University Press, 1982.

Kramer, Dale, *Thomas Hardy: The Forms of Tragedy*, London: Macmillan, 1975.

Kramer, Dale, ed., *Critical Approaches to the Fiction of Thomas Hardy*, London: Macmillan, 1979.

Laird, John, *The Shaping of* Tess of the d'Urbervilles, Oxford: Oxford University Press, 1975.

Lawrence, D. H., *Study of Thomas Hardy* (1914), in Edward D. McDonald, ed., *Phoenix* (1936), London: Heinemann, 1970.

Lea, Hermann, *Thomas Hardy's Wessex* (1913), St Peter Port: Toucan Press, 1969.

Leavis, F. R., *New Bearings in English Poetry*, London: Chatto & Windus, 1932.

—— *Mass Civilization and Minority Culture*, Cambridge: Minority Press, 1930; also in *Education and the University* (1943), Cambridge: Cambridge University Press, 1979.

—— *The Great Tradition* (1948), Harmondsworth: Penguin, 1962.

—— *D. H. Lawrence/Novelist* (1955), London: Chatto & Windus, 1967.

—— *The Common Pursuit* (1962), Harmondsworth: Penguin, 1978.

Lodge, David, 'Tess, Nature and the voices of Hardy', in *The Language of Fiction*, London: Routledge & Kegan Paul, 1966. Reprinted in R. P. Draper, ed., *Hardy: The Tragic Novels*, London: Macmillan (Casebook), 1975.

—— '*Thomas Hardy* as a cinematic novelist', in Lance St John Butler, ed., *Thomas Hardy After Fifty Years*, London: Macmillan, 1977.

—— *Working with Structuralism*, London: Routledge & Kegan Paul, 1981.

Longhurst, Derek, 'Shakespeare in education: reproducing a national culture', *Red Letters*, 11, Spring 1981.

—— 'Not for all time, but for an age: an approach to Shakespeare studies', in Peter Widdowson, ed., *Re-reading English*, London: Methuen, 1982.

Lucas, John, *The Literature of Change*, Brighton: Harvester, 1977.

Madden, Paul, 'The tide of fate', *The Listener*, 9 March 1978.

Marcus, Jane, 'A Tess for child molesters', *Jump Cut*, 26 (December 1981).

Maxwell, J. C., 'The "sociological" approach to *The Mayor of Casterbridge*', in Mack, M. and Gregor, I., eds, *Imagined Worlds* (1968). Reprinted in R. P. Draper, ed., *Hardy: The Tragic Novels*, London: Macmillan (Casebook), 1975.

Millgate, Michael, *Thomas Hardy: His Career as a Novelist*, London: Bodley Head, 1971.

—— *Thomas Hardy: A Biography*, Oxford: Oxford University Press, 1982.

Milne, Tom, 'Tess', *Monthly Film Bulletin*, May 1981.

Mitchell, Juliet and Oakley, Ann, eds, *The Rights and Wrongs of Women*, Harmondsworth: Penguin, 1976.

Morrell, Roy, *Thomas Hardy: The Will and the Way* (1965), Oxford: Oxford University Press, 1978.

Newbolt, Sir Henry, *Board of Education Report, The Teaching of English in England*, London: HMSO, 1921 (the 'Newbolt Report').

Newton, Stella Mary, 'Thomas Hardy', 'Writers and their times, 1', audio-visual filmstrip: Cheltenham: Visual Publications, advertising pamphlet, 1987.

Orel, Harold, ed., *Thomas Hardy's Personal Writings* (1966), London: Macmillan, 1967.

O'Sullivan, Timothy, *Thomas Hardy: An Illustrated Biography*, London: Macmillan, 1975.

Pacey, Ann, 'Alas Miss Christie, less than Victorian', *Sun*, 17 October 1967.

Page, Norman, ed., *Thomas Hardy: The Writer and His Background*, London: Bell & Hyman, 1980.

—— *The Thomas Hardy Annual*, nos 1–6, London: Macmillan, 1982–

Paterson, John, *The Making of The Return of the Native*, Berkeley: University of California Press, 1960.

Phillips, Philip, 'The man who sold his wife', *Sun*, 21 January 1978.

Pinion, F. B., *A Hardy Companion*, London: Macmillan, 1968.

—— *Thomas Hardy: Art and Thought*, London: Macmillan, 1977.

Polanski, Roman, interview in *Continental Film Review*, 26, 5 (March 1979).

Price, James, '*Far From the Madding Crowd*', *Sight and Sound*, Winter 1967/8.

Purdy, R. L., *Thomas Hardy: A Bibliographical Study*, Oxford: Oxford University Press, 1954.

Purdy, R. L. and Millgate Michael, eds, *The Collected Letters of Thomas Hardy*, 7 vols, Oxford: Oxford University Press, 1978– .

Rissik, Andrew, 'Laurels for Hardy – but less for "Tess"', *Films Illustrated*, 10, 117 (June 1981).

Roud, Richard, 'Taking the sex out of Wessex', *Guardian*, 17 November 1979.

Sarne, Mike, 'Tess', *Films*, 1, 6 (May 1981).

Schlesinger, John, interviewed in 'Schlesinger: "Crowd" an "epic" challenge', *The Film Daily*, 22 September 1967.

Sinyard, Neil, *Filming Literature: The Art of Screen Adaptation*, Beckenham: Croom Helm, 1986.

Skilling, M. R., 'Walk round Dorchester (Casterbridge) with Thomas Hardy', Thomas Hardy Society Pamphlet, 1975.

—— 'Walk round Weymouth (Budmouth) with Thomas Hardy', Thomas Hardy Society Pamphlet, 1983.

Stevens Cox, J., ed., *Thomas Hardy: Materials for a Study of his Life, Times and Works*, St Peters Port: Toucan Press, 1968.

—— *Thomas Hardy: More Materials for a Study of his Life, Times and Works*, St Peters Port: Toucan Press, 1971.

Stewart, J. I. M., *Thomas Hardy, A Critical Biography*, Harlow: Longman, 1971.

Stubbs, Patricia, *Women and Fiction: Feminism and the Novel 1880–1920* (1979), London: Methuen, 1981.

Tanner, Tony, 'Colour and movement in *Tess of the d'Urbervilles*', *Critical Quarterly*, 10, 1968. Reprinted in R. P. Draper, ed., *Hardy: The Tragic Novels*, London: Macmillan (Casebook), 1975.

Taylor, Richard H., ed., *The Personal Notebooks of Thomas Hardy*, London: Macmillan, 1978.

Taylor, Richard H., 'Thomas Hardy: a reader's guide', in Norman Page, ed., *Thomas Hardy: The Writer and His Background*, London: Bell & Hyman, 1980.

—— *The Neglected Hardy: Thomas Hardy's Lesser Novels*, London: Macmillan, 1982.

Tomalin, Claire, 'Hardy's perennial', *Radio Times*, 21–7 January 1978.

Totterdell, Ann, '*Tess*: a second view', *Films*, 1, 7 (June 1981).

Vaines, Colin, 'Hardy task for Roman in love', *Screen International*, 24 (February 1979). Contains an interview with Roman Polanski.

Vigar, Penelope, *The Novels of Thomas Hardy: Illusion and Reality*, London: Athlone Press, 1974.

Wain, John, ed., *Selected Shorter Poems of Thomas Hardy* (1966), London: Macmillan, 1975.

Walker, Alexander, 'What's a swinging 1967 girl doing in Hardy's Dorset?', *Evening Standard*, 19 October 1967.

Wallace, Melanie, 'Tess', *Cineaste*, 11, 1 (Winter 1980/1).

Weber, Carl, *Hardy of Wessex* (1940), revised edition, London: Routledge & Kegan Paul, 1965.

Weiner, Martin J., *English Culture and the Decline of the Industrial Spirit, 1850–1980* (1981), Harmondsworth: Penguin, 1985.

Welsh, James M., 'Hardy and the pastoral, Schlesinger and the shepherds: *Far From the Madding Crowd*', *Literature/Film Quarterly*, 9, 2 (1981).

Widdowson, Frances, *Going Up Into the Next Class: Women and Elementary Teacher Training, 1840–1914* (1980), London: Hutchinson, 1983.

Widdowson, Peter, ed., *Re-reading English*, London: Macmillan, 1982.

Widdowson, Peter, 'Hardy in history: a case-study in the sociology of

literature', *Literature and History*, 9, 1, Spring 1983.
—— 'The anti-history men: Malcolm Bradbury and David Lodge', *Critical Quarterly*, 26, 4, Winter 1984.
—— 'Hardy, "Wessex" and the making of a national culture', in Norman Page, ed., *The Thomas Hardy Annual*, vol. 4, 1986.
Widdowson, Peter, Stigant, Paul, and Brooker, Peter, 'History and literature "value"': *Adam Bede* and *Salem Chapel'*, *Literature and History*, 5, 1, Spring 1979.
Williams, Merryn, *Thomas Hardy and Rural England*, London: Macmillan, 1972.
Williams, Merryn and Williams, Raymond, 'Hardy and social class', in Norman Page, ed., *Thomas Hardy: The Writer and His Background*, London: Bell & Hyman, 1980.
Williams, Raymond, *The English Novel from Dickens to Lawrence*, London: Chatto & Windus, 1970.
—— *Politics and Letters* (1979), London: Verso, 1981.
Wilson, Cecil, 'Darling Julie is sexy even in those Victorian skirts', *Daily Mail*, 17 October 1967.
Wotton, George, *Thomas Hardy: Towards a Materialist Criticism*, Dublin: Gill & Macmillan, 1985.

NB Many miscellaneous items referred to in the course of this book are not listed above. These can be found in the notes to individual chapters, and include: reviews and essays reprinted in R. G. Cox, ed., *Thomas Hardy: The Critical Heritage*, op. cit.; other unsigned reviews and articles from newspapers, magazines, etc.; information from the BBC programme catalogue; secondary and tertiary level examination papers from many boards and institutions; student 'study guides'; tourist brochures; advertising blurbs; films and television productions.

Index

Index